MW01233201

THIS BOOK WILL SHOW YOU HOW TO MAKE
A MILLION DOLLARS
IN THREE YEARS OR LESS

TWO YEARS FOR
FREEDOM

Author:

Bill "Tycoon" Greene

P.O. Box 408

Mill Valley, California

94941

Preview Edition, November 1978

Sold out in one month !

Hardcover (First) Edition, May 1979

Sold Out Prior to Publication !

Second Edition , Revised & Expanded, June 1979

Sold Out in Two Months !

Third Edition, January 1980

Self-Published by:

BGTC,Inc.

Reno, Nevada

To Order Addional Copies, see order form on Page 168 or On Last Page.

Library of Congress Catalog Card Number: 79-53914

ISBN 0-934668-02-7

TWO YEARS FOR FREEDOM!

TWO months to write - Two hours to read

This book can make you financially
independent two years from today.

Is it worth two hours of reading, followed by
two years of effort to be financially free?

Are you willing to give yourself

?

LIBRARY OF CONGRESS
CATALOG CARD NUMBER: 79-53914
    Greene, Bill "Tycoon"
        TWO YEARS FOR FREEDOM.
    1. Real Estate Investment 2. Investments
    3. Tax Avoidance
    CA : BGTC, Inc. , PO Box 408, Mill Valley, CA
    94941; 307 Pages, 60 Illustrations by Edward
    Barker.   .
     ISBN 0-934668-02-7
    7906   790627

TWO YEARS FOR FREEDOM

MULTI-MILLIONAIRE AND MAVERICK TYCOON BILL GREENE SHOWS YOU HOW TO ELIMINATE TAXES AND BECOME INDEPENDENTLY WEALTHY

Original Cartoons

by

Edward Barker

London

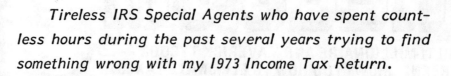

DEDICATION

to

Dale and Larry

Tireless IRS Special Agents who have spent countless hours during the past several years trying to find
something wrong with my 1973 Income Tax Return.

You travelled the far corners of the hemisphere
spending perhaps a million in public funds investigating my affairs. You
carefully interviewed my ex-girl friends. When no dirt was uncovered, you
sought out MOTHERS of ex-girl friends.

You declined to come to my free public lectures, but you cleverly infil-
trated my $250 "Tycoon Classes" with undercover agents. You paid full
price and didn't apply for the couple rate.

Finding nothing sinister, you had the government pay for a 4,000 mile
trip to interview my childhood playmates. You induced an uninformed informant to mail you a false "tip" then used it to justify an expanded investigative
budget. You harrassed my parents, friends, tenants, employees and rela-
tives. You intimidated my accountant and banker. You issued summonses
and subpoenas in paper blizzards that caused my lawyers and other to lose
another million in productive time and money.

When I think of the five hundred homes or other useful products lost to
society by this diversion of resources, I consider what might have been:

You might have found an error on my 1973 Tax Return. You might have
had me indicted for tax fraud. You might have won a conviction. You might
have won the appeals. You might have had me sentenced to a one year
retreat in Southern California. During the six
months until parole, I'd have improved my tennis
and horsemanship at the Lompoc Correctional
Facility (cost to government, about $200 per day).
There I'd have enjoyed the company of Nixon's
White House Aides and other soon-to-be-famous
authors.

I'd have finished this book a year earlier.

Thanks, Dale and Larry, for trying to help!

Confessions of a real estate tycoon

Condensation: 9/28/78 Feature Article by Kevin Cody, Editor

Maverick Tycoon Bill Greene, America's most interesting multi-millionaire?

Five years ago Greene was broke. Three years later he owned over 60 pieces of property in Marin, with a total value of over $4 million.

"And I haven't paid a penny in taxes. I think it's unfair; the system is very unfair. But everyone is ripping off the system, so you might was well do it too. Greene is unabashedly dedicated to making money as a means toward happiness. Somewhere ("Not at my home"), he has a room with a million dollars in gold bars.

What makes Greene somewhat unique among people dedicated to making vast sums of money is that he has a messianic compulsion to teach others his methods. Though his critics claim his "Tycoon Class" is just another money-making gambit, Greene points out he could make much more money sticking with real estate investment.

"Two hundred years ago, doctors had one cure for everything—bleeding. A hundred years from now people will look back on this socialistic era, and taxes will be viewed the way we view bleeding today. Taxes are government's cure for everything," claimed Greene, who says he was a Libertarian before he knew there was such a thing as a Libertarian party.

His real estate investment classes are intended to help "the common guy with a job get into real estate."

"The general feeling among people is that they're being squeezed out of the home buying market, that they're being screwed by the system. So they think rich people are evil, and they turn to things like rent control, which is a disaster.

"The standard approach to buying a home is to go to a broker. But if the cheapest dump in town is $75,000 you'll need over $15,000 down—if you can get financing. $15,000 down is too much for a guy who makes $20,000 a year.

"I'm saying you don't have to go that way, that you can buy property with no money down and for significantly less than market value.

"The short of it is that a lot more properties are available for sale than are on the market. I teach how to locate these properties, and how to convince their owners to sell for no money down.

"One technique is to go to the tax assessor's office and look for out of town property owners. About fifty percent of them will accept a reasonable offer. Also look for people who are delinquent in paying their taxes.

"Why don't these people put their property on the market. Because, as we know if we examine ourselves, most of us are lazy and want someone to solve our problems for us.

"Phase two is how to buy with no money down. You have to know the tax law. Armed with this knowledge, go to the seller and show how he can keep more of his profits if he agrees to sell to you with no money down. One way is to have the seller refinance his home. On an $80,000 home he could get a $50,000 loan. You agree to make his loan payments. Were he simply to sell his home and make a $50,000 profit he might have to pay as much as 65 percent in capital gains taxes.

"California law is unique in regard to real estate loans," Greene pointed out. "Loans on properties of one to four units are 'non-recourse.' The lender's only recourse, if you are unable to make payments, is to go after the house. He can't attack your other assets. It makes real estate loans a no-risk proposition for the borrower."

Greene doesn't have a realtor's license, and would consider one a handicap. "One reason is the money you make selling property, if you have a license, can be taxed as high as 85 percent because it's classified as income. The second reason is a licensed salesman is required by law to tell a seller what the true market value of a home is. A salesman can be sued for making a profit off a customer by acting as a principal. Another reason a license is a handicap is that brokers are not allowed to 'trade up,' though they have ways of getting around that.

I asked Greene if he thought "the bubble" in real estate was going to burst.

"But real estate values aren't going up, at least not at the 25 percent people think they're rising at," he answered. "What's happening is that the dollar is sinking. And inflation has to continue because there are no restraints on the spending by politicians. Property values may not continue to outrace inflation by the same margin, but the bubble is never going to burst," Greene said.

Greene made his first million (on paper, where he prefers to keep his money for tax purposes) in the early 60's in the stock market.

"I got in early on the electronic stocks boom. But I got out late, I was a millionaire at 20 and broke at 24. So I started American Equities Group. I tracked down unknown heirs and lost stock holders—people who had assets due them but didn't know it. I traveled all over the world. But after a while, one dusty road begins to look like another. So I bought a dumpy mansion in San Francisco and restored it. I found using my hands much more satisfying, and creative, and also healthier. Then I found out you could carry back real estate losses five years. I got $50,000 back. So I started doing more real estate deals."

Greene is not concerned that revealing his methods for locating buyers willing to sell below market value, and for no money down, will exhaust the supply.

Beach People's EasyReader

A Revealing Look at Marin's Richest Landlord

By Dorothy Kelly

Even before we meet for our interview, I have formed an opinion of real estate tycoon, Bill Greene. I imagine that any thirty-nine-year-old bachelor with as much money as he has and who is willing to make it a public fact, must be arrogant, flashy and . . . probably lecherous.

His secretary lets me into a huge old redwood log house on his four acre estate in Mill Valley. She tells me that Mr. Greene has not yet arrived. The rest of her conversation is drowned by a deafening roar outside as a car races into the drive. "Bill Greene is a Porsche," I predict, smug because I know I've got him tabbed. Instead, a dented 1973 Chevy pickup truck pulls up and out jumps a cuddly guy with big brown eyes and a warm grin. He apologizes for being five minutes late and hands me a bottle of red wine, "home brew," as a gift.

I like him instantly.

Greene jokingly refers to himself as "the financial guru of Mill Valley." He has made three separate fortunes from scratch and estimates his worth at between two and three million. "There is no magic key to making lots of money," he insists. "Anyone can do it, within one to three years. All that is necessary is to decide that you sincerely want to be independently wealthy. And then get out there and hustle."

To make it even easier, Green offers a course on how to become a millionaire in real estate. He passes on principles that have helped him amass his own empire.

The elimination of consumption in order to accumulate capital is one of his most important rules. "It need only be temporary," he says, "But it will influence your whole outlook. Once you get into the habit, you will probably never want to go back to needless spending again."

But needless spending to Bill Greene means hardly any spending at all. "In my view, you never have to buy anything," he says, "I acquire things free or in trade. The hot item in my course is my fashion show. I get up there and show off my clothes. They are either cast-offs from friends of left behind by tenants." His black naugahide sofa was a discard, too. So were a couple of rather worn looking easy chairs. The Oriental rugs he got as security on a loan that failed to pay off. Greene's living room may never make the pages of *House and Garden*, but the total effect is pleasing and comfortable.

Some may accuse him of carrying his principles to the extreme, but to Bill Greene, it's all part of playing "the game." The game of acquiring money. I argue that instead of buying things, if one waits for them to come along as he does, then they will never get exactly what they want. Green says he loves the surprises and the challenge of it.

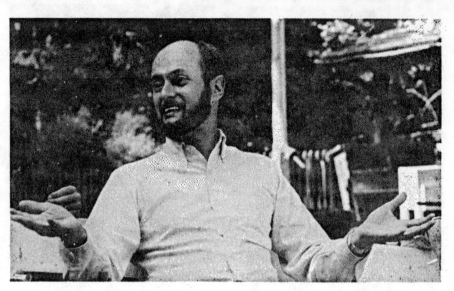

Another way of playing the game is learning to use your own assets to get ahead, no matter what they are. "If you are a woman," says Greene, "that may be sex appeal. Or maybe you have a chance to be the token black for a company. Next year black may not be in. So take the opportunity this year and make yourself valuable for your other qualities."

Greene also advises spending only five per cent of your gross income. The rest goes back into investments. "This may be hard when you are making $100 a month and spending three hundred of it on rent," he admits, "but there are ways to do it. One is to manage an apartment building and live rent-free. My ways are not the only ways," he adds, "its just a matter of imagination and realizing that it is possible to do things like this."

A broken love affair was responsible for the course Green teaches on how to be a real estate tycoon. Lonely and depressed, he found it difficult to find another woman who shared his mania for real estate dealing. "My idea of a great weekend is to get up early Saturday morning to look through the classifieds and spend the rest of the time out looking for properties. Most women don't see it this way, however." He cleverly solved the problem by advertising a class for women only. An endless supply of dates resulted.

Greene even managed to find a way to dine free by trading an evening of consultation to any woman willing to take him out to dinner. "But I also gave a few scholarships," he adds with a wink. "I was giving a valuable course," he says, "so those that did not care for me personally at least got a lot of practical information."

The course has expanded from informal sessions on his front lawn to a (money back guarantee if you're not satisfied) seminar for both sexes

It will cover everything from how to collect rent from reluctant tenants to how to make deals and get financing.

"My course is not a mind trip," Greene emphasizes. "It's full of a lot of practical, very useful information that most people don't know about. It is for people who would like to get up in the morning and not have to go to a job they don't like. For those who want to change their lives and would like to acquire some material signs of their transformation."

Every year, Greene takes off for two months to do something "totally wierd." Once it was Andalusian dance classes in Spain and another time he visited France to study French cooking and literature.

Why, I want to know, is Greene ready to put so much energy into these classes when he is already so rich. His answer is that after five years in real estate he is ready to try something new. And it's also exciting for him to see his students doing well, much better than he had even imagined. "I began to realize that a person does not have to be born with an incentive to make money," he told me. "It can be awakened. And *that* is my job."

BILL GREENE'S TYCOON CLASS

P.O. Box 408
Mill Valley, CA 94941
(415) 383-3229

Excerpt: Bay Area Lifestyle

'Profit Prophet' shares his tips

By Tricia Crane

You too can make one million dollars. That's right, one million dollars, no money down. All you have to do is follow in the footsteps of real estate entrepreneur William (Bill) Greene.

"If you give a hungry man a fish you get a dependent," says the prophet of profits. "But if you sell him a hook, line and sinker on an installment plan, you get a friend."

The moral?

"The point is that our government is set up to create a lot of consumers to support the social system," says Greene. "There's no way you can get ahead working for a salary. What's the difference whether you are recapping tires in Russia or in Los Angeles?" he asks. "If you continue to follow the conventional wisdom you will continue to foot the bills for millionaires like me."

And why is this Mill Valley resident visiting "our" Valley? In Greene's own words, "to spread the gospel," by promoting his do-it-yourself tycoon seminar, a two-day crash course for which he charges $295. He is offering free, two-hour introductory classes this coming Monday and Wednesday evenings at Sportsmen's Lodge in Studio City in an effort to lure prospective students into his course.

Dressed in clothes that are "either cast-offs from friends or left behind by tenants," Greene is characteristically generous in outlining the basics of his formula for effectively and lucratively bucking the system.

The 40-year old tycoon-turned-teacher is convinced, as well as convincing, that true freedom is of the financial variety and that real estate is one sure-fire way to get rich quick and escape the dreaded nine-to-five work drudgery.

Born in the Chicago slums and raised during the Depression by a father who was a "fuzzy thinking" socialist state representative, today Greene is a multi-millionaire who claims not to have paid income taxes for the last ten years. "And I expect to never have to," he boasts.

His secret?

"It's no secret," he insists. "I just stopped being a wage slave. I started to let my investments work for me. Invest in real estate, where the government's inflationary and unfair tax policies will actually help you.

"Use spare time and spare money you are using on consumer goods to buy investment, rental property. Wage slaves work pretty hard, but life doesn't get any easier. You get raises, but your standard of living keeps going down. Why? An average income buys less and less.

"Assume you make $20,000 a year," he continues. "The tax bite is about $6,800. Inflation pushes up costs of rent, coffee, sugar and bread about 10 percent a year. So in year two you end up with $13,200 but you're left with only $11,880 in purchasing power.

"This explains why your real standard of living keeps dropping," Greene says. "Even if you get a cost of living raise, the government raises taxes. As you get a raise, your tax bracket is raised. Even with a $2,000 wage increase you suffer as tax bracket goes up and dollar goes down in value. And that doesn't even take into consideration new Social Security taxes."

An attorney who also was graduated from the prestigious Wharton School of Finance, Greene claims "more academic degrees than a thermometer."

He took three years to complete a four-year course in urban land economics and finance, traveling to Mexico, Europe and the Middle East to study. Yet he insists "I didn't start making money until I tore up my degrees."

One of the original members of the Proposition 13 committee, Greene is also honorary Consul General of Senegal, ghost writer of magnate William Zeckendorf's autobiography and founder of the American Equities Group, an agency that tracks down unknown heirs, lost stockholders and people who have assets due them.

Having made three million dollars in California real estate within the last four years, Greene believes "our government discourages people from getting out on their own two feet. It's built into the system. It is set up to create a lot of consumers to support the mammoth social system. But we are still a free country."

But can a person make a real estate investment with no money to invest?

To begin the Greene-way to "true financial freedom," he suggests:

● Learning to live on five percent of your gross salary.

● Acquiring detailed knowledge of the local real estate market.

● Accumulating unlimited credit and borrowing to the hilt.

● Forgetting about waiting around for red ribbon deals.

● Deferring or altogether eliminating paying income taxes.

"You first have to get over a fear of the unknown," he cautions. "Then it's just hard work.

"Most people feel secure with a nine-to-five job. But how secure is it when you can be fired any time, unless you own the company?" asks Greene. "What has done very well for the investor, uninterruptedly since 1776? Homes and low income property.

"Therefore," he continues, "real estate is the answer. Even in the worst depression in U.S. history, low rent housing did very well. And if an investment goes sour? In California lenders cannot come after other assets because there is no personal liability on purchase money mortgages on one to four units. If it goes sour you can walk away from it. The lenders can't come after you for the money."

How do you get into a real estate career and buy your first investment property?

"Confucius will tell you how to get rich quick," promises William Greene, real estate tycoon. "And the best way to make your money grow fast is to buy one house, then another, then another..."

Get out a newspaper and look at properties, Greene says. Evaluate them, but don't buy until you've looked at least one hundred.

"My rule of thumb for finding out how much a property is worth is to take the monthly gross rents and multiply it by 80. Take, for example, a duplex that rents for $200 per month per unit. The two ($400) multiplied by 80 will give you $32,000.

"If you can buy it for that it is a good price. That may seem low, but in many areas that is the going price. If you want to make money you can never pay more than 100 times the gross monthly rental. Real estate agents will say 'I never saw a deal like that.' In my opinion, most of them are not too much help."

Greene says that all his ex-students make at least one deal every six months, and you should be able to close at least one deal every week once you are actively into the business.

How to find your first investment property?

"Simply walk around a neighborhood and get to know the people. Don't be too disappointed too soon. I'll make 20 visits to one person. It takes a lot of persistence. If people in the neighborhood like you, you'll probably get a decent price.

"Next, prepare yourself. Take a basic accounting course and perhaps a real estate course. Of course many of the teachers only go by the books. They have never been out in the real world. Take my tycoon class.

But why would a seller take a no-money-down deal?

"Because what is a no-money-down deal to you, as buyer, is not necessarily that to a seller. Many a seller owns a hundred thousand dollar property with no mortgage on it. If you bought it from him subject to obtaining an 80 percent first loan then he'd get $80,000 from the first financing and you might get a no-money-down deal if that same seller agreed to lend you the additiional $20,000 needed to buy his property.

"The typical real estate broker doesn't like the no-money-down deal," Greene continues, "because he wants a 6 percent or a $6,000 cash commission. And of course that 6 percent has to come from somewhere. So it is much harder to make a no-money-down deal with a broker than if you are dealing directly with the seller.

"Sometimes the seller may be concerned that you might walk away from the property because you have nothing to lose." According to the "real estate tycoon," it might take a little convincing to show the seller that your motive is to keep and improve the property. And of course that should be your motive. You give the seller the security he needs."

And taxes? One of the concepts is to get to the point where you never have to pay any. Financial independence is the objective, one which real estate tycoon William (Bill) Greene calls "true freedom."

REAL ESTATE FEATURE SERVICES

P. O. BOX 6710
SAN FRANCISCO, CALIFORNIA 94101

INTRODUCTION

If you enjoy dull, theory-filled books about real estate, Bill Greene's TWO YEARS FOR FREEDOM isn't for you. When I got my copy, I couldn't put it down until I finished it at 2 A. M. Its pages are filled with Greene's practical, profit-motivated, and realistic philosophy about real estate investing today.

This is a lively how-to-do-it book which explains in simple, easy-to-understand language, how real estate can be your vehicle to accomplish your financial goals. Whether you just want to buy your own home or become a real estate tycoon like Greene, you'll find this is a "fun book" which is deadly serious about what's involved - gaining your financial freedom in today's inflationary world.

Greene's story of how he started in real estate and acquired over $1,000,000 in property equities is outlined on the pages of this book. His style of telling how the reader can accomplish the same thing is unique. By use of funny cartoons and lively writing, Greene explains why real estate ownership is the best (and perhaps the only) way to (1) legally avoid paying income taxes and (2) build your estate and financial security at the same time.

This book is autobiographical. But it shows how the reader can apply the same principles that Greene used to acquire and profit from real estate. Greene's unusual personality comes through to the reader; by the time you finish the book you'll feel you've known him all your life. The important result, however, is the reader is made to feel that if Greene can accomplish real estate success, then anyone can.

While this book is entertaining, its main purpose is to give the reader a blueprint of the steps to acquire and profit from real estate today. Whether you're a real estate novice or a long-time professional property investor, you're going to enjoy and profit from this book.

                                        Robert J. Bruss
                                        Syndicated real estate columnist

CONTENTS

The Buck Starts Here   11
Embryo Tycoon Award (FREE)   20
Acquiring Financial Independence   27
The Stock Market - A Game for Fools   39
The Tycoon Mentality   45
How to Profit From Inflation   51
You & Your Banker   73
Fuzzy Thinking Leftists !   83
Your First Investment Property   87
Depreciation   113
Get Yourself Organized   115
The Tycoon's Credo   143
Finding Super Deals   144
Negotiating Tips & Ploys   169
The Magic Question   173
Buying Property Without Money   181
Nice Guys Finish Last   201
How To Use A Contract of Sale   203
Installment Sales   215
Managing Property & Problem Tenants   217
Pay No Taxes Ever Again, Legally !   230
"1031 Exchanges" -Buying & Selling
    Tax Free   255
Becoming An Insurance Company   285
When The Good Times Are Over   288
New Directions   294
Reading List   297

Start Here!

Getting rich is fun. More fun
than being rich. That's why we'll
start with a game.

Sit down in a comfortable place.
Pretend that someone you know
and love is giving you $200.00

What will you do with it?
How will you enjoy it?
There is no right answer.
Just close your eyes. Take
a while. Do not turn the page
until you have mentally spent
that money.

Drift off...daydream...
Spend that money...

Have fun!

NOTES

Is This What You Did With $ 200 ?

A GOOD DRUNK ?

NEW CAMERA, NEW WATCH
WEEKEND VACATION ?

NIGHT ON THE TOWN?

GET HIGH?

WOULD YOU SPEND IT ON A TERRIFIC CAR AND A TRIP AROUND THE WORLD?

Now suppose that someone gave you
$2,000,000.00

Yes, TWO MILLION DOLLARS.

What would you do with it?

Think about it.

On the next page is the answer most of my students gave...

NOTES

"GIVE IT TO THE BANK TO MANAGE!"

BUT IF A TRUST OFFICER IS SO GOOD AT INVESTING,

HOW COME HE'S A WAGE-SLAVE?

NOTES

PROBABLY YOU WERE A DUMMY!

There are <u>right</u> answers!

All the answers you saw were wrong!

Daydreaming about how you will spend money will

assure that you stay on the

wage-slave treadmill all your life.

If you are not financially independent now, part of

the reason is that you squander seed money --

on trips, presents, consumer goods, trinkets and junk

you don't need.

THE FIRST BARRIER BETWEEN YOU AND A NET WORTH OF

A MILLION OR MORE IS THE "CONSUMER MENTALITY."

In the real world you can get $200 ahead with ease.

But if your first thought was how to "consume" your

first $200 you'll never be worth $20,000, or $2 million.

NEVERMORE THINK OF WHAT YOU ARE GOING TO SPEND MONEY ON!

SMALL SUMS ARE THE SEEDS THAT GROW INTO GREAT FORTUNES.

CONCENTRATE ON:

What useful products can you produce?

What services can you provide?

What needs can you fill?

THESE THOUGHTS WILL HELP MAKE YOU A MILLIONAIRE.

FREE

The
"EMBRYO TYCOON AWARD"

Goes to you if you put the "pretend money" into deals or projects that would triple your investment within the year.

For humorous diploma, suitable for framing, plus a one hour cassette personally narrated by Bill Greene entitled "Think Like A Tycoon," send $10 to cover costs, postage and handling to: Bill Greene's Embryo Tycoon Development Department, Box 408, Mill Valley, California 94941. Allow up to six weeks for delivery. If you don't want the tape, just send a stamped, self-addressed 8½ x 11 envelope and you get the diploma <u>FREE.</u>

If you write me, for any reason or no reason at all, you're on our mailing list for a free newsletter.

Bill Greene

"I DON'T KNOW THE <u>PURPOSE OF LIFE</u>, BUT

I AM SURE THAT GOD DID NOT INTEND FOR

YOU, ME OR ANYONE ELSE TO SPEND OUR

LIVES ON EARTH BEING POOR OR UNHAPPY"

Bill Greene, Hon. D.D.
Pastor,

CHURCH OF FREEDOM,
SAINT OF THE
UNIVERSAL LIFE CHURCH

Become independently wealthy in one to three years

Decide that you sincerely want to be independently wealthy.

Get out in the real world and **talk** to property owners and people you'd like to emulate.

Realize that in order to accumulate capital you must eliminate consumption and taxation. **Dedicate** yourself to the full-time accumulation of untaxed wealth. Use the 5% Rule!

Prepare written plans. Schedule your time. **Establish priorities** and stick to your plans. Don't drift. Don't deviate, regardless of what other people say, do or think.

Establish relationships and maintain credibility with bankers and other financial backers.

Educate yourself. Take a basic accounting course. Take a basic real estate course. Use the '100 House Rule.' Find a "Yuck House" for your first investment.

Put your plan into effect. Establish wealth-building tax shelters with carefully selected, low down payment real estate. Use the Minimax Technique.

Develop a reputation for extreme dependability in financial matters. Follow through on your plans with the determination of a marathon runner. Let the momentum of your achievements and success build until you are well beyond your goals.

Maintain a low profile to keep the IRS, bureaucrats and fuzzy headed leftists out of your hair. No bribes, but remember The Small Gift Rule.

Avoid sucker investments. Remember the Red Ribbon Rule.

Have Complete Confidence in yourself. Recognize that because you are well prepared, well organized and have a plan, you cannot fail to achieve your goals.

Be alert for changes in the economy and profit from them. **Check and revise** your written goals every six months. Don't get stale.

After you are financially independent, ask yourself, "What would I do if I only had six months to live?" Then do it!

Protect yourself by diversification.

Anyone who can read this page can be financially independent in one to three years.

BILL GREENE'S TYCOON CLASS

P.O. Box 408
Mill Valley, Ca. 94941

IF YOU READ THIS BOOK FROM COVER TO COVER,
AND DO EVEN HALF OF WHAT I TELL YOU TO DO,
YOU WILL BE FINANCIALLY INDEPENDENT TWO
YEARS FROM TODAY. POSSIBLY SOONER.

Bill Greene

WARNING!

As this book goes to press, some idiot who attended a free lecture is threatening to sue me. He quit his job to become an overnight real estate tycoon after hearing me on the radio. Without job, money, credit (and I might add, brains) no one has been willing to sell him his first property. In my Tycoon Class and here I say, DON'T GIVE UP A REGULAR JOB OR INCOME UNTIL YOUR REAL ESTATE EMPIRE HAS GROWN TO SUFFICIENT SIZE TO SUPPLY THE CASH FLOW YOU NEED TO LIVE ON AND SUPPORT YOUR FAMILY. YOUR OUTSIDE INCOME PROVIDES STABILITY AND BORROWING POWER NEEDED AT THE EARLY STAGES.

All of the opinions given here and in my talks are based upon my personal experiences and research. When applied with common sense, I believe many of my ideas will be very helpful. BUT THE READER MUST NECESSARILY PROCEED AT HIS OWN RISK. Opinions expressed herein are often unconventional and controversial. It is recommended that BEFORE MAKING ANY DEALS OR CONTRACTS INVOLVING LEGAL OR TAX CONSEQUENCES, PROFESSIONAL ADVICE AND COUNSEL BE OBTAINED. Don't sue me if they throw you out of the casino.

Sincerely,
Bill Greene

PROCEED IN THE GAME OF LIFE AT YOUR OWN RISK.
IF YOU LOSE YOUR CHIPS, DON'T EXPECT
TO SUE BILL GREENE

NOTES

Acquiring Financial Independence

What is financial independence? To me it's the wonderful feeling of getting up in the morning without having to go to a job I hate. It's living <u>where</u> I want to live - not where I can afford. It's living <u>with</u> people I love -- not someone I'm stuck with because they are supporting me. Financial independence is never worrying about rent money, grocery money, or doctor bills. It's going out and having steak or lobster once in a while. It's having basic needs and even a few luxuries, without being a wage-slave or doing prostitute work. It is in a word, FREEDOM!

Some would equate financial independence with servants, a summer home in Monte Carlo, a Rolls Royce. But to me that is <u>show</u> not FREEDOM. Financial independence WILL buy freedom from a boring job. It will buy time to pursue your own interests: freedom to travel, to read, to write, to create, to play or do your life work whatever it may be. Not necessary to be fashionable, chic, or Jet Set. A mansion, poodles, servants and Rolls Royce only tie you down. I know. I've tried that life style.

The <u>Political</u> freedom we have (to a limited extent) is nice. It's wonderful to be able to write your congressman. You can even climb on a soap-box and call the president names. You can complain. I wouldn't want to take away that sort of freedom. But what value is freedom to exercise your vocal chords or pen if you are stuck in a daily inescapable rut of earning a subsistence living. The only worthwhile freedom we, as individuals, can hope to achieve in America is FINANCIAL INDEPENDENCE.

I am going to tell you how to get this freedom in less than three years. It will take all your spare time and energy. I will show you how to use your energies to effectively accumulate wealth. I'll show you how to work for maximum results. With a hell of a lot of effort you can make your first good deal. And one good deal can make you thirty thousand bucks. In a few months you may be able to do that once or twice a week. If you are willing to work very hard you could be a millionaire in a year. Using my methods you should be able to make your million in less than three years.

After you have your first million, then you've got freedom. It won't be exactly what you imagined, because a million dollars isn't what it used to be. A millionaire today is about the same as being worth $100,000 after World War Two. But a million still spells financial freedom for a small family.

With a million invested conservatively to yield 7% or $70,000 per year, there may be only about $20,000 spending money left after federal and state income taxes. Rent of $1,000 per month hardly buys the sort of apartment that one associates with millionaire status, and rent alone can take more than half a millionaire's income. About $8,000 per year is left for food, entertainment, medical bills and supporting the family. Since a first class maid or butler commands a salary of $20,000 per year, obviously there are going to be no servants, Rolls Royces or summer homes in Monaco even if you have a million in the bank.

But if you've got a million dollars, you do have freedom. You don't need an expensive apartment and you don't need to put on a show for anyone else. But you can afford to live where you want. Not regally perhaps, but comfortably. I think I will convince you, if you are not already convinced, that buying real estate -- primarily investment (or rental) property, is a policy of MINIMUM RISK, MAXIMUM RETURN. It's the best thing you can do with your time and SMALL AMOUNTS of money. It can make you a million dollars in less than three years. You can never hope to save anywhere near a million (in today's dollars) working for someone else.

Most of my disciples start out being what I call wage slaves. They work at a 9 to 5 job. If you are a wage slave maybe you don't understand why it seems impossible to save and harder and harder to get by on what you earn.

THE WAGE-SLAVE MENTALITY

Each year, though you MAY work harder, and even though you get decent raises, your standard of living seems to be going down. FACT IS, it doesn't only seem that way. It's true. THE AMERICAN STANDARD OF LIVING IS DROPPING! At the same time the real standard of living in places like inflation free Switzerland is going up drastically. Here in America, after 50 years of having the highest per capita income in the world, we have dropped to a miserable 6th place. By the time you read this even the average Chinese Communist may be able to afford more goods and services than you can! Right now Germany, Switzerland, Japan and even Sweden, Denmark and Norway's workers do better than Americans. Why? Our inflation-eroded highly taxed dollar simply buys less and less good things than it used to.

Let's assume you are lucky enough to make $20,000 a year. The tax bite on $20,000 at a 34% effective tax rate for single tax-payer is about $6,800. That leaves you with $13,200 to spend. Now, let's assume in the following year you don't get a raise. You still make $20,000 a year but inflation has pushed up prices of normal things you buy at a minimum of 10% a year. I'm talking about rent, coffee, sugar, bread and just about everything else. Since prices are going up a minimum of 10%, in year 2 you end up with the same $13,200 but the purchasing power of the $13,200 WITH a 10% inflation rate leaves you with only about $11,880 in purchasing power. So, if you made $20,000 last year you had roughly $13,000 in purchasing power. But if you made the same amount of money this year, your purchasing power went down to below $12,000. This little mathematical exercise explains why your real standard of living IS dropping drastically every year.

Now, suppose for a second example you are lucky enough to have received a cost of living 10% raise. Next year, your salary is $22,000. But guess what? The government raises your tax bracket from 34% to 36%. Remember, every time you get a raise your tax bracket gets a little higher. So, therefore, when you deduct the new higher taxes from your $22,000 salary your new tax is about $7,920 leaving you with a net of around $14,000. Giving effect to the 10% inflation you take off $1,408 to arrive at your real purchasing power which is a net of $12,680.

Remember, in year 1 you earned $20,000 and your net purchasing power after taxes was $13,000. But with a $2,000 raise in year 2, your purchasing power is down to $12,000. So you have taken a loss of over

$500 in your purchasing power even with a $2,000 wage increase.

Why is that? Because your tax bracket went up at the same time the dollar went down in value. And that doesn't even include the extra 10% bite that's going to be taken out of your wages for new social security taxes. Nor do we consider state and local taxes that have been rising at an average rate of 15% per year.

In view of this situation, many people want to find a scapegoat. Some say (with a degree of accuracy) it's the "politicians" that are just taxing us to death. Therefore, the answer of some irate citizens is to become a Tax Resister. Break the law! Don't pay any taxes! Go to jail. I don't like that "solution" because if you go to jail, the government will just raise the taxes of the rest of us to keep you there.

Some other would say (also with accuracy) America has a terrible social-istic government and what we ought to do is immigrate to a real free, good country like Switzerland where they don't have such a big bad government and such terrible inflation. Well, I'm an American, you're an American and unfortunately we are stuck here because "real good countries" like Switzer-land in general don't want us. We have to make the best of a bad situation right here.

From my point of view, the best thing an American can do is to invest in well selected, income producing real estate. Done right a real estate invest-ment program will make you a millionaire in a few years. With real estate, the government's inflationary and unfair tax policies can actually help you -- probably because a lot of congressmen and senators own real estate. Since politicians seldom pay any taxes, partly because of their real estate holdings, they haven't gotten around to taxing real estate incomes. It would hurt most politicians too much.

If real estate is so good and so sure fire, why isn't everyone into it? Virtually all rich Americans are into it. But what about the non-rich? Let's look at how the great unwashed masses spend their time and view their future.

Most people, and that may be you, have a 9 to 5 job. You MAY feel pretty secure while you are in the job. It's not too bad a job. And after a day at the salt mines, sitting down to dinner and watching TV, is about all you have energy for. The weekend with the spouse (and more TV?) goes by so fast you don't have time to think about any financial plan, much less have time to do anything constructive. Besides, the average Joe feels reasonably secure in his RUT of a wage slave job. He feels secure for up to 20 or 30 years. Right until the day the pink slip comes and he's fired, he feels secure. It's a false security: The vast majority of retired or laid off older workers are destitute.

It's not uncommon to see people fired after 30 years. And when they look into the pension plan that was going to take care of them in their old age, there is a loop hole: If fired before retired, they don't get anything. So, don't you be mislead into feeling that there is any security in a job working for someone else. You can be laid off at any time, unless you're the one who owns the company. And as far as pensions and Social Security are concerned, I'd call most people's retirement plan, SOCIAL INSECURITY.

Though government and your pension fund takes more and more out of your income, they give you back less and less. You get back inflation eroded dollars when it comes time to retire. Social Security allowances or pensions won't give you enough to live on with any style or even dignity. But if you wait until you're 65 to retire, statistically, you'll be dead within two years anyway. In my view two years of doddering retirement when you're too old to enjoy many things is no decent reward for forty-five years of work.

Let's suppose that you want to provide for your "golden years." You hope to live in a reasonably comfortable manner. The most common choice is a savings account. Banks and Savings and Loan Associations are now paying about 6 - 8% interest. This is only 2 - 4% after taxes. But we're running at a 10% annual inflation figure. That simply means that with the value of the dollar going down 10% a year you lose 6% per year or more on money left in savings accounts.

Many economists predict that we will be faced with triple the present rate of inflation in the next few years. Well, I don't have a perfect crystal ball for predicting the future. I couldn't give you a definite figure but can observe the inflation rate going up at an ever increasing rate. I would guess that 10 to 15% per year inflation in the next few years is the MINIMUM we can look forward to. Keeping money in dollars has to be nothing less than economic imbecility.

WHAT THINGS MAY COST	1962	1977	Compound Annual Rate of Increase 1962-77	6% What it would cost assuming same rate of increase as '62-'77 1987	1997	Assume 10% Rate of Increase 1987	1997
One-Family Home	$17,600	$54,400	7.8*	$115,290	$244,327	$141,097	$365,971
35-Foot Cabin Cruiser	21,500	49,900	5.5	85,234	145,593	129,426	335,697
Annual College Costs-Harvard	2,650	7,060	6.8	13,631	26,316	18,311	47,495
Chevrolet Impala-4-door	2,529	4,887	4.5	7,590	11,786	12,675	32,877
Annual Social Security Deduction	150	965	13.2	3,334	11,520	4,257**	18,779**
Two-Week London Vacation	893	990*	0.7	1,061*	1,138*	- -	- -
Auto Insurance Premium	87	245	7.1	486	966	635	1,648
Man's Wool Suit	130	215	3.4	300	420	558	1,446
Monthly Electric Bill	8	26	8.2	57	126	67	175
Prime-Rib Dinner	4.65	9.75	5.1	16.03	26.36	25	66
Haircut	1.00	3.00	7.6	6.24	12.98	7.78	20.18
Paperback Novel	.95	2.25	5.9	3.99	7.08	5.84	15.14
Hamburger	.60	1.20	4.7	1.90	3.01	3.11	8.07
Pizza (Slice)	.15	.55	9.0	1.30	3.08	1.43	3.70
Gasoline Per Gallon	.31	.64	5.0	1.04	1.70	1.66	4.31
Hershey Bar	.05	.20	9.7	.50	1.27	.52	1.35
Daily Newspaper - N.Y. Times	.05	.20	9.7	.50	1.27	.52	1.35
First-Class Postage Stamp	.04	.13	8.2	.29	.63	.34	.87

*Assumes Laker Airways low air fare.
**Assume 16% increase

Sources: Bureau of the Census, Chris-Craft, Harvard University, General
Motors, State Farm Insurance, Hart Schaffner & Marx, Edison
Electric Institute, Howard Johnson.

WHAT YOU MAY EARN	1962	1977	Compound Annual Rate of Increase 1962-1977	What you would earn assuming same rate of increase as '62-'77 1987	1997
Corporate Attorney					
Gross Earnings	$16,440	$38,828	5.9%	$68,881	$122,196
Aftertax Earnings*	12,872	27,459	5.2	40,153	63,851
Constant $ - 1977	25,829	27,459	0.4	22,634	20,289
Aftertax Earnings as percent of Gross	78	71		58	52
Production Worker					
Gross Earnings	5,021	11,740	5.8	20,631	36,255
Aftertax Earnings	4,420	10,137	5.7	16,012	24,787
Constant $ - 1977	8,869	10,137	0.9	9,112	8,027
Aftertax Earnings as percent of Gross	88	86		78	68

*Assumptions: Married taxpayer joint return, two dependent children, standard deduction, no change in 1977 tax
structure for subsequent years; gross earnings less net tax liability, state and local income taxes (assuming the
same proportion of state and local income taxes to federal income taxes); Social Security tax for 1987 estimated
from pending legislation.

INFLATION CHEWS UP YOUR LUNCH MONEY

Another "investment" mistake is putting money in stock. Did you realize that since 1967, about ten years ago, the quoted value of the average stock is down around 20%? Many individual stocks are down 70%. Now this 20-70% decline is not adjusted for inflation. We are talking about dollar figures. If you adjust for inflation, the stock market performance has been abysmal! Virtually every stock is down 50% with many down over 95% in real or constant dollars. Next is insurance. Buying insurance is the absolute worst thing you can do with your money.

Insurance gives you about a 2% after tax return on the "investment" feature. That translates into a 8% annual capital loss after inflation. So, unless you need some term insurance to take care of youngsters who are unable to support themselves in case you die in the first year of your investment program, stay away from insurance entirely. If you need insurance to provide for dependents, stick with term life insurance. This has no "investment" feature but it will pay back substantial sums if you die unexpectedly at an early age.

Then there are "tax shelter" syndicates. These are package investment deals that stockbrokers, real estate brokers and promoters put out for the unwary, wrapped in a red ribbon: Complete with printed brochure and smooth salesmen. In general, they stink! My own personal survey of real estate syndicates and other tax shelter deals indicates that only 1 or 2% of those deals ever return the investment, much less any profits.

There are, of course, a few worthwhile promoters and syndicators who have good long term records. Almost everything they touch makes 10 to 30% a year for their investors. But an ordinary real estate deal that you can make yourself should return over 300% a year tax free on your investment. The best syndicators won't be advertising or going to look for you with a smooth sales pitch. They won't be advertising because they have their own following and don't need or want your business. There is a lot of money around, but few good Red Ribbon deals. And only if you know where to find them. You don't. You can only buy turkeys.

With everything else so bad, what has done very well for the investor almost uninterruptedly from 1776 to 1977? I'll tell you what. Homes and moderate to low rent income property. Even during the most inflationary times in Germany, when money was worthless, and rent controls went into effect, real estate worked out well for people who owned a home they turned into a rooming house. Equally good was a two or three unit, low-rent apartment building.

Suppose you had a hundred thousand dollars ten years ago. Instead of investing in the stock market or a savings account to lose most of your capital you might have bought four ordinary three bedroom, two bath homes in any desireable major city of California. In those days a nice above average tract house cost $25,000. Now, 10 years later, that same home will be worth a MINIMUM of $100,000. You could have bought four homes then for $100,000 but today you could only get one. The future will probably produce similar or greater price increases.

But what if we have a depression? In the worst depression the United States ever had, 1929 to 1935, this is what happened to real estate:

In those days, when a low rent apartment went for $10 a month, those low rents went up from $10 to $14 per month. Why? Because people moved out of their expensive $40 apartments and doubled up in the cheaper places. So low rent housing in fact did very well as an investment during the last depression

Now of course some people in those days, like today, bought expensive high rent properties with negative cash flows. They went bankrupt. Some people do lose money in real estate. I will talk at length about the "No Money Down Deal". It should be obvious that if you put little or no money of your own into a real estate deal, there isn't much to lose. Some uninformed people would say that if you have big mortgage debts and you owe money to a lot of people, then those lenders can come after your other assets if you default.

In California, and many Western States that just isn't true. There is no personal liability on purchase money mortgages on one to four units.[1] If a real estate deal goes sour, the buyer can just walk away from it and tell the lender to take the property. That's all they get. They can't come after you for the money. So, in a "No Money Down Deal" which I'll show you how to do, there's absolutely no downside risk.

For all practical purposes there is no personal liability on any real estate loan in California because a lender has two choices:

1 See C.C.P. 580b and related California statutes.

a. In the event of default he can take back or sell the property in 110 days at a trustee's sale, but only if he lets the debtor off the personal liability hook.

b. If a lender wants to enforce personal liability he must go thru a complex, expensive and impractical <u>JUDICIAL</u> <u>FORECLOSURE</u>. There the deadbeat debtor must be left in possession for a year, and then for another year the deadbeat can still <u>redeem</u> the property for the amount of the loan balance.

Let me show you how to buy your first investment property. Every journey starts with a first step. But before you take your first steps to financial independence, let us look at one detour you <u>shouldn't</u> take: The Stock Market.

NOTES

THE STOCK MARKET

A GAME for fools

Most people feel that the stock market is a bad bet just because historically, over the past ten years, it has been so lousy. Money put into an average portfolio of stocks ten years ago is worth slightly less than if it had been kept in cash. That means that (after adjusting for inflation) an average investor who put $10,000 into reasonably good stocks ten years ago has purchasing power of about 40% to 60% of what he started out with. But to make a judgment about the future ONLY from looking at the past can be a shallow and misleading analysis. When "most people" feel that a particular investment is good and shows great promise, that is usually the signal for the astute -- for the Tycoons -- to sell out. But when everyone is depressed and articles in the media bear pessimistic titles like the one above, the smart money can move in and pick up bargains.

With that said, you might expect me to reverse the thought of the title and tell you that NOW, while the stock market is still depressed, is the time to plunge. I can't do that. At almost any price level the stock market as an investment is a worse bet than putting your money "on the line" in a gambling casino. My thoughts may be easier to understand if we compare a $10,000 cash investment in stocks with a similar investment in real estate.

Let's assume that you buy 1,000 shares of Growth, Inc., a company that in its way, is one of the best prospects in the market. Its sales and earnings growth are far better than the national average. Its particular business prospects are good, and best of all the price of the stock is depressed. On todays' market it may be one-third or more below what it was selling for ten years ago. We can assume that just as you would go out of your way to find a really good four unit apartment building, you did the research necessary to find an extra-ordinary growth stock. And we will further assume that the income, market value and all other aspects of your stock investment perform at least as well as an assumed real estate investment of the same dollar amount.

All other things being equal, the stock in our theoretical example should perform exactly as well as the real estate investment. Naturally, in a stock you don't have the element of control that has made real estate so profitable for diligent property owners. But we won't consider that. We will assume that the strangers running the corporation are just as competent as you would be yourself. It quickly becomes clear from the comparisons below that the TAX POLICIES of Federal and State government have made the stock market a "no-win" investment. And it is those policies combined with the effects of over-regulation, government inspired inflation, and labor problems that make investment in securities strictly a fool's game.

REAL ESTATE INVESTMENT	STOCK MARKET INVESTMENT
Earns $1,000 [rents less expenses]. Investor keeps $1,000, totally tax sheltered.	Earns $1,000 in net profits. Average Corporate tax: (State and Federal) $600. Maximum possible dividend to a typical professional person is taxed as Unearned Income at 85% combined State and Federal rate or a tax of $340
NET CASH AVAILABLE TO THE INVESTOR	NET CASH TO THE INVESTOR
$1,000	$60

THE ABOVE ILLUSTRATES THAT THE NET CASH RETURN TO THE INVESTOR IN THE STOCK MARKET IS ONLY 6% OF THE AMOUNT RETURNED TO THE REAL ESTATE INVESTOR IN A SIMILAR INVESTMENT.

IT REQUIRES OVER 14 TIMES AS MUCH MONEY INVESTED IN THE STOCK MARKET TO PRODUCE THE SAME RETURN AS AVAILABLE FROM REAL ESTATE!

In view of the foregoing, it is extremely unlikely that 100 shares of Growth, Inc. will ever go up in value at all -- because who would want to invest in a deal that is 14 times worse than what you can get elsewhere.

But for the sake of this example, let's assume that a few years later the market price or value of both the stock and the real estate have exactly doubled.

REAL ESTATE
Assume investment in "average" four-plex with "average" leaverage.

STOCK
Assume investment in stock with maximum permitted leverage during "average" period.

Cost $100,000
Loan   90,000
_____
    $ 10,000 Equity or
    Starting Investment

Cost $20,000
Loan   10,000
_____
    $10,000 Equity or
    Starting Investment

We assume that ten years later, both investments appreciated 100% in dollars with no adjustment for inflation.

REAL ESTATE

Selling Price: $200,000
    Less Loan   90,000
    _____
        $110.000 Profit
            Before
            Taxes

STOCK

Selling Price: $40,000
    Less Loan   10,000
    _____
        $30,000 Profit
            Before
            Taxes

The above illustrates that because of tradition and legally imposed restrictions on the amount of money that can be borrowed, much higher leverage is available in real estate than for stock market investments. Although not illustrated on the chart, the interest rates for real estate loans tend to be lower than for stock market margin loans.

TAXES ON REAL ESTATE PROFITS ASSUMING RE-INVESTMENT IN REAL ESTATE

Profit $110,000
Taxes   -0-
_____
    $110,000 Profit

TAXES ON STOCK MARKET PROFITS ASSUMING RE-INVESTMENT IN STOCKS

Profit $30,000
Taxes at highest combined California and Federal rates, approximately 45%
NET: $16,500 Profit

The preceding illustrates that with a profitable investment, it would apparently take ten times the initial cash investment to produce the same after-tax capital gain available in real estate, or looked at another way, a stock would have to increase in value ten times the amount that a building would have to go up to yield the same net return after taxes.

To visualize something overlooked by analysts, let's assume that the stock of Growth, Inc. <u>did</u> go up ten times as much as comparable real estate.

Cost	$ 20,000	
Selling Price	$200,000	or 100% per year increase for ten years
Less Loan	$ 20,000	
Profit pre-tax	$180,000	
	84,000	less 45% Cap Gains Tax
	$ 96,000	Net After Tax (Cash)

Because of the tax bite, it is apparent that to equal the net-after-tax performance of real estate, a stock market investment must do <u>considerably better</u> than 1,000% of what the real estate does in order to yield the same after tax return.

What general rule could be a guide to when real estate prices have gone so high, and stock market prices have gone so low that switching from real estate into stocks would be a good bet?

Due to the fact that real estate investors WILL have to pay capital gains taxes on the sale of real estate in order to get into stocks, the strategy indicated would seem to be this:

1. No matter how great the disparity, NEVER sell real estate to purchase stocks - rather <u>borrow</u> against the real estate to invest in stocks.
2. The signal to begin shifting assets from real estate cash into stocks will come only when securities can be purchased for approximately 1/20th of the value of real estate earnings. In down to Earth terms, if a property, after paying all expenses exclusive of loan amortization yields $1,000 per year, you would be wiser to invest in a corporation owning similar property only if it were paying a dividend of $20,000 per year.

On a pure numbers investment basis, one would shift from real estate into stocks if there was only a ratio of $1 to $14, on pre tax earnings, but the greater regulation of companies, the greater possibilities of lawsuits, labor disputes, higher business taxes, and the general outlook for private enterprises causes me to look at stock only if it earns twenty times better than real estate.

These recommendations apply only if real estate retains its current favored status being both relatively unregulated and effectively tax exempt. If rent controls or tinkering with the existing tax incentives was a possibility, I would borrow heavily against real estate, invest in hard assets like gold or art works and make plans to abandon properties. This was the only path open to thousands of investment property owners in New York City or London when rent controls inflicted terminal cancer on the real estate markets there.

NOTES

THE TYCOON MENTALITY

If you sincerely want to become a Tycoon, you must THINK LIKE A TYCOON. You can think like a Tycoon by reading this chapter very carefully. Though I will be talking mainly about real estate, the principles covered here apply to all forms of managing your money. Living a good life or being exceptionally successful in business requires more than a can of beer, a T.V. set, and thou.

TYCOON is a Japanese word meaning TY - great, and COON - shogun, a military leader. A Tycoon is someone with ambition and drive who has placed himself in a position of importance. In the case of a great general like Patton, or the great boxer Muhammed Ali -- or anyone great, one characteristic is universal:

GREAT PEOPLE THOROUGHLY ENJOY WHAT THEY DO.
TO BE GREAT AT WHAT YOU DO,
YOU MUST BELIEVE THAT WHAT YOU DO IS GREAT FUN.

An episode of the 'Peanuts' cartoon strip once showed Charlie Brown playing with half a yo-yo. It was broken. But he was having a good time dangling it, bouncing it up and down the wall, and playing 'fetch' with his dog Snoopy. Suddenly Charlie Brown's girlfriend Lucy comes along: "You stupid dummy," she says, "you can't have a good time with half a yo-yo. Everybody knows that." Poor, dejected Charlie Brown throws his toy on the ground. "I'm sorry," replies the little boy. "I didn't know I could not enjoy myself with a broken yo-yo."

The story has a moral for prospective Tycoons. Fuzzy thinking leftists and other depressing types like Lucy have convinced many people that making money these days is abnormal -- or at best, dull. They would like to make us capitalists feel guilty for becoming rich and - shudder - actually having fun making it.

Ignore these people. Fuzzy thinking leftists fail to realize that capitalists don't just rake in money and count it -- bank tellers do that. A Tycoon is involved in something creative and beautiful: He (or she) must invariably bring forth upon the world a product or service that people want. A 'something' that people willingly part with their earnings or savings for. He's not ashamed to take their money because (unlike forcibly extracted tax money - which pays for dubious social services or more tax collectors that nobody wants), a capitalist exists for The People. He works for The People. He serves them only so long as his products or services meet their needs. A Tycoon needs The People as much as they need him. However, being creative -- like an artist, musician, or new mother, a Tycoon has more fun at living than the wage-slave at his routine job. Tycoons enjoy doing what they can be Great at -- providing an abundance of goods and services that people want and can afford. Every Tycoon has an invisible directive flashing like a neon sign in his brain:

FIND A NEED AND FILL IT

FIND A NEED AND FILL IT

FIND A NEED AND FILL IT

A Tycoon doesn't count his money every day to measure his success. Dollars are just evidence of votes from the previous day, votes of confidence in the particular goods or services that the Tycoon is providing. But a Tycoon gets his confidence from within himself, not through these dollar votes. Any businessman who wants to keep on being successful, however, must continue to deliver needed goods and services, or the people will vote their dollars for a new Tycoon.

Some individuals, of course, can never become Tycoons. That's because they thwart themselves right from the beginning. They make excuses: "I'm not smart enough. I don't have enough money to start. I have no business sense." These are all cop-outs. Anyone, including you, can become a Tycoon with the right attitude. If you think you're dumb -- relax. Most Tycoons have average IQ's. The straight-A students are too busy getting PhD's and looking for teaching jobs to make it in business. You can begin with little or no money, and become a multi-millionaire. Most of today's industrialists were poor a few years ago. So not having any money, the second excuse, doesn't wash either. As for having no business sense -- well, you're reading this book. That's pretty sensible. Whatever acumen you lacked before today, you'll have by tomorrow.

Other individuals wait until they are ALREADY Tycoons before they thwart themselves. All people should learn from their own mistakes, but you can more cheaply benefit from other people's mistakes. Look at what some successful Tycoons who failed have in common: Businessmen who have made it big once and then go downhill have frequently overexpanded. They got careless and didn't attend to emergencies or details. They didn't have time anymore. In contrast, a successful Tycoon leaves nothing to chance. He makes time to watch over his investments or hires competent help to do it for him. It's much easier to be extremely successful on a small scale when you're starting out in familiar territory, than it is when you have the riches of a Howard Hughes or a J. Paul Getty. Does that surprise you? Allow me to illustrate: Once a real estate deal was proposed to me in Reno, Nevada. The big selling point was that one of the richest men in the world, J. Paul Getty, (who made his fortune in oil) had taken 25% interest in it. Therefore (I was told) I should be willing to take

47

10% (ten 'points' in Tycoon talk), because Getty was pretty smart and wouldn't have had a 25% interest in a deal if it wasn't any good. The deal went sour shortly after that. I should have known it would! Now when I hear that <u>extremely</u> rich people have an interest in a project, I run the other way.

That sort of deal usually is a tax shelter that won't make money for anyone but the promoters. Super-rich people seldom have time to investigate new ventures; they are too busy keeping what they have to be effective in fields outside their immediate area of expertise. I am sure that if J. Paul Getty had a good oil deal that he investigated and put together personally, he would have taken all of it for himself and not sold any points to outside investors. But the fact that Getty, a super-rich Texas oilman, living in London, was investing in a Nevada real estate deal, probably meant that he relied on someone else's judgement. That 'someone else' would not have sought me out as an investor if it was a super deal.

Tycoons who have been very successful <u>often</u> make bad investments. They don't attend to the details of investigating a situation as thoroughly as they would have done when they were starting out. The best deals are the deals that you go out and find yourself. Not prepackaged 'no work, no worry deals' all wrapped up with a Red Ribbon. Where all you do is write a check, that Red Ribbon will only tie you in financial knots.

> THE RED RIBBON RULE:
> If a deal sounds to good to be true,
> it <u>is</u> too good to be true!

Another common characteristic of a Tycoon destined to go downhill is he feels 'too important' to attend to humble work. He passes by one of his properties, for example. In the old days he would have taken time to pick up junk spilled by the trash collectors and put it in proper cans. At the very least he'd have given the janitor or the tenants a gentle reminder to clean up their act. But now, looking at the mess, he doesn't notice. He's too busy whizzing off to negotiate a pie-in-the-sky deal. A lack of pride in ownership means the start of decline -- the beginning of the end. When you're no longer concerned with detail (and willing to see to it yourself), you're heading for trouble. If an owner doesn't care anymore, his business goes to pot.

Another characteristic of ageing Tycoons is a sudden fear of competition. When new at the game, competition was a challenge. The embryo Tycoon stole his competitors' best ideas and avoided their mistakes. Determined to beat the competition one way or another, the upstart had to come up with innovative methods. He worked at it all day and Christmas too. However, once on top, some Tycoons start to worry about all the young upstarts moving into 'their' backyards -- as if it was an exclusive preserve. In the case of manufacturers it is 'cheap foreign goods! "Why," they worry, "are those Sayonara Sleeping pills becoming more popular than my Yankee Doodle Doze?"

Instead of trying to produce a new or better product, some old Tycoons retreat into deep leather chairs at the Union League Club. Old, has-been Tycoons never die, they just become ineffectual aristocrats. At worst, a formerly successful Tycoon these days becomes a 'gold bug'. A 'gold bug' is someone who buries or stashes most of his assets in a Swiss Bank in gold. Of course in a nation run by irresponsible politicians who print and spend money like toilet paper, building personal gold reserves, to a reasonable level, is only prudent. But when you start concentrating on reducing the size of your business operations and finding ways of becoming 100% liquid, then you can produce no products, no progress, and no profits. The entire French Nation nearly collapsed economically in the pre-De Gaulle era because a large number of French people, (perhaps for good reasons) chose to take their wealth, convert it into gold coins and bury them in their gardens. Buried gold coins (while providing some degree of safety and security in times of political turmoil or revolution), will not make you rich. A business operation is like a vine. Once it stops growing, it dies.

What are characteristics which help a Tycoon succeed? A Tycoon on the way up is always able to motivate his staff, partners and the people who work with him. When he is big, an enthusiastic, loyal staff will be needed more than ever. But sometimes a Tycoon forgets his staff. Don't forget, when you become valuable in terms of dollars, your staff becomes equally so in terms of support. Some employees respond best to praise and titles. Others, to money. Imaginative gifts or bonuses can score you more points than money! How about a round-trip ticket to Hawaii for your secretary or property manager? The successful Tycoon always keeps thinking of ways to put a smile on the faces of his Team.

Some Tycoons believe that inspiring fear in their associates is an effective method of getting them to work. I strongly disagree. Fear is only good for incompetents, because only incompetents are afraid of getting fired. If an employee or business associate is good enough, he can always find work with the Tycoon down the road. Thus, if you can't make the work situation pleasant for those who contribute to it, something is wrong. You can never get the best out of employees through fear. Remember: Motivation is better accomplished by the carrot than the stick.

On the home front, the same rule applies. Keep the peace. Give recognition and daily compliments to the people around you - your children, your spouse, your friends. Make the people you know feel good about themselves. If they feel good about themselves, they'll work harder and feel better about you. If you're making a compliment, don't make the mistake of taking it back. I've heard people say things like "Gee, you look younger. Are you dyeing your hair?" Say it and feel it. If you personally get a compliment, don't argue. Accept it graciously; a simple "Thank you" will do. So make the people in your family and organization feel secure. If you feel it, say "I love you." Give praise and recognition generously! Tell them, "I really like being with you." Or, "I like working with you." Give the reasons. Your own life will be better if those you live and work with know that you like them. Tell them often. If you have to be critical, try to be positive in your criticism. When the toast is served burned to a crisp, say, "I really enjoyed the breakfast, honey, but next time around could you set the toaster a bit lighter." For business associates just substitute different words. Try it - it works!

HOW TO PROFIT FROM INFLATION

These are inflationary times, and the promise of having a million dollars twenty or thirty years from now should not dazzle you. It should not even be one of your goals, since you don't know exactly what a million dollars will be worth in terms of buying power in twenty or thirty years. If the present rates of inflation continue, by the year 2010, a million dollars will probably be one year's salary for a street-sweeper (the ones in San Francisco get $18,500 already!) Thus you don't really want Money. You want Things. Preferably things to own or to control that can be rented out which will earn money while you own them. And preferably things that will not wear out, break up, or fall down too fast. In inflationary times it isn't money but wealth in other forms you want to accumulate. Anyone who keeps their money in money is getting poorer -- at any interest rate they can hope to earn.

Therefore, you want plenty of debt. You want to borrow money to acquire things and also to acquire education in developing saleable skills. The fees and commissions earned as a doctor, lawyer or plumber in your ordinary job and the rents received from your property should keep pace with inflation until the time comes when you're rich enough not to need an ordinary job. In the meantime, the money debts you have accumulated can be paid off with ever more worthless dollars. Let me explain more about debt.

Suppose you borrowed 100,000 eggs to buy an apartment building this year. With a typical loan you have thirty years to pay those eggs back. It's easy to see why real estate is such a good investment. You can estimate that thirty years hence the property may be worth a million eggs, but the debt used to finance the property will have been paid back with 20,000 eggs instead of the 100,000 eggs originally borrowed. Get the point? Borrow dollars today to buy an asset today. You pay back a lot less than you borrow in terms of real money.

Due to inflation, the quoted dollar value of all property will increase dramatically, yet you pay back debts with cheaper and cheaper dollars. With each passing year, all other things being equal, the debt you owe becomes less and less burdensome, while the property you bought becomes more and more valuable. Obviously the less money you put down to make a deal and the greater portion of the price borrowed, the more deals you will be able to make. The more buys you make, the wealthier you become. The nitty-gritty of my technique 'how to buy property for little or no money down' is fully covered in the other chapters of this book.

So, in these inflationary times, a Tycoon must acquire as much property and as much debt as possible. Needless to say, there will be occasional disappointments. How can you deal with them effectively? If in real estate, you are trying to buy property, and a deal you've been negotiating falls through, there is a game or mental trick that can be played on yourself, to feel better. Say this: "Had the deal closed it would have made me at least $20,000. But if ten of my no-money-down deals are rejected, I know that at least one out of twenty deals I negotiate for will eventually work out. Thus, every failure, every deal that falls through, amounts to a $1000 experience. And that's pretty good going for one morning's work." If you can think positively about what others might consider failures, the next failed deal will only encourage you to get on with it. Not dwelling on what you did wrong, but thinking about what you did right will soon have you scanning the classified ads again. There's an old Scottish proverb: "No man ever died from overwork." But people do die and certainly get sick from emotional problems such as anxiety, or worry. These lead to ulcers and other diseases. So one of the best habits a Tycoon can develop is to laugh at his problems. Many times things will go wrong, but if you can manage to grow a funny bone, your body will never develop ulcers or high blood pressure. Take life easy. Remember, money should be thought of as gambling chips -- and life only as a game.

Look back at the big tragedies of your pre-teenage life. Not winning the pitcher's position in the Little League - it was so important then. But does it matter now? You can laugh about it. When you were a teenager and got stood up by the Prom Queen, or were rejected as a Hamburger High cheerleader, you were miserable, right? But now it's funny. If you can cultivate the ability to laugh at your predicaments at the time they occur, you will be way ahead of other people who spend their time worrying, dwelling on their failures and feeling sorry for themselves.

Laugh a lot. Don't take yourself or your money too seriously!

My father once knew an Italian gent name Joe Garibaldi. Joe had come
to the States as an orphan, and worked at a Chicago newsstand when he was
only eleven years old. In twenty years time that first stand had grown into
a chain of newsstands. Joe, finding himself wealthy and lusty at age thirty-
one, sent for a mail-order bride from his home town. She duly arrived and
enjoyed living in America, being the wealthiest lady in her immigrant neighborhood. By 1929, Joe Garibaldi, like all other newspaper dealers, tailors,
and barbers of the era, fancied himself an expert in the stock market. He
took the profits from his newspaper stands and everything else that he could
borrow, and invested in stocks.

We all know what happened in 1929. Joe Garibaldi went through the
wringer, and by 1931 was back selling newspapers at good old newsstand
number one. He took his losses like a Tycoon, realizing that it would only be
a matter of time before he could repeat the wealth-building process and recoup
his fortune. Yet, all around him people were jumping out of windows. They
didn't realize they should have thought of money only as gaming 'chips'. If
they lost their chips, the game wasn't over. Joe Garibaldi knew how to
Think Like A Tycoon. To him, losing a hand meant accumulating more chips
by selling papers again. He'd find another game to play someday. Not poor
Mrs. Garibaldi. Joe's bride was unable to face the neighbors after having to
sell the Cadillac and take in boarders. She went crazy, was put away, and
to this day has never recovered from the fact that Joe lost their fortune in
1929. She didn't know how to think like a Tycoon.

Joe adjusted quickly. He merely reduced his expenses, got back to work
and within half the amount of time it took him first time around Joe was once
again prosperous. Like all Tycoons, Joe knew it's easier to make a million
the second time around.

THE MILLION DOLLAR A YEAR DIFFERENCE

Tycoons always have goals. Some weeks it's possible to make progress
towards these goals, but some weeks, due to circumstances beyond your
control, it isn't. Having no goals at all, however, is like starting in the
middle of nowhere without a road map. It's impossible to know where you
are or where you're going unless goals are selected, and a plan is established
to give your life some positive direction. Any goal is preferable to just drifting. Selecting financial independence as a goal and thinking like a Tycoon

will get you there. The first step of the Tycoon plan, then, is to decide that you want to be independently wealthy and that you'll do what it takes to achieve that goal. If that first decision is made, you will be independently wealthy in 1 to 3 years.

About a year ago, two people took my San Francisco TYCOON CLASS. One was Clara, a girl who sold wholesale soups to grocery stores. She did well in her job and was very effective at pushing clam chowder. Twenty-three years of age and she made $20,000 a year. A great start! At the same time, a boy we'll call Gunslinger took my class too. He got very enthusiastic about using the Tycoon techniques in real estate. He had no job, was a school drop-out, and had no real direction in life until he took the Bill Greene Tycoon Class. Clara was less enthusiastic about becoming a Tycoon. She continued to do well pushing fish stew, but she didn't do much about real estate. In a year, Clara looked at a total of three condominiums and eventually bought a pleasant middle-class condo apartment for $55,000. She moved into it. Period. Of course the girl was better off than had she done nothing. But two years have now gone by. Clara still owns the one condominium she bought on a '20% down' standard deal. She now makes soup commissions of $22,000 per year, and saves little or nothing. She has an unrealized profit of $10,000 in the Condo. Nothing wrong with that, but its hardly spectacular.

Gunslinger, on the other hand, followed my program like a fanatic. Real estate seemed to become his reason for living. He looked at hundreds of properties and once he knew the market, began making ridiculously low or no-money-down offers on every deal he saw. Today he owns approximately eighty different buildings in central California. One year into the game, Gunslinger was a bona-fide 22-year-old millionaire. One year it took him! Is that the American Dream or not?

Two people took the same class. They had the same information, the same level of intelligence. (Actually, Clara was a bit brighter). The one you'd expect to have been more successful, a girl already earning $20,000 a year, now owns one property and has a net worth of $20,000. The boy who had no job and no assets was a millionaire in twelve months. What accounts for the difference between them?

Gunslinger got off his fanny, looked at many deals, and made lots of offers. He had motivation! Big but realistic plans! Gunslinger's goal was to be worth thirty million by the age of thirty. He acquired large amounts of property for little or no money down. A day did not go by where he didn't make three or four offers on properties. Clara, in contrast, already considered herself successful and didn't want to change her life drastically. She only made one offer in an entire year. As a result, she made only one deal. On that one investment she doubled her net worth. She made more than she'll save in ten years. She's very proud of her one real estate deal and is glad to have been inspired to "get into real estate" by the TYCOON CLASS. Compared to Gunslinger she's hardly a Tycoon. But who knows, maybe she'll become the first lady president of Campbell soup some day.

If there's any moral to be drawn, it's that reading books like this one and taking courses isn't going to make you a dime. But getting off your fanny, setting goals, and doing what has to be done to make it happen can result in a Million-Dollar difference. How much money you earn is solely up to you. Luck is for other people. When should you start this program of achieving the goals you set for yourself? I'll tell you when. Today! Every day is a new beginning, and once you have written goals, life has a purpose. Every day should be a pleasure and a challenge.

DO IT TODAY!

As I said before, most people's problems come from over-worry and not over-work. They agonize about what happened in the past. But the past is over; it's finished. So forget about it and concentrate on what's happening NOW. Other people worry about the future. Equally unproductive! Get on with it. If worry can't be eliminated, try channelling it in constructive directions. Estimate what percentage chance there is that what you are worrying about will actually occur. For example, what is the percentage chance there will be an earthquake in California? My research shows there has been an earthquake about every sixty years. Therefore, viewing the situation optimistically, the possibility that it will happen next year is about one in sixty. If these odds are precarious enough to make you feel you should acquire earthquake insurance or should avoid brick properties

55

likely to tumble down in an earthquake, then take action. Get insurance.
Buy wooden houses. Taking sensible precautions in view of a reasonable
estimation of risk makes sense. But worrying about something uselessly
is a waste of energy. Worry and fear easily translate into paralysis and
no action at all.

DON'T WORRY ABOUT IT. DO SOMETHING!

Along with worry, another thing that will get in the way of success is
fear of change. Change or innovation is always uncomfortable. Even going
on vacation in some foreign country is a lot less comfortable than staying in
Normal Town, Idaho. But if you want to grow intellectually and if you want
your fortune to grow, you have to not only accept change, but seek it out.
Sure, the results are not definite. When you're a Tycoon there's no steady
paycheck waiting for you at the end of each week. Tycoons must not be
plagued with feelings of insecurity. If you only feel secure in a steady job
which offers nothing in twenty years but a pension and a gold Timex, you
are not thinking like a Tycoon. A Tycoon thrives on insecurity. He can
achieve financial success in a few years far beyond what a wage-slave can
expect in a lifetime.

Security is more feeling than reality, anyway. It's a state of mind.
Don't forget, the pension a wage-slave earns won't support a decent standard of living at the time it becomes payable. Social Security is even worse.
That's why I call it Social Insecurity. Subsistence isn't living. It isn't living
or worth living for. Social Security provides only for a poverty-level exi-
stence. The Tycoon who goes out and acquires large amounts of income property will have the real thing: An income that keeps pace with inflation.
Like love or happiness, security is a state of mind that nobody else can give
you. It's a state of mind that only you can give yourself. Go out! Get a
piece of the action going on all around you!

The feeling of being in a comfortable rut is not what a Tycoon wants.
Naturally, there is always the problem of conflicting goals. A fat man might
say, "I want a beautiful and healthy body, but I'm not going to give up
eating bon-bons and potato chips. And I am not willing to exercise or diet."

Obviously, if you're not going to do what is necessary to achieve a goal, you're not going to get it. It's that simple. If you can't give up a nice secure rut or a hobby that makes you feel good for a good chance of making a million dollars, then you may never get the million dollars. You can't say, "I'd like to make a million, while keeping my present job, and still spend all my evening and weekends sailing." If you're going to become independently wealthy within 1-3 years, your time must be allocated ruthlessly and you should expect to spend virtually all your spare hours on achieving financial independence.

Can you go half-way? Sure! It will just take longer. If, for instance, in real estate you decide to spend only Saturdays looking at new properties, it may take ten or fifteen years to get rich instead of one or two years. To my way of thinking, if a million dollars can be made in one or two years, it's worth spending all your spare time and energies on achieving that goal. With the present boom in real estate, the time to start acquiring is NOW. But DON'T quit your income producing job until your real estate income is big enough to replace it.

A Tycoon always prepares written plans. He (or, as always, she) will schedule time, establish priorities and will stick to those objectives both long and short-term. A Tycoon should have both a Life Plan and a series of five-year goals. The first five year plan should outline what he hopes to achieve in half a decade and how he is going to do it. It should then break down into more detailed periods for the first year, namely, a monthly plan, a weekly plan and a daily plan.

One man-with-a-plan was Frank Harris, who lived in the 19th Century. One day at the age of fifteen, he sat down and mapped out his lifetime goals. He made a list of five hundred ridiculous things he wanted to do before he died. He set up his goal list in order of priority and one by one, as the years passed, he proceeded to work on them. Sometimes they were prosaic goals like learning German. But other times they were glamorous or exotic things most people only dream about, like visiting every country in the world; becoming an internationally known journalist; seducing five thousand of the world's most beautiful women; becoming an American cowboy. At a ripe old age, Frank Harris died, having accomplished 90% of his five hundred objectives. His story is told in a spicy Victorian classic called 'My Life, My Loves'. Good reading -- even though Harris never was, nor wanted to be a business success.

But Frank Harris was undoubtedly a success at knowing how to get the most out of life. How did he cram the adventures of five hundred men into one lifetime? By setting goals! By planning ahead! By plotting and working steadily to achieve those goals.

Now maybe travel bores you. Or you're allergic to horses. All you want is to be the richest man in Duluth, Minnesota. To do it, all you need is a reasonable plan. To achieve that goal your daily activities should always be related to achieving your objectives. Eventually you'll make it. If you schedule time, establish priorities and stick to plans, there is no way you can not achieve your goals. To think like a Tycoon, however, once your plan is in effect, you must stick to it. You must acquire the patience to see it through, plus the flexibility to alter it if the original premise on which the plan was based changes.

There always have been, and always will be, negative people who say, "These things can't be done." Or "You're doing it the wrong way." What you want is too "abnormal" or whatever. Remember Charlie Brown and Lucy? You must not drift, deviate or be discouraged, regardless of what others say, do, or think about you and your goals. YOU know best. Success speaks for itself. Remember, Tycoons like us are the "doers" of the world, the caretakers of life's abundance.

Capitalists do a lot of good too. We create jobs for people less creative or dynamic than we; we produce better products, better places to live. We achieve more good than "social" engineers, academics, theorists, do-gooder social workers or fuzzy thinking leftists. Any, or all of whom, by the way, will criticize our actions.

The Communists should only know how much they would benefit from Tycoons. If ever you visit the Soviet Union, that neon light in your head will start flashing overtime; the needs are shocking. Most apartment buildings are in the same bad shape as our worst public housing projects. Driving between Moscow and Leningrad there are no decent places to eat even borscht, much less get a cheeseburger. Oh, for one MacDonald's. Functioning gas stations are hundreds of miles apart on even the most traveled roads.

Consumer goods of all types are in dreadfully short supply. If you're looking to buy chewing gum, ballpoint pens, an alarm clock, or 99% of the consumer goods we take for granted -- forget it!

Of course, while I have few kind words for the Communist governments which are the most oppressive and meet the fewest needs of their citizens, I don't have too many kind words for our own government. At this point, government officials are confiscating a big percentage of our Gross National Product in the form of taxes. And the things taxes pay for are almost always pure waste. What could be more useless than the billions we spent in Viet Nam? The equipment abandoned there and now owned by North Viet Nam represents the third largest arsenal in the world. If some Tycoon could arrange to buy all this army surplus back from Viet Nam and resell it to the U.S.A. (as some Tycoon eventually will do), he could make several billion on the deal. Then the U.S.A. could give it away again!

GET A LITTLE HELP FROM YOUR FRIENDS

Have you ever heard of Reverend Ike? Reverend Ike is a black preacher who operates mostly out of New York City and talks to his congregation about material success, prosperity, and making money. One of the things he says is that you should go out of your way to cultivate successful, power-ful, intelligent people. People who are the way you'd like to be. The Bible according to Reverend Ike, says: If you hang around street-corners with losers, you are a loser. You are judged by the company you keep and you'll end up with values of your peer-group.

Where can you get role models if your friends are all deadbeats or jail-birds?

Interestingly enough, I found that most successful people have avidly read the biographies of other well-known people in the fields in which they are interested. One example was Mr. "L", an almost legendary figure on Wall Street. I was privileged to be his house guest many times and to get to know him fairly well, because his son was my college roommate. While at his house one day I was surprised to see his personal library consisted almost exclusively of the biographies of men and women who had made a success of themselves in finance, on Wall Street, or in Europe. No trashy novels for him.

59

When I asked Mr. "L" about his choice of reading matter, the man replied,
"Many of my best ideas were variations on deals I read about in historical
biographies of Tycoons." Mr. "L" also told me that he learned something
special from these biographies: "Virtually everyone who made a big success
of themselves had been the protégé of a winner!" In his own case "L" made
an effort to become the protégé of the senior partner of a big respected Wall
Street firm. Mr. "L" came up with some good ideas in the field of arbitrage--
that is, buying and selling the same stock or commodity in two different
places at the same time to take advantage of international price differences.
He made the firm big trading profits by borrowing an idea from the biography
of Bernard Baruch who'd made similar deals thirty years earlier. Soon Mr.
"L" became a senior partner of the most prestigious firm on Wall Street. He
later became chairman of the Board of Governors of the New York Stock
Exchange.

Mr. "L" owes a lot to the Tycoons he met only in books. Maybe you will
too if you read some of the selections on my book list. Reading a selection
of these books is recommended for important reasons. Potential Tycoons can
not only apply the same principles these people did to make the right deals,
but with the benefit of hindsight, profit from where these Tycoons went wrong.

In reading historical biographies, you should gain greater understanding
of economic history and the role of the Tycoon or entrepreneur in history.
You'll learn that the possibility of acquiring great wealth in this country
has only been around for the last hundred years. Before then, you had to
be born with a silver spoon, or you ended up in a poverty trap. Virtually
all fortunes today are made from scratch - the aristocracy's dwindling contributions to the economy consist of donating funds to the Daughters of the
American Revolution. Prior to the Civil War, then, there were only about
five or ten self-made millionaires in the entire U.S.A. They made their money
shipping, whaling or slave trading. Perhaps the first national property
Tycoon in America was a woman named Hetty Greene. She invested her small
whaling fortune in industrial slums all over the U.S.A. Her real estate was
low-grade, low-rent tenements. Hetty was such a tough negotiator and
tightwad, she earned the nickname "The Witch of Wall Street" - the title
of her biography.

Another early real estate developer was Vincent Astor, who got his grubstake together as a fur trapper. His motto was "Never Sell the Land". He bought only first class property in busy business locations. Both Hetty and Vincent made a hundred million dollars, when a million was really worth something.

The Civil War caused great industrial expansion in the North. Building boomed in the cities. It was a period of rapid social and economic change. The stagecoach was replaced by the iron horse as railways crisscrossed the United States. But money was made mainly by people "out of railroads" (like stock promoters) rather than by people "in" them (like investors). Bankruptcies and lawsuits were common, and wealth changed hands rapidly.

Land up until this time, don't forget, was incredibly cheap by today's standards. Roads were poor and there was so much property around that the government gave away millions of acres to homesteaders. To buy several thousand acres near a city was no big deal. But railroads meant mobility and changed the nature of the real estate market. Urban land prices soared as people moved out of the country into sooty American cities where good paying jobs were available in steel mills and other new industries. Cornelius Vanderbilt made his first million transporting these newly mobile masses. He sent his "clipper" sailboats from Europe to New York City and from New York to California via Nicaragua. The discovery of gold near Sacramento caused the California Gold Rush, a stampede the likes of which America never saw again. Vanderbilt found a need and filled it! He made a deal with the locals to allow his passengers to cross overland on his trains and transfer to another Vanderbilt clipper waiting on the other side. The Vanderbilt clipper was faster and cheaper than going overland, and much safer than going by covered wagon. Vanderbilt made it easy for would-be Bonanza Kings to get from the East Coast to California.

Now we come to my favorite book, The Robber Barons. The most colorful robber baron of the 19th Century was Big Jim Fisk. He was a complete opportunist. Dumb. Crude. No special talent except for making money. Jim eventually took over the Erie Railroad, and being especially fond of lady singers, built the opera house in New York City so he could become its "casting director". Unfortunately for poor Fisk, one day he got it on with a cute soprano, and ended up murdered by the lady's lover. Moral: Tycoons should steer clear of sopranos. Or anyone else with jealous lovers.

In this same era, another Robber Baron, John Rockefeller, made half a million dollars in the leather business. Like all great Tycoons he then diversified. He bought oil wells and started selling kerosene, which was used for lamps. Those were the days before cars. Finding he wasn't making enough profit from kerosene -- did Rocky give up? Of course not. He put his brains to work and came up with a deal that thousands have been copying ever since. What was he trying to sell? Kerosene. What uses Kerosene? Lamps. So Rockefeller gave away the lamps. All over the world. The customers were so delighted with their free gift that they bought their fuel from -- you guessed it -- Rockefeller's Standard Oil Company. Gillette did the same thing with razor holders. And then sold his blades by the billions.

This is a valuable lesson for all modern Tycoons. Both Rockefeller and Gillette saw a need. How to fill it? By giving away another product which depended on refills that only they sold.

This technique is still used today. Melitta coffee pots were originally designed to use no other filter papers than their own brand. So anybody using the cheap Melitta coffee pot has to buy their filters from -- Melitta. The same with Hoover and their vacuum cleaner bags. Have you made your fortune today? Get your free ideas from people who have!

Biographies exist on hundreds of great Tycoons, and I highly recommend you read some of them. These men and a few women had several characteristics in common. They stole the ideas from each other. All found a need and filled it. In the case of some cosmetics magnates, they created needs. Most started from scratch. Historical biographies of Tycoons who made it are inspirational. Practical. Fun. They're also free if you go to the public library.

Besides cultivating and studying people who can do them good, admirable characteristics of many Tycoons are: They speak well of other people. There is an old saying: "If you can't say anything good about someone - keep quiet". I've found that to minimize the number of enemies and keep friends to a maximum, it's a good idea to praise people wherever possible. If you can give someone a sincere compliment, give it! If talking about ex-lovers, ex-employers or ex-business associates, try to be positive, not negative about them. Even if the experience you had with a particular person was unpleasant, if you speak well of them, it might get back to the person in question. They will then be more likely to speak well of you. To paraphrase the Golden Rule: Speak about others as you would have them speak about you.

Tycoons must be optimistic. About friends, about finance, about the future. That does not mean that you should ignore obvious risks, but given a choice between visualising a future of rosy progress and one of gloomy fiascos, you will be better off viewing the future positively, and acting accordingly. The most visible business pessimists, led by Harry Browne and other predictors of disaster, are the "gold bugs". Remember them? Usually right-wing lunatic fringe types who think that the world-as-we-know-it is about to come to a grinding halt. The way to survive into the future, say the most fanatic "gold bugs", is to leave the country now or take to the hills. Bury stashes of gold coins and an arsenal or two of automatic weapons.

In my opinion, there may be a time for all that someday, but these guys are missing the biggest real estate boom in the history of the United States Sun Belt. Since the odds of a 1980-1985 economic collapse are, in my view, about 10%, I would spend only a very small portion of my energies on disaster preparation. I'd much rather believe that over the next five years things are going to get better - that profits will continue to be made in the free enterprise system and that the taxpayers revolt which we see taking place in the United States today will actually lead to a new era of prosperity. A trend away from the welfare state we've been drifting into during the last fifty years.

DO IT, DON'T TALK ABOUT IT

Another thing you will notice about the way Tycoons think and act, is that they avoid unnecessary conversation. Some time-wasters merely sit and shoot the breeze for hours on end. They discuss the weather. The state of Coors beer. "And hey -- did you hear that Mabel went home with Henry last night? Robin was so upset she took downers and then Blanche came in..." Tycoons don't gossip. They don't "make conversation". Silence gives the impression of strength and knowledge. But when they do speak, they have something important to say. A Tycoon does not brag about himself, either. He doesn't have to toot his own horn. Success speaks loud and clear.

MOST FOLKS STAND AROUND WATCHING OTHER PEOPLE ACQUIRE WEALTH.

THEY'D BE AMAZED AT WHAT THEY COULD GET BY MAKING AN OFFER !

How about a '1031 Exchange' tonight baby ?

THE TYCOON'S MORALITY

Much of the business inspirational material I've read has made a great deal of "morality". Many people feel that being a "womanizer", a drinker, or a dope-smoker are pit-stops on the road to failure. But, based on the Tycoons that I have known, the fact that they indulged in occasional immoral delights has had no effect on their financial success. Of course the key here is moderation. If entire energies are devoted to close encounters of a physical kind, then obviously there isn't enough time in the day to be successful in business. But spending a moderate amount of time on "vices" or other interests won't, I don't think, affect the outcome of your future. Of course, a "vice" can be viewed in many ways - and when people talk about drinking too much, I always remember the story about the Temperance League.

Once, in an anti-drinking demonstration, the Temperance League lady took a can of worms and put half the worms in one glass and poured water on them. Then she took the other half of the worms and poured ninety-proof Vodka on them. The worms in water wriggled around, but the worms in Vodka curled up and died instantly. The Prohibitionists ended the demonstration by asking the question, "Now what did that tell you about drinking?" Someone stood up in the audience and shouted "If you drink a lot, you'll never have worms."

You can see that what is considered a vice by some may be considered beneficial by others. So try to be tolerant. Remember: As a real estate Tycoon you might one day find yourself buying a house from somebody who drinks too much. Lecture to them about the evils of drink and you'll blow the deal. A reasonable amount of missionary zeal for your favorite cause outside of business hours however, should not inhibit your business success. Who knows - it might even add to it. Take religion for instance....

BECOME A TRANSCENDENTAL TYCOON

Don't laugh. A few words on meditation isn't as out of place in a real estate book as you might imagine. Some years ago the Harvard Business School recommended it for relieving stress in executives. And who can argue with the "B" school? You don't have to wear white robes or chant exotic mantras; you can meditate effectively right now. Here's the secret.

Whenever you have a problem or just lack a sense of well-being, place yourself in a horizontal position in a darkened room. Get comfortable. Eliminate distractions, and banish all thoughts. Breathe in a regular manner. Concentrate on relaxing each part of your body, from toes to ankles to calves and so forth, until you have consciously relaxed all your body. At the same time concentrate on breathing. Silently repeat a meaningless word. It should be a word that has no particular association, such as "abracadabra" or "Sears & Roebuck". Softly, silently, chant this word over and over. Do it in rhythm with your breathing. For instance, breathe in - abra, breathe out - cadabra, abra, cadabra... If you can do this successfully in a quiet place, with near total relaxation, you will achieve a particularly satisfying state of mind. Some would call it a religious experience.

Meditation can be utilized a number of ways. Use it simply to get to sleep. Or practice it in the middle of the day instead of a cat nap. It'll clear the mind and you might even find solutions to many of the troublesome problems of the day. A "natural high", some call it. But whatever it is, it's an altered state of consciousness that is invariably beneficial. It's cheaper than alcohol or dope and like I said, not just me, but Harvard Business School recommends it.

In case you're now too relaxed to remember, here's a quick summary: Persistence and enthusiasm are a Tycoon's most important tools. You only learn how to do something right by doing it wrong first, so view all mistakes with a sense of humor as experiences that will do you some good. Every mistake, every "failure" is a valuable experience. Problems are just exciting challenges. LAUGH A LOT.

Pay no attention to negative people. Ruthlessly cull the people who tell you "it can't be done" from your address book. When you're really depressed, don't dwell on failures. Think about what you did right, not what you did wrong. Never worry! If you use meditation to clear your mind, you will often find that your subconscious will work out creative solutions that will magically surface when you come out of your higher consciousness.

No one ever made a big success of themselves without failures. Winston Churchill, in World War I, was the instigator of a disastrous plan to invade Turkey at Gallipoli. It was such a massive failure that Churchill was forced to retire from public life in disgrace. He wrote, studied, and made no attempt to come back for many years. But he was preparing to be a leader again. He did not give up. Remember your biggest successes will come after your biggest failures. A Tycoon is never a quitter!

A Tycoon is always alert for changes in the economy. He always asks, how can I profit from the coming events? A real estate example: If you see for one reason or another a major employer in your area is having problems, like Boeing did in Seattle, that means the lay-off of a lot of people. That could cause a temporary depression in the market. It might be the time to sell or trade property while prices are still up and to build up cash reserves to acquire property when everyone is depressed. Property sells below replacement costs during depressions. The Tycoon knows it pays to buy when every one else is panicking. In San Francisco and Los Angeles during 1977/78, prices got a little crazy, went up too much too fast, and intelligent investors reduced their holdings to look at better deals available in other parts of the country.

A Tycoon always has historical perspective, you see. He knows that a big boom is almost always followed by a bust. After a very healthy rise in the stock market or the real estate market there's a period of leveling off or even declining prices which is called a "correction". During that "correction" (bad one is called a depression), the Tycoon must be ready to move on to more lucrative areas. Even different countries, if necessary. When the stock market died in the United States around 1968, people who stayed with it wasted ten years of their lives. They didn't know what you know: A Tycoon is ready to go where the action is.

AVOID BEING A CONSUMER

Finally, I must outline the most important rule for being a Tycoon, and that is: DON'T BE A CONSUMER. If your mind is always focused on how to blow the next few hundred dollars, you'll never accumulate the capital you need to be successful.

These are my three rules to avoid being a consumer.

If you see IT in a store and are about to buy IT, ask yourself:

1) Can I live without IT?

2) Is there something I can trade for IT?

3) Can I get IT cheaper in another store?

Hopefully the mental process you go through with those three questions will make you forget about IT, and will cause you to look for more productive uses for your money. Like where to invest a dollar and get back two. Not where to spend a dollar and get back nothing except an expensive memory. Whenever possible, don't even think about consumer goods like cars, vacations, pet rocks, or any sports requiring expensive trappings. You're independently wealthy only when you've enough money coming in from your investments to enable you to quit working. Then, the surplus left over from paying for basic necessities can be spent on consumer goods.

Not only does a Tycoon not consume, he generally pays little or no taxes. The government under our confiscatory tax schemes is theoretically our 50% - 70% partner. All Tycoons (and I personally) don't pay any income taxes because we spend (far too much) time figuring out how to legally shelter income. I do this by making business deals that bring me tax losses (on paper) in excess of the money I put into the deal.

The way many corporations avoid taxes is by charging more for their product. The fuzzy thinking leftists of the world don't realize that General Motors, although it seems to pay about 50% corporate income tax, really passes its taxes along to the consumer.

Take the Chevrolet, for instance. It could be sold for $3,000. But does it? Of course not. "Consumers" shell out $8,000. Why? Because $5,000 is needed for taxes, and corporations must always raise the price of their product to cover all costs. This way they get the needed return on their investment. Corporations don't pay taxes, people pay taxes. In reality, taxes are always just another add-on cost for the consumer. If the Feds cut out real estate tax incentives, rents would merely go up 50% to pay the new taxes.

If you're in real estate, at least for now you can set up your deals in such a way that income is sheltered and taxes are deferred into the distant future. The average middle class wage-slave has no way of avoiding taxes relatively legally. If he makes $30,000 a year he'll pay about a third in taxes. He could avoid the whole thing if he took the time to read my chapter "Pay No Taxes Ever Again, Legally". If you're going to be a Tycoon, you will have to keep clear not only of taxes, but of flakes, frauds, and Red Ribbon deals. The Red Ribbon Rule is to avoid a deal presented to you all wrapped in a Red Ribbon, your only requirement being to write out a check, sit back and watch the profits flow in. Don't do it. The deal will never happen. Avoid sucker investments.

The best business deals are the ones you create, where YOU personally see a need and are willing and able to do what it takes to fill it.

DOUBLE ESSERS

No matter how good a deal sounds or what guarantees you're offered, never get involved with a person of bad reputation. That person will find a way to do a "Double S" on you. Screw and Sue, in other words. "Double eSSers" are people who want to get something they are not entitled to. They get you into lawsuits which are a waste of much money and valuable energy. Always find a way to settle quickly with a "double eSSer", then never have anything more to do with him. Go on to something more productive.

Women in a divorce situation are often Double eSSers. One lady I knew, let's call her Sue Screw to make the point, was married to a wealthy fellow named Sam. The marriage fell apart and Sue hit Sam with a Vengeance. She contacted famous divorce lawyer "S.S. Castrator" who wanted a court order for Sam to pay alimony of $1,000 a month. Sam refused such a high sum. He offered $600 per month as an out of court settlement. Was Sue Screw satisfied? No. She would rather fight! Things dragged on for years, with Sam refusing and Sue screwing, but Sue fought on. Sue didn't realize that 80% of all alimony orders are in default anyway within two years after the alimony award. Eventually the case was decided, five years and $20,000 in court costs later. Sue Screw was awarded her $1,000 a month alimony. Sam moved to Israel and became a kibbutznik. She never got a dime. If only she had accepted Sam's original offer. Sue could have bought real estate and been a lot richer both financially and emotionally. So: The Bill Greene Ruling on Double eSSers is: Forget it. Stay out of court - settle quickly. Do something productive instead. The only one who wins in a lawsuit is the lawyer. Double eSSers exist in business too and they come in all three sexes. So always be sure the people you rely on in a deal are dependable and of super reputation. The same rule applies to you:

DON'T BE A DOUBLE ESSER !

DON'T BE A DOUBLE ESSER!

From time to time for very good reasons, you may have to be technically dishonest. But never by taking what isn't yours. It's just that sometimes the laws of the country or a community make no sense. Number one priority has to be "look to your own survival". When a place like Rhodesia prevents Rhodesians from simply picking up their chips and moving to safety, it may be necessary to circumvent the law. Governments are immoral, cynical, and inhumanly interested in their own self-perpetuation. Always at the expense of their citizens -- sometimes at the expense of their citizens' lives.

On a less dramatic level, if the building code in Atlanta, Georgia makes it impossible for me to complete a necessary repair or alteration on one of my buildings, I may find it necessary to make that repair anyway and take my chances of getting caught. Economic survival on a day-to-day level is as important as my personal survival. My feeling is that you should respect the laws of your country or community where you can, but when they get ridiculous, follow your own conscience.

On that score, every Tycoon reading this book should realize that the free enterprise or capitalistic system is fighting a losing battle for survival all over the world. Only political involvement by us may preserve it for our children. Consider joining all local property owners' groups. Consider the Libertarians. It's a new political party in America, dedicated to fiscal conservatism in government, plus maximized individual freedom. The interesting and usually wealthy people who've joined this party feel there are just too many laws and too much taxes for anybody's good. They feel that the public sector - namely government - has over-expanded and has become dangerously all powerful. The Libertarian Party, which is a behind-the-scenes mover in the current tax-payers' rebellion, is a group you should consider getting behind. Membership is about $20 per year and their number should be in your telephone book. If not, write to "Libertarians" P.O. Box 71383, Los Angeles, Ca. 90071. They will forward your letter and get you on the mailing list. At the very least you'll make some interesting contacts.

I remind you again, that every Tycoon, certainly when he starts out, should prepare written plans. Set forth your goals and what it is you want to accomplish. The world steps aside for a man (or woman) with a plan.

Have complete confidence in yourself in whatever you're doing. Recognize that if you're well-prepared, well-educated, well-organized and have a plan, you will not fail to achieve your goals.

After you become a Tycoon and are financially independent, ask the question: What would I do if I had only six months to live? Then do it. With financial independence, you finally have the power to do whatever you want. Real power, i.e. the freedom to determine your own destiny. While on one level I talk about how to make money, at a deeper and more philosophical level, I'm talking about this freedom. You only get freedom when you don't have to work at a job you hate or live with a spouse just because he/she is paying the rent.

When you have no money problems, you can enjoy life infinitely more. Enjoying your family more might be one of the unexpected benefits, because the reason you will be with them is because you want to enjoy them, not because you have to.

Once you've made a lot of money, look around and think about protecting your fortune by diversification. Remember, real estate in the Sun Belt, that whole Southern area between San Francisco and Atlanta, Georgia, has been booming for some time now. It will probably continue, but you must be ready at any time to transport yourself or your business into other areas, even other countries. It never hurts to start your diversification of investments program from a position of success.

Don't wait for the Boom to bust: While still doing well in real estate, set aside funds to establish reserves or even better, look for different business ventures. Anyone who can relate to what I've discussed in these pages has the capacity to become financially independent in one - three years. And to keep it, you don't need luck. Luck always comes to those who think like a Tycoon. At my TYCOON CLASSES which have now been attended by over 2,000 graduates I often end my lectures by telling my students "look to the right of you and look to the left of you. Including yourself there are three people. In a few years one of you is going to be in essentially the same economic position you're in today. And the reason will be that you did not set goals and get off your fanny. Another one of you will be much improved, and will probably own a couple of properties. You'll have doubled your present income. The third person will be a millionaire, and a real Tycoon."

The choice of whether you do nothing, apply yourself moderately, or make it big is yours! America with all its defects is still the land of opportunity! "Life is a banquet", said Auntie Mame. "But most people never get near the table."

The choice is up to you.

Are you ready?

Let's take Step One of the Tycoon Plan.

Tomorrow morning, at 9 a.m. go to see a banker.

You And Your Banker

Bankers must all go to a class where they learn the basic rule of their trade: <u>Never lend to anyone who needs money.</u> In the old days before I learned the secret, I walked into a bank cold and asked to borrow. They requested collateral in the form of some asset worth <u>more</u> than I was asking to borrow. They asked me to pledge bank accounts or marketable stock worth double the amount I needed.

In those old days I tried to explain that if I <u>had</u> a savings account for more than I wanted to borrow I could use my own money and would not have to borrow. If I had stock of double the value of the hoped-for loan, I could sell half my stock to get the money I needed. Several times my unsecured loan requests were refused, and I was left frustrated. But that was a long time ago, before I learned how to get unlimited money - whatever I wanted, from any bank.

Let me share the unbelievably simple secret that will get you a million or more in unsecured credit, whenever you need it.

Before I learned how to do it myself, I made some wrong assumptions about how unsecured loans were made. I figured that family ties, school contacts or some clubby-social considerations made the difference between outsiders like me and the favored few who were extended unsecured credit. I was very wrong. Banks are interested in making loans to almost anyone.

The only reason they refuse to make a loan is they are worried about getting the loan paid back. If you can convince a banker there is no risk, you will get the money. If your ability to repay is an unknown or in doubt, you get the cold shoulder. Here is how you can establish credit.

First, open a checking account at a large commercial bank - not a Savings and Loan Association which, by law, can not make unsecured loans. Put enough money in your checking account so there will be no service charges. Be sure your new checking account is classified as a business or commercial account. Do that by calling yourself "John Yourname and Associates."

Once your account has been opened wander over to the platform -- that section where the bank officers sit. You'll notice the two flashing neon signs that say, "SMARTIE DESK" and "IDIOTS REPORT HERE." You may have trouble seeing these signs because they are invisible to the uneducated eye. But, if you ask, "Who handles consumer loans?" and "Who handles commercial loans?" someone at the bank will tell you.

Consumer loans are used to buy consumer goods, like vacations or a new car that will be a worthless, rusted hulk in five years. The interest rate for foolish pleasure loans on disposable consumer products is often double the interest rate on commercial loans. IDIOTS REPORT THERE. Commercial loans are used, or at least should be used, to invest in deals that will bring you back $2 for every $1 that you borrow. Now do you begin to see the flashing lights?

Walk over to the SMARTIE DESK, the chap or lady who makes commercial loans, and say something cute. Like, "Hi there, I'd like to have a relationship with you." After their initial puzzlement subsides, you explain that you are starting the Joan Yourname business. While you do not want a loan immediately, you want to establish rapport today. You want to know their commercial credit requirements. Explain further, that you want your potential banker to know you and to be aware of your needs for credit.

Establishing rapport with an intelligent and reasonable bank officer on your wavelength is of the utmost importance. If you are an attractive young lady-tycoon-to-be, perhaps your best banker will be an old Fuddy-Duddy. You can flatter him with your attention and charm. Fuddy-Duddy might turn

a wheeler-dealer like me down in an instant, but the attractive Miss Leggs could do very well with him. A young and aggressive black man might do better by seeking out a female loan officer with an Afro than Mr. Fudd.

Unfortunately some prejudices both positive and negative do exist. It is up to you to exploit them to your own advantage. A chinese Vice-President, for instance, might be more understanding to a Chinese customer than a closet Neo-Nazi who feels non-Germans are inferior beings. But racially prejudiced bank loan officers are relatively rare in my experience. The old school ties, family connections - all these things may help but are by no means a major factor. It is important that the bank officer starts out liking you. As I said, try to get one on your wavelength.

It may appear that I am telling you, "Forget your principles and pander to the base instincts of dirty old men," (in the case of Miss Leggs), or "give up your legal rights to equal treatment," (in the case of Mr. Afro). That is one way of looking at it. You could as a female or black, seek out a bank officer who instinctively dislikes you and vice versa. Then when he refused to make a loan, you could sue. Ten or fifteen years later, your civil rights case might be decided. You might win. You might lose. But many years would have gone by, and your program of becoming a millionaire would have long been sidetracked.

This book is about the world as it IS, or at least how I perceive it. It's not a fairy story of how it should be. Getting ahead will definitely involve being agreeable, even charming, to people that socially you might have no use for. It will involve going around obstacles rather than fighting staunchly for "your rights" and thereby spending your life waiting for your case to be decided in courts of law. More than anything else, it involves the constant application of common sense. If your goal was to be a great medical doctor, kissing the fanny of a hospital administrator who is balky about signing your certification, may be necessary if you don't want to go back to driving a cab. Once you have the certification you have the freedom to proceed according to your own values.

This book is about FREEDOM, and a net worth of a million dollars buys FREEDOM. Making a million in a few years is not easy. It may involve compromises and sacrifices you don't feel should be necessary. It will involve dealing with people you would rather not deal with. It will involve exploiting every talent you have and every opportunity you come across. Thus, the example of a black friend of mine who refused an executive partnership because it seemed his potential partners wanted him as their <u>token</u> <u>Negro</u>. He was a fool! You must get the job, deal or loan first. Then you prove how good you are. The boss, partners or bankers will soon become color-blind. If you have the tycoon mentality, you will exploit all your assets to the fullest.

Getting back to the narrower issue of loans. Whatever your financial needs are, do not be afraid to shop banks and loan officers until you find one or more you can relate to. Bankers are just employees trying to do their job. That job is to make solid loans to reliable people; to get the loans paid back as agreed: on time, with interest.

A bank couldn't stay in business for a month if it was not able to lend out its capital and deposits. That's their business. They <u>need</u> borrowers. They <u>want</u> you to succeed. But no matter how charming you are, and how much your new banker likes you, their job is to keep alert for telltale signs that will indicate how reliable you are likely to be. Do you bounce checks? If you do, forget about ever borrowing a dime - or change your habits. A person sloppy enough to be frequently writing overdrafts is automatically labelled <u>irresponsible</u> and a poor loan risk.

Do you make regular deposits to your account that indicate a steady source of income? Do you make occasional larger deposits indicating that you are a successful <u>wheeler dealer</u>? You should. If you appear to have a regular income or are a successful person with a cash flow, this establishes credibility. The record established at your neighborhood branch bank with the bank manager, and ultimately with the big shots at "head office," is what gets you a million dollars, unsecured. If you think it can be done in a week, forget it. This is a one to three year program. Patience and the approach outlined here will get you all the credit you need. But it could take a couple of years.

After establishing rapport you are ready to apply for your first loan. Remember the bankers' rule is, on first loans <u>you will not get it if you need it</u>. Thus, your first small loan of say $500 is only to establish credibility, you want to establish a record that you pay back on time or, better yet, <u>early</u>. If you do not have any good deals to invest in, <u>create</u> a not too fanciful story about ten cases of rare wine you can purchase at a bargain price in a nearby town, and sell to local wine connaisseurs at a 100% profit. Or perhaps you can invent a deal involving an antique dining room set that you can buy for $500, refinish in your basement, and resell for $1,000.

When applying for your first loan, offer to transfer $500 from your checking account to a savings account to stand as security for the $500 you want to borrow. Or be ready to put up some shares of stock.

Remember, even when you borrow 100% secured, the loan is still to _you_ and if the loan officer suspects he will have to grab the security, he would rather not make the loan. Bad loans are a headache, cause public relations problems, and if you do not service your first loan as agreed, you might as well move your account somewhere else and start all over again. You also might just as well forget about being a Tycoon without the backing of a banking community that perceives you as a responsible and worthy customer.

RULE: DURING YOUR FIRST YEAR OF BORROWING PAY OFF EVERY LOAN EARLY!

Assuming you have made that all important first bank loan for a term of three months; go in and pay it off in three weeks.

THE SMALL GIFT RULE. A small or token gift can be given _after_ some service has been rendered. It is not a bribe. You already got your loan. You go into the bank on pay off day with your check. You effusively thank the banker for his help and tell him about all the money you made on the Chair Deal or the Wine Deal. You happen to have with you a sample chair or bottle which you give the banker to show him the product you were trading or producing. You say, "By the way, that's an extra (or factory second). Why don't you keep it?"

Once I (really) invested in a soap factory. When the loan was paid off everybody in the bank got a bar of cucumber flavor glycerine soap. To this day, the tellers, clerks, and loan officers remember me as the "soap guy." I get super service at that branch. The most important thing about the SMALL GIFT RULE is that your banker will remember you. You stand out among the sea of supplicants he must listen to every day. Effusive thanks or buying you banker lunch is a variant on the SMALL GIFT RULE. It psychologically conditions your banker to expect a goodie or some strokes for himself at the safe time he collects for his employer. Verbal praise can mean as much as a material thing to some individuals.

For your second loan, which should be requested soon after the first has been paid, ask for at least double the amount of money of the first loan. Have another "good deal story" ready. You may have to do the "Savings Account as Security" bit again, but its likely that if your checking account balance is for more than the amount borrowed, you can, for loan number two, merely informally promise your banker that you will keep your checking account balance over the amount of the loan.

Before the loan is due, handle the payback, small gift, and effusive thank you scene as before. The third, fourth, and each succeeding loan should be for more money, longer terms, and with less security than previous loans. You may have to provide financial statements, copies of income tax returns, and so on once you get over $5,000: But by then the banker with whom you have established rapport will help you prepare documentation that will look good to higher-ups.

Your loan officer should be a firm ally within six months. You can even confide in him that your first loan was not really used for a wine deal, but you were just establishing credit and your relationship with him. He will confide in you that he too read this book, and knew what you were up to all the time. Needless to say, by your third loan, you should have found some uses for borrowed money. The whole purpose of this exercise is to establish a credit line so that you can pick up bargain deals, products or businesses for cash when opportunities present themselves.

Around the time of your third or fourth loan, consider going through the whole process of establishing rapport with another banker at one or more different banks. You should not tell the first banker about bank number two and three unless he asks. Bankers do not like what they call Double Borrowing. But here is how it works.

Assume you went through the same process of building confidence with a series of secured, then unsecured loans of increasingly large sums at a second bank. While you will have to meet interest payments out of personal funds you can borrow $10,000 from bank Number one. When it is due, you repay it with $10,000 loan from bank Number two. When that comes due, pay if off with a new loan from bank Number one. If you want to get complicated, pay that loan off with a loan from Number three.

The result is that your $10,000 loan is always rolling over between banks. The full $10,000 can be in deals out there working for you - - hopefully earning 100% per year or more, while your loan interest is only around 10% per year. As mentioned, banks do not particularly like this double or triple borrowing mode of operation. Yet all big companies and all Tycoons operate on borrowed money from multiple lenders in much the same way. This handbook is just making you aware, as a future tycoon, of what is going on in the Real World. Once you make your first deals with borrowed money, refinements in your system of paying loans back will come from your own experiences. Your borrowings will be scheduled in accord with your own needs, and in line with the requirements of your banks or other financial backers.

WORDS OF CAUTION: Always try to be liquid enough to clear up all your short term loans at least once every year or two. If your double or triple borrowing is discovered, admit what you are doing, honestly and candidly. You may be surprized, as I was, when banker Number one said to me: "You don't have to go through all that nonsense with three banks, we will give you whatever you need, up to a million, if you just clear the decks every now and then and continue to show us that you have the ability to pay off all your short term loans from time to time."

After that, for several years, I did all my short term commerical borrowing with one bank, and they did indeed give me whatever I wanted. It took me three years, but by paying my debts on time, taking my banker to lunch, and establishing social and personal contacts with higher-level bankers in the same bank, I eventually got carte blanche. If I could do it, so can you.

Bankers now invite me to lunch and ply me with small gifts. If times get tough and it's impossible for you to repay a loan on time, don't be afraid to ask for an extension of the payback time. If this happens on your first, second or third loan, it will be harmful to your credit. But, after a dozen loans or a year of dealing with the same banker, you will have established enough credit and credibility to call your banker and say things like, "I have written a check for $50,000 to acquire a property worth $100,000. On line with our previous agreement, will you cover it with an unsecured loan until I line up a long term loan? I'll have you paid back in three months." With established credit, you can make a partial payment in three months and get the loan extended for another three months if necessary.

The most common way of handling a cash flow or bouncing check problem is the worst. At the first sign of trouble the deadbeat puts a pillow over his head and does nothing. Even worse, he disappears. Goes fishing. His phone is disconnected for non-payment of bills, and mail is returned to creditors, unopened. As a result any normal banker gets all upset, makes a bad debt report to the Higher-Ups and the borrower has Zero Credit. Even if at a future time the borrower belatedly pays back the loan, the sour taste of irresponsibility remains. How much better and simpler it would have been if the embryo tycoon went to his banker, explained the problem, received the standard permission to extend the loan, and then made token payments, until conditions improved.

If you can not meet a loan payment, or cannot resist an opportunity to make a deal with what would otherwise be a bouncing check, you MUST always call or stop in at the bank and explain quite truthfully what has happened. More importantly, you must tell your lender what you are going to do about it. If over a period of years a businessman never had any temporary cash binds he'd be a most unusual character indeed. You become an even better risk if you show skill at extricating yourself from occasionally difficult positions. Obtaining a long term savings and loan secured mortgage (due in twenty or thirty years) is my favorite way of paying off short term debt. If you own real estate or a business, getting a mortgage or doing a sale-leaseback can usually raise needed cash.

Bankers hate lawsuits and foreclosures and would much rather give you a chance to settle up on terms you can live with. They do not want to terminate a good relationship with a bad lawsuit. To sum up, this is how to borrow a million unsecured:

1. Always borrow from the commercial loan department. Never have anything to do with consumer credit.
2. Establish relationships at one, then several, banks.
3. Borrow money you don't really need on a secured basis to establish credit and credibility.

4. Establish credit at more than one bank.

5. Always borrow more than you need.

6. Always pay back your first loans early.

7. Each time you apply for a loan borrow more than your previous loans, even if you don't need it.

8. Deposit unused funds in another bank, as reserves.

9. Always keep cash reserves of at least 25% of your loans.

10. Establish bank friendships on levels that are appropriate for your level of operations. You should aim to be on a first name basis with the bank president within one year.

11. Meet your obligations punctually. . Remember the small gift rule.

12. In times of difficulty, after you have established credibility, never appear irresponsible. Never disappear. Always stay in contact. Prepare and show them your plans for solving any problems. If you are reasonable, a bank will always grant extentions. Occasional financial difficulties are an expected part of all business operations.

HIGH FINANCE IS NOT A MYSTERY. It involves the steady build-up of the unsecured credit for the apparently credit worthy person. You, as a tycoon, can use other people's money in many ways, as explained in other chapters. With a good line of unsecured credit you can take advantage of special situations that less credit worthy individuals can't handle. Cash is king, and when a financially troubled company or disgusted property owner wants to sell in a hurry, you will be able to pick up bargains. You cannot be a Tycoon without a substantial line of unsecured credit. Take Step One. Visit the Smartie Desk today.

Fuzzy Thinking Leftists!

The first fuzzy thinking leftist I recall in my life was Mr. Stanley, a very brilliant high school social studies teacher. He had reputedly inherited a small fortune from his wealthy Eastern family, and he imbued us all with the the desire to make the world a better place in which to live. At the time - 1955 - this meant joining the United World Federalists and wearing a green feather to symbolize opposition to Republicans, Joseph McCarthy and the military-industrial-corporate conspiracy.

Mr. Stanley's parents had placed his inheritance with the trust department of a major New York bank. This gave him a monthly check. He had the disdain for private property that only seems to come with a regular welfare or trust fund check. His parents were wise because Mr. Stanley would have given it all away to worthy causes, had he been able to.

He mobilized many generations of privileged upper-middle class kids to support all the favorite leftist-liberal causes, from civil rights in Georgia to Ecology. As far we we were concerned Mr. Stanley was as right as anyone could be. He was clearly a good man: Quaker, a pacifist and a man who got behind all benevolent causes -- sometimes even before they became fashionable.

I remember him telling us in class "There's nothing more stupid than nations going to war over how to distribute God's bounty -- and how to distribute it -- that's the only argument between the Capitalist and

Communist world."

He influenced us all. No one in the class considered going into business as a career. We all hoped to go into teaching, government service or the professions. We were determined to "help people". It never occurred to us that the production of goods and services for profit might be of more help to the world than becoming a political scientist or social worker.

Our Mr. Stanley was multiplied by fifty when I got to college. Even at the Wharton School, supposedly a bastion of capitalistic education, I never received an hour's positive exposure to Libertarian thought. Laissez-faire was presented all right, but as a long dead, no longer applicable 19th century philosophy. On our first day of orientation at Wharton, one of the many Fuzzy Thinking Leftist Academics I was to come into contact with there announced the purpose of our education: "We are going to turn you into good administrators, so that when the revolution is over, they'll still need you to run the business, whether or not you control the stock."

In those days there was a lot of talk about "People's Capitalism" and how our form of government was becoming more Sovietized, just as the Communists were discovering the "profit motive" and becoming more American- ized. It was predicted that within a decade or two we'd truly become "one world". None of the Academics mourned the passing of the Free Enterprise System. I didn't know there was a choice or that there <u>was</u> any wave of the future outside of Socialism.

It took me another twenty years of dealing with the Real World and real people to look at things differently. I still feel that the Mr. Stanleys had OK moral positions in matters of individual liberties, civil rights and such- but they were dead wrong in their anti-business attitude. The Fuzzy Thinking Leftists made us all believe there was something wrong with owning property and producing goods and services for profit. As a result, govern- ment was allowed to erode the economic freedom of the individual with progres- sive confiscatory taxes and incredible regulatory burdens. The result was a shift of interest and employment away from the private productive sector into "public service". Today nearly two out of every four people are directly or indirectly government employees. Of the remaining two, one spends full time coping with red tape and tax planning required by the public sector. That leaves one person to support three drones and their dependants.

Thus has the Fuzzy Thinking Leftist Vision of Utopia been fully implemented by total government control over almost all segments of the economy. Real Estate is the last bastion of capitalism and free enterprise. That's why Americans are the best housed people in the world. Despite the great job private real estate owners are doing, it could be the next to go. Trouble is, socialism doesn't work economically, and as the result of our "welfare state" there is far less individual freedom in the United States now than there has been (in any peaceful era) since 1776.

NOT ALL FUZZY THINKING LEFTISTS LOOK LIKE THIS. THEY JUST THINK THE SAME.

NOTES

YOUR FIRST INVESTMENT PROPERTY

Let's go to kindergarten! The first thing you must do is to toddle out into the real world and see what's on the market. There is a lot of property out there. Much of it is for sale, at a price. The prices or availability of only a tiny fraction is known to your potential competitors - other buyers. What's "advertised" or openly listed with brokers is like the tip of an iceberg. Most people in real estate never get below the tip. You'll soon learn about the vast untapped market below the surface in "Ferreting Out Super Deals" - but for now just buy a magic marker and your local weekend newspapers. The tip of the iceberg will be quite enough to keep you busy for the next four weeks.

Once you've bought the papers don't waste time with the sports pages or news. Throw out everything but the classified section. Turn to the property ads. Circle every ad for investment property located within half an hour drive from your home. Look at them carefully. Go over expense and income figures with sellers or their agents. For at least a month, look at a minimum of 25 offerings every weekend.   Spend weekday time after work looking at more deals if you can. This first exposure to the conventional market is your kindergarten. Don't get carried away. Don't buy anything. You are not educated yet - - not until you have seen one hundred properties. Just look! Ask questions.

Assume that sellers and their agents are lying to you. They are! Values and rental incomes will be exaggerated. Expenses will be grossly understated. But you can ferret out real figures. Check everything. Don't be afraid to call up the county tax assessor for actual taxes. Go over to the garbage people for debris collection rates. Review tenant's leases. Follow up "for rent" ads. Pretend to be a prospective tenant to discover true rent levels in your chosen area. Make no serious offers until you have looked at at least one hundred properties! THEN MAKE A LOW OFFER OR A NO MONEY DOWN OFFER ON EVERY DEAL YOU LOOK AT! After looking at 100 properties you will then recognize an outstanding deal when you see it.

Until you become an expert, here's one rule of thumb to tell what property is worth. Take a monthly gross rent. Multiply by 80 to get "the value". For example, let's talk about a duplex that rents for $200 per month for each unit. That's a total of $400 per month. Now to apply my rule of thumb, take those monthly rentals of $400 per month and multiply by 80. That will give you $32,000; $400 times 80 is $32,000. In many areas, if you shop you can buy a two unit property earning $400 per month for $32,000 in an average neighborhood in average condition. That may seem like an incredibly low price to those who have been looking at property in Beverly Hills, but in many parts of California and certainly in much of the sun belt, 6.5 times the gross annual rent or 80 times the gross monthly rent is the going value. It is necessary to pay a premium in areas perceived as more desirable than average. In places where landlords pay high fuel bills, like Boston or Chicago, even that 6.5 multiple would be high.

If you expect to make an income from any property, you should never pay more than 100 times the gross monthly rental. The $32,000 property we are talking about must be purchased for under $40,000. If bought for more than $40,000, it would be a bad deal and it would need cash from your pocket each month to meet expenses and mortgage obligations unless you could raise the rents quickly and substantially.

Naturally, the rental figures that you use in this rule of thumb should be realistic rents you can expect to collect - - not actual rent. Actual rents could be too high or too low for the existing market.

Many investors use a multiple of the annual gross rents as their rule of thumb. You can earn a positive cash flow with a price of from five to seven times the annual gross rents. At prices above eight times the expected annual gross unless it is a spectacular location - - PASS THE DEAL! There are still many properties available at bargain prices if you know how to find them. In my "hey-day" in Marin County, I was making about three deals a week. Most required little or no cash investment. All were scheduled to break even or produce a small cash flow within a few months.

If you want to judge your own performance, if you are closing less than one deal every six months, you are not operating at anywhere near TYCOON levels. It may take six months for you to get rolling in the business. One deal a month should be your initial goal. One deal a month will make you a millionaire in 2 - 5 years.

Now concerning the No Money Down Deal, some real estate brokers will say, "I've been in the business 20 years and I never saw a deal like you want!" The unfortunate fact is that most real estate agents would not know how to make a No Money Down Deal if it fell on them. Agents seldom know how to create anything but very standard financing arrangements: 20% down payment, and 80% financing from a Savings & Loan association. In my opinion, most real estate agents won't be much help because they just aren't very creative at their trade. Probably 5% of the real estate agents in any locality make 90% of the local commissions.

Until you've become a serious buyer the best ones, who have all the good deals and could arrange "No Money Down" purchases won't want anything to do with you. So before I tell you how to select a good broker and get them to feed you their secret listings and super terms, let me tell you how to make good deals without the help of a real estate agent.

Besides following all the for sale by owner ads, simply walk around a neighborhood you feel comfortable in. Particularly in springtime. You'll see people working, painting houses, planting in yards. You can be sure it is not a tenant! Tenants never work in their houses or gardens. Anyone doing beautification is probably an owner. Ask a person working in his yard about his place. Particularly if he's older and near retirement, once you start talking you may find that he has some interest in selling and moving. Don't be too disappointed if in your first few conversations no deals materialize. It could take six months until you get rolling. But if in six months you haven't bought anything, you are doing something wrong.

Expect to make 100 cold contacts to get 5 hot prospects. Five prospects may yield only 2 deals. To make your first super real estate deal will take much effort and persistance. Getting acquainted with older people in your neighborhood is another good way to spend part of those first months. If they like you, you will make many useful contacts. Eventually you'll get several direct (no broker) deals at reasonable prices with good terms.

During your educational or looking phase, don't neglect to prepare yourself intellectually. Finish reading this book. Take an elementary Federal Tax Course and also Basic Accounting. Consider going to a community college for an evening real estate course. Be extroverted and expand your contacts. You might also consider good real estate seminars like my Tycoon Class. It's one of the best. I cram into one weekend all the basic information you'll need. But similar information is available in books like this, or in my cassette lectures.[1] As mentioned, you can get courses at local colleges. They are not expensive. The problem is, many college instructors go by the books. They learned from the books and have never been out in the real world. I know few teachers who make their money wheeling and dealing. That's why after you've learned the basics the best ideas will come not from books or courses but from looking at many properties and negotiating in the field. Very much secondary are the courses. To repeat, in the order of importance it is accounting, real estate and Federal Taxes that you should be interested in. Courses will do you more good and give you more usable ideas after you have educated yourself and understand what opportunities are on the market.

Now let's talk about "No Money Down Deals." Why would a seller ever want to take a no money down deal? I'll tell you why. Because what is a no money down deal to you as buyer will not necessarily be a "no money received" deal to the seller. Say a seller owns a $100,000 property with no mortgage on it. If you bought it from him subject to obtaining an 80% first loan, then he gets $80,000 cash when the deal closes (from the new financing). If you owe him $20,000 that's only a small 20% of the sales price not in cash.

You, as a buyer, might make a no money down deal if a second mortgage lender agreed to lend the $20,000 down payment. Thus, what is a no money down deal to you may yield the seller 100% of his sales price in cash. But many sellers, particularly older people, like to hold high interest yielding mortgages.

1 See order form at back of this book for "home study course."

Typical real estate agents or brokers do not like a no money down deal. They expect a 6% commission in cash. Look at a $100,000 deal. A broker wants a $6,000 cash commission when the deal closes. And of course, the extra $6,000 has to be generated somewhere. So, usually, it's harder to make a no money down deal with a hungry broker in the picture than if you are dealing directly with the seller.

For the moment assume that we found a good property and a willing seller (a little old lady with a nice four-plex in a neighborhood you have decided is convenient and desireable). You negotiate a price with her: $100,000. The terms are no money down; an 80% bank loan with the seller carrying $20,000 at 10% interest for 10 years.

Sometimes a seller or lender will give you the argument that if you don't have any money in a deal, you are likely to walk away if times get tough. Supposedly you have "nothing to lose." It may take a little convincing to overcome that fear on the part of the seller. You have to show the seller, the little old lady in our case, that perhaps you have had the same job for quite a long time and you are a steady person; a family man. Whatever works! After 20 visits, a few small gifts and a lot of conversation, hopefully you can convince the seller that your motive is not to get her property and then walk away from it but rather to keep it and improve it. Of course, that truly should be your motive. You must convince the seller you will provide the dependable monthly checks she needs.

Of course, if you do not pay the $20,000 debt back, she can always take back her property and sell it to someone else. That is what a second mortgage is all about. It is not as if the seller is getting "nothing". She is getting $80,000 cash from the proceeds of the first mortgage and an additional $20,000 note from you. The note itself has a cash value and could be resold at a discount by the seller for between $16,000 and $18,000. Discounts on second mortgages typically range from 20% to 40% of the face value. So there's only a limited risk in making a no money down deal with you. Still you always have to convince sellers and lenders that you are reliable.

Now let's analyze a typical deal. We'll take the $100,000 four-plex and asume the fair rents are $300 a month each on the four units that you just bought. An income of $300 for four units is a total of $1,200 per month. Eighty times that is $96,000. So $100,000 fits my rule of thumb as the fair market value of that particular property. I told you that the gross rents per month for all the units combined is $1,200 per month. If you multiply that times 12, you will get an annual gross rental income of $14,400 per year. Six and ½ times the annual gross is about $99,000.

Your payments on the first mortgage would be at least $10,000 per year. Your real estate taxes in that deal would be under $2,000 while your upkeep and maintenance would be another $2,000 per year. The reason I'm throwing these figures out now is because there are certain rules of thumb that you should know.

Figure real estate taxes in most Western States are going to be just about 20% of your gross rent.* Other expenses in round numbers will be about 20% depending on the age and condition of the building. The rest of the rental income will go to the amortization of the loan. And that figure of course will be different in every case depending upon what arrangement you made for financing. But in the case we are talking about, the loan amortization payments would be about $10,000 per year. The expenses and taxes altogether would be about $4,000 a year; total $14,000. With a gross rental income of $14,400, the net cash flow would be only $400 per year.

Seeing this small figure you might ask what's so terrific about spending a lot of time negotiating a deal, running the property, putting out a lot of work and effort, improving the property, collecting rent. Maybe if you are lucky and have no vacancies or major repairs you take out $400 a year. You say to yourself, "I didn't put up any money but what's so terrific? $400 a year? That's peanuts. How is that kind of deal ever going to get me financially independent? I can see that it might possibly make me a millionaire in 3,000 years - - but what's with this two years Greene talks about?" Well, the cash flow in real estate so long as you break even, is the least important consideration. Let's talk about what's really important. How do you make money? The first invisible profit is the benefit you get from depreciation. Depreciation is an artificial bookkeeping or accounting figure that the Internal Revenue Service with it's Alice-In-Wonderland rule book says you are allowed to offset

*Under the recent Jarvis-Gann Amendment in California, real estate taxes should be about 1% of what you pay for the building, or $1,000 per year in our example. In Nevada, taxes are also about 1% of value. Check actual figures by merely calling your friendly county tax assessor.

92

against your other income when you own real estate. The government assumes that when you buy a $100,000 property, the land will not depreciate. The land in our example may be worth $20,000. They will let you assume that the structure is worth $70,000. Now you see, the land value and the structure value that's a total of $70,000 and $20,000; $90,000 in all. What happened to the other $10,000? The other $10,000 can be allocated to personal property. That's stuff like carpets, drapes, refrigerators and so on. Who allocates? You do.

You can depreciate a building and its contents but not the land on which it stands. You are allowed to depreciate a structure in as little as 10 years, if that building is old, decrepit, falling apart, wood frame, and low rent. That type of building is my favorite investment because it can always be assigned a relatively short remaining life for IRS purposes.

Who sets that life? You as the tax payer are responsible for estimating that remaining useful life of any building you buy. If you said to yourself in good faith "this building would need a major remodeling after 10 years to stay competitive and rentable", you would be entitled to use a 10 year life and a 10 year depreciation schedule in computing your income tax. That 10 years would be divided into the price of the property, 10 into $70,000 equals $7,000. You would then get an "artificial loss", a depreciation figure of $7,000 per year. That is the depreciation on the structure, $70,000 spread over 10 years. That figure alone would go a long way to save and possibly eliminate your Federal and State income tax.

THE MAIN BENEFIT OF BUYING REAL ESTATE IS NOT THE CASH FLOW. (CASH FLOW IS WHAT YOU HAVE LEFT FROM YOUR RENTS AFTER YOU PAY THE MORTGAGE, TAXES AND OPERATING EXPENSES.) THE MAIN BENEFIT YOU ARE GOING TO REAP DURING YOUR FIRST YEAR IS A TREMENDOUS TAX REFUND WINDFALL.

Here is a bird's-eye view of how you get the tax refund. You bought that $100,000 building. You start year one taking straight line depreciation over a ten year life, meaning $7,000 per year. As explained, depreciation is an artificial loss. In the real world your property can double or triple in value. Still, for tax purposes it is treated as if you really lost money. Remember, depreciation occurs only for tax purposes and for accounting purposes. There is no real loss. But for IRS purposes it's <u>as if</u> you had a business loss of $7,000 out of pocket.

So you start out with that benefit of $7,000 a year loss being the depreciation on the <u>structure</u>. There was also $10,000 worth of carpets, drapes, stoves, fixtures, refrigerators - that sort of <u>removable</u> or detachable category of thing the IRS calls personal property. Personal property can be depreciated over a much shorter life than the structure itself. The IRS says, for old appliances, carpets, drapes, a 3 to 6 year useful life would be reasonable. That would give you up to $3,333 worth of depreciation on the personal property the first year that you own the building. But IRS say "Take another 20% on top of that for your depreciation of personal property in your first year." Why? That's the rule. With a 6-year life and accelerated depreciation you get an extra 20% first year depreciation on furnishings and fixtures. Don't question a gift from the IRS!

So, when you add that to your depreciation of the building, you are taking $7,000 depreciation on the structure and a total of over $5,000 first year depreciation on the personal property. That is over $12,000 a year deductible from your other taxable wage-slave income.*

If you have another job and you happen to be making wages of $10,000 a year, this depreciation of $12,000 coming in from your first real estate deal will result for U.S. Federal and State Income Tax purposes in your reporting a net income of less than zero. That will translate into at least a $3,000 a year tax savings.

For a plumber or brain surgeon with $250,000 of earned income and $250,000 of unearned income, the first year tax savings resulting from the purchase of larger amounts of property could be well in excess of a quarter million dollars.

Clearly, the main benefit of buying a few run down buildings for little or no money down will be a magic wand to eliminate current and future taxes forever and absolutely! Equally amazing: You are entitled to a refund of taxes you have paid during the prior three years - plus interest.

Yes, best of all, you can carry these artificial real estate losses back 3 years and get a refund of every bit of income tax you have paid in the last 3

*The mechanics of how to figure depreciation are explained in detail in our companion volume, <u>Landlording</u>. See order form in back of this book.

years. Not only that, you get up to 21% interest (7% per year) on the amounts refunded from the government.

The U.S. government will subsidize your entry into the real estate game to an almost incredible degree. The income tax refund check you get from the treasury could be $10,000, $500,000 or more depending on how much you paid in taxes during the past three or four years. The more you paid, the more you get back.

The next benefit you get from owning real estate is the dollar appreciation resulting from inflation. We talked previously about the negative effects of a 10% inflation rate on the worker, saver or rich person with money in the bank. The same 10% decline in value of money or a wage-slave's purchasing power will make the buildings that you bought for $100,000 worth at least $10,000 more paper dollars a year later. The real value of the property may be the same - but because of your high indebtedness you make out like a bandit. When you bought a building for no money down in year 1, in year 2 with 10% inflation you would be able to sell that building for a $10,000 real money cash profit. Since that $10,000 would be taxable you'd no doubt prefer to refinance the property and pull out $10,000 in tax free cash by borrowing, yet keeping the property.

Let's consider the tax free borrowing power that will be yours once you own property. You bought a $100,000 duplex a few years back. It's gone up in value to $150,000 just as a result of inflation. It was a very average deal. Nothing special. You did no work - made no physical improvements. Because it has gone up in dollar value from $100,000 to $150,000 you will be able to borrow around $40,000 more against the property. That maneuver is called "refinancing".

How does refinancing work? Once you borrow that money, the bank isn't concerned with what you do with it. You can spend it on a lover or give it to the Red Cross. You can fly around the world, buy yourself a yacht, or do whatever turns you on. Refinancing proceeds are like income because you can spend the money any way you want. But because it is borrowed, the IRS doesn't consider it taxable income. BORROWED MONEY IS NEVER TAX-ABLE INCOME! So one of the best things about real estate, it gives you more and more borrowing power as the years pass. The more inflation we have, the better it is for the real estate owner.

The next logical question is, if you borrow money, don't you have to pay it back? The answer is you don't have to pay it back because your tenants will pay it back. What's more, with rents increasing at the rate of 10 to 20% a year, inflation will in a few years time make the rest of the loan appear insignificant.

After inflation the next thing to consider is your due reward for creativity and good management; initiative and skillful negotiating. Many times, a property you buy will be run down and painted an ugly color. You may choose to paint it with super-graphics or give it charm by adding geranium window boxes and bright shutters. Cosmetic improvements, tastefully executed can make your property worth infinitely more than it was when you bought it. Then too, the fact that you looked at considerable amounts of property before you committed yourself to any particular one means that you probably bought "right", or slightly below market value. If you also negotiated hard and received good financing terms, a good long term loan in and of itself makes the property worth more: most buyers do not expect to get a no money down deal, and if you got 100% financing, other buyers will beat your door down to take the deal off your hands for a premium or profit to you above the loans. If you did not get better than average terms, you should have been able to negotiate the seller down to a price of at least 10% below market.

As you can see, the real benefit on our $100,000 deal is not the pitiful $400 cash flow you have available to spend, but will be the invisible benefits:

DEPRECIATION - The magic wand that eliminates present and future taxes; and gets you a refund of whatever you have paid during the past 3 years. Projected value on your first deal: $10,000.

CREATIVITY & MANAGEMENT - The reward you have earned by carefully improving your property, and managing it well. Possible resulting improvement in value on your first property: $10,000

INITIATIVE & NEGOTIATION - Real estate is an "imperfect market" says the Economists. As a result, if you search carefully, and negotiate hard, it is to be expected that properties you acquire will be bargains worth $10,000 more than what you paid.

INFLATIONARY PRICE INCREASE - In a highly leveraged real estate deal, because of the decline in the purchasing power of the dollar, the fixed debt amortization payments become less of a burden because they are made with upward rising rents. The

underlying market values of income properties increase at
something more than the inflation rate. Assumed one year
gain on first deal: $10,000

Total up those four factors and you will see a possible increase in your net worth - - one year after your very first deal - - of $40,000! While this figure is arbitrary, it represents a composite - - and a very conservative composite - - of typical results. Total idiots - - people who can't chew gum and drive a car at the same time achieved similar results over and over again.

If you could make $40,000 on one "no money down" deal, what would you make on 50 or 100 deals? Get used to multiplying and having your results come out in million dollar plus figures -- because you'd make between one and two MILLION.

Can YOU do it? The answer is unquestionably, YES! You don't have to do it in one year by making two deals a month. Take it easy. Just do one a month. You'll be a millionaire in two years.

Now skeptics will say, "You can't do that. It's not that easy." But if you own an ordinary home or if you know anyone who has bought an ordinary home in the last few years, just ask them. Ask any homeower! A place I bougnt about 5 years ago when the price of a home was $25,000 required a down payment of $2,500. The average loan was for $22,500 at 7% interest. Just look at it today. The average selling price of that same property is close to $100,000. But the loan I took out 5 years ago is now paid down to $18,000.

What is the equity in such a home? Equity is the market value less the loan balance or the anticipated net cash receivable if you sold. In this average deal, the equity is $82,000. Thus, $2,500 invested 5 years ago in a very average home has turned into a $82,000 equity. And it's the easiest money that I or all those other homeowners who bought 5 years ago made in their lives. If they had bought a dozen homes five years ago, all you'd have to do is multiply $82,000 by 12 times. Owning a dozen dinky homes makes you a millionaire.

Will it happen again in the next five years? If inflation keeps increasing at it's present rate of increase, instead of looking at $82,000 in equity you'd probably be talking about much more appreciation in similar properties bought today. But if inflation does not continue at the same rate and drops to half you'll only make $33,000. That would not be too bad a return on a $2,500 investment without a risk.

As you can guess, most people who invested $2,500 in a home purchased five years ago probably did not shop too hard. They didn't know the secrets or tricks of the trade explained here: How to eliminate closing costs for instance. They were not good negotiators. They had low ambitions. They had no motivation to make a fortune in real estate. They just wanted a place to live! They didn't have the drive to look at 100 deals a weekend and pick out only the three best ones. Still, the average home owner picked up from $70,000 to $80,000.

What did that same guy save at his wage-slave job? What did you save while working at your eight hour a day job? The average guy was lucky to save $1,000 a year! In 5 years that totals $5,000. Five years ago that could have bought a new Cadillac. Today you barely get a Volkswagen for $5,000.

The moral should be clear. In an inflationary era, you can't get ahead working for a wage or salary. But you can make a great deal of money using borrowed funds to buy real estate. I've done it; my associates are doing it all over the United States and you can certainly do it! If this sounds inspirational, like a pep talk, that's what it's meant to be. Because negativism is sure defeat. If you feel you can't make it, that attitude will bog you down and prevent you from taking the first step.

You can make big money in real estate without quitting your present job and without risking anything except time you would be wasting anyway. If you go into the real estate market place with a positive attitude and if you make enough offers, you'll be surprised at the exceptional opportunities just waiting like ripe fruit on trees. But you must get out there and circulate. You must get out there today and start looking at properties. There's no way that you can fail! There's no risk!

If you put little or no downpayment on properties, the most you can lose is your time. If you put 10% down you can soon get your money out in the form of refinancing. Of course, if you put 'no money down' in the first place, there's no risk at all. In California, lenders, for technical reasons, cannot go after your personal assets if you default on a purchase money real estate loan used to buy 4 units or less. Now I'm not telling you to default. But if the world turns to ashes and we have a quake, or the worst depression we've ever had hits, it's comforting to know you <u>can</u> walk away. You can walk away and still hold on to whatever else you may own.

Can you make a lot of money in real estate today? Probably, yes. Not everybody can do it. If you are very rich, you may have problems. Rich folks are usually not hungry enough to get out in the rough and tumble market and make deals. Rich people always seem anxious to make a big down payment. Or maybe to pay all cash. They are conservative. In inflationary times that is not the way to do it. If you bought a $100,000 property for all cash and it went up in value 10% a year, all you get is a 10% profit on your money. But if you buy ten $100,000 properties for 10% down and they each go up 10%, you make a hundred thousand dollars. Over 100% on your money. Rich people do not seem to understand that using leverage or debt is how you make money from inflation. Creditors lose their shirts. Rich people are usually of the creditor class. They are wiped out by inflation. To make big money you can't be too smart or too intellectual. If one thinks too much about the pro's and con's, and intellectualizes endlessly over "to buy or not to buy" a particular property, someone else will turn the deal before you even make a decision. Action, not thoughts, make Tycoons.

You cannot be lazy. If you have a problem with a stopped up drain, or some tenant complaint, you have to get out there and snake it. If you don't keep your tenant happy, it's "curtains." If you just sit back and pay no attention to your properties; if you let the rents get behind; if you don't stay on top of the collections - real estate will not work out for you. Keeping up with properties, getting along with your tenants and doing simple repairs promptly is very simple. Very necessary!

Real estate is not a lazy person's business. Sure, after you've been in it a few years, then you can hire managers, bookkeepers, handymen. They will be your buffers. But, for the first few years you will have to work like you have never worked before. If you are too lazy to get off your fanny and look at properties and keep them up once you own them, you won't make it.

Quit watching soap operas on television. Take that T.V. set, put it in the closet. Leave it there for three years. Get out, start looking at property this weekend. The first step is to get out into the real world. Inertia is the greatest problem. Get off the time wasting, T.V., Time magazine treadmill. Quit wasting time. This month look at 100 properties! All your spare time should be devoted to looking at properties, starting now. After you've looked at 100 properties, then make a low down or no money down offer on every single property that you look at. You can make low offers and know that you are doing right because once you have looked at a hundred deals you will know what every property is worth. Being successful in real estate is like being an athlete. The more you work at it, the better you get. If you get out there and you look you'll get an education and many contacts. If you make a lot of offers you'll own property. Once you become a landlord, if you make the effort to effectively manage your property, you will get very rich, very soon.

The heart of this little pep talk to repeat for the tenth time is that you should get out there. Now! Live, sleep, think, eat and talk to everybody you run into about their real estate. Talk to everybody that knows anything about real estate. That way you will be getting a very good education. After looking at all the property on the market in your community, you will be as good an appraiser as anyone else. And once you've looked at 100 deals, you'll develop a very good sense as to what things should sell for. When a bargain comes up, you'll be able to recognize it. That's probably something you can't do right now.

I want to end this section by actually writing up a deal with you. Let's use a form I recently put together. This OFFER TO PURCHASE REAL ESTATE can be used when you attempt to buy any type of real property. If you don't like my form, or on general principles, you should write for sample forms to: PROFESSIONAL PUBLISHING COMPANY, PO Box 4187, San Rafael, CA 94903. They have agreed to supply my "Tycoons" with a thick sample pad of all their real estate forms for $2-. I'm sure these forms will give you many good ideas ! You should never be afraid to modify a printed form to fit your own needs -- by changing the language, crossing out paragraphs you don't like, or by cutting and pasting. It's YOUR contract and must be tailored to fit YOUR needs.

OFFER TO PURCHASE REAL ESTATE

RECEIVED FROM: *Bob Buyer, Yourtown, Yourstate* TELEPHONE: *(333) 444-555*
or his assignee, hereafter "Buyer" THIS SUM RECEIVED AS A DEPOSIT: *$1,000*
( ) Personal Check, ( ) Cash, ( ) Cashier's Check, ( ) Deposit to Escrow,
(X) Other: *Note* ON A TOTAL PURCHASE PRICE OF: *One Hundred Thousand Dollars*
For real property situated in the city of *Bigtown* county of *Globe* state of *California*
ADDRESS: *1 Bargain Ave., a duplex with 3 garages, assessor's parcel # 12345*
SUBJECT TO THE FOLLOWING TERMS AND CONDITIONS: *Buyer to assume existing*
$70,000 loan from XYZ Savings & Loan Association. Seller to carry back $30,000
second loan at 10% interest only for 10 years. Escrow to be at Founder's Title
Company, Yourtown Office.
Note: Buyer is acquiring property for long-term investment purposes, not for resale.
ADDENDUMS: *The attached "Exhibit A" is part of this agreement.*
PERSONAL PROPERTY INCLUDED WITH THIS REAL ESTATE: *Drapes & wall to wall*
carpeting in living room, 2 gas stoves, 2 GE refrigerators, washer & dryer,
assorted garden tools, 6 potted cactus plants on front deck.
ENCUMBRANCES: All liens against property including bonds or assessments are to be
paid by the seller. Taxes to be prorated to date of sale. Clear title to be provided
by seller.
CLOSING COSTS: Escrow charges and "points" to be paid by the seller.
DEPOSIT INCREASE: Not applicable.
TITLE INSURANCE POLICY TO BE PAID FOR BY: ( ) THE SELLER (Binder Rate)
( ) THE BUYER.
OCCUPANCY DATE: ( ) _____ (X) UPON RECORDATION OF DEED
The date of closing shall be *Feb. 2, 1980*. If seller remains in possession after the
closing and buyer has performed fully, seller shall pay buyer $ *30.00* per day from
date of recording to date possession is delivered. Seller shall leave in escrow
$ *750.00* as a security deposit for cleaning, damage and rent payment in the event
possession not delivered at closing.
RISK OF LOSS: Shall be Seller's until date of closing.
PRORATIONS: Shall be made as of date of closing as per custom in the area.
MAINTENANCE AND CONDITION: Seller agrees to maintain and deliver all heating,
sewer, electrical, plumbing appliances & equipment in good working order, to maintain
and deliver the grounds and property in clean condition with no broken or cracked
glass & all debris and personal property removed.
CODE VIOLATION: The seller warrants that he has neither created nor has any
knowledge of legal violations relating to this property.
PEST CONTROL: Inspection report to be obtained at expense of: 1. ( ) Seller;
2. ( ) Buyer; 3. ( ) Seller agrees to have all needed pest control work done at his
expense and to deliver to buyer a termite cleared property; 4. ( ) Property is to
be taken in its present condition subject to buyer's approval of termite report.
TIME IS OF THE ESSENCE IN THIS CONTRACT.

Bob Buyer	*Barbara Buyer*
DATED: *Jan. 1, 1980* TIME: *9 a.m.*	BUYERS

************************************ACCEPTANCE************************************

The seller accepts the above offer. At the closing, seller agrees to pay a real
estate broker's commission of *none* for services rendered. In the event legal
action is instituted to enforce this contract, the prevailing party is to receive
attorney's fees. The seller acknowledges receiving a copy of this contract.

I acknowledge that the buyer and
seller signed this document in my
presence and in the presence of
each other:

Sam Seller

Sally Seller

SELLERS

Norah Notary DATED: *Jan. 1, 1980*
NOTARY PUBLIC

DATED: *Jan. 1, 1980* TIME: *9 a.m.*

Now there are timid souls out there reading this book and they think that if you offer $100,000. on a property and things do not work out you will have big problems. By not working out I mean you've changed your mind and don't want to buy. The timid souls think you could lose 'everything' just by making an offer. 'They' would come and 'they' would take home, bank accounts, and car.

Nothing could be further from the truth. When you make an offer on this form (and you make it right) and the seller accepts it, guess what? The seller must sell to you. But if you do not want the property before the deal closes you can walk away from the deal with no loss, no penalties, and no cost whatsoever. In most real estate deals, done my way, even after the deal <u>closes</u> you can walk away from it with no loss whatsoever. So let's get into a sample offer right now. Let me show you how to fill out a standard purchase agreement. You can do it in a way to tie up the property so the seller can't get out of the deal. <u>But you can.</u>

First of all, fill in the line <u>Received From</u> with you name, Bob Buyer; your address, your town and your phone number. In every real estate deal there is a lot of communication that has to do on and if the seller does not have your address and does not know how to get in touch with you, all sorts of things can go wrong. It can blow a deal out of the water. These days everybody thinks they are a celebrity and has unlisted phone numbers. If you can't get in touch to arrange for the lender to get in to appraise, it's very frustrating indeed. Naturally you want the seller and any real estate agents involved to have your name and number <u>just as you need the seller's</u> and his agent's name, address and phone number. The best way to keep that information handy, right at the start of negotiations, is to put everybody's name, address and phone number on the offer and acceptance form.

The next thing for you to fill in, is where it says <u>Sum Received As a Deposit</u>. You do not want to give the seller any deposit if you don't want to tie up $1,000 of real money just because a broker says it is "customary." Not at all. So where the box that says personal check or cash or cashier's check appears, you mark the place that says "Other." You write in "Note."

A note is something you can make up or get at any stationery store.
This is what your note might look like:

STRAIGHT NOTE

$ _1,000.00_   _Modesto_ , California, _January 1,_ , 19_80_

Upon closing of deal on 1 Bargain Avenue _____ after date, for value received,

I promise to pay to _Sam Seller, only if needed to close this real estate deal_ _____

_____, or order, at

the sellerstown office of St. Paul Title Company as escrow agent _____

the sum of _one thousand_ DOLLARS.

with _no_ interest from _date_ , until paid at the

rate of _- 0 -_ per cent per annum, payable _in full at the closing, if_ _____

required under terms of attached purchase agreement and deposit receipt dated

January 1, 1980

Principal and interest payable in lawful money of the United States of America. Should default be made in payment of interest when due the whole sum of principal and interest shall become immediately due at the option of the holder of this note. If action be instituted on this note I promise to pay such sum as the Court may fix as Attorney's fees.

_____ (Signed) _Bob Buyer_ _____

This is what a California Trust Deed looks like:

RECORDING REQUESTED BY

Bob Buyer

AND WHEN RECORDED MAIL TO

Name `1 Bargain Avenue Partnership`
Street Address `Your P.O. Box`
City & State `Yourtown and State`

——————————— SPACE ABOVE THIS LINE FOR RECORDER'S USE ———————————

SHORT FORM DEED OF TRUST AND ASSIGNMENT OF RENTS   A.P.N

This Deed of Trust, made this **1st** day of **January, 1980** between
the 1 Bargain Avenue Partnership

, herein called TRUSTOR,

whose address is **yourbox, yourtown**
(number and street)   (city)   (state)   (zip)

St. Paul Title Company, a California corporation, herein called TRUSTEE, and

Sam Seller , herein called BENEFICIARY,

Witnesseth: That Trustor IRREVOCABLY GRANTS, TRANSFERS AND ASSIGNS to TRUSTEE IN TRUST, WITH POWER OF SALE, that property in County, California, described as:

Insert legal description of 1 Bargain Avenue

TOGETHER WITH the rents, issues and profits thereof, SUBJECT, HOWEVER, to the right, power and authority given to and conferred upon Beneficiary by paragraph (10) of the provisions incorporated herein by reference to collect and apply such rents, issues and profits

For the Purpose of Securing: 1. Performance of each agreement of Trustor incorporated by reference or contained herein. 2. Payment of the indebtedness evidenced by one promissory note of even date herewith, and any extension or renewal thereof, in the principal sum of $ **30,000** executed by Trustor in favor of Beneficiary or order. 3. Payment of such further sums as the then record owner of said property hereafter may borrow from Beneficiary, when evidenced by another note (or notes) reciting it is so secured.

To Protect the Security of This Deed of Trust, Trustor Agrees: By the execution and delivery of this Deed of Trust and the note secured hereby, that provisions (1) to (14), inclusive, of the fictitious deed of trust recorded in Santa Barbara County and Sonoma County October 18, 1961, and in all other counties October 23, 1961, in the book and at the page of Official Records in the office of the county recorder of the county where said property is located, noted below opposite the name of such county, viz.:

COUNTY	BOOK	PAGE	COUNTY	BOOK	PAGE	COUNTY	BOOK	PAGE	COUNTY	BOOK	PAGE
Alameda	435	684	Kings	792	833	Placer	895	301	Sierra	29	335
Alpine	1	250	Lake	362	39	Plumas	151	5	Siskiyou	468	181
Amador	104	348	Lassen	171	471	Riverside	3005	523	Solano	1105	182
Butte	1145	1	Los Angeles	T2055	899	Sacramento	4331	62	Sonoma	1851	689
Calaveras	145	152	Madera	810	170	San Benito	271	383	Stanislaus	1715	456
Colusa	296	617	Marin	1508	339	San Bernardino	5567	61	Sutter	572	297
Contra Costa	3978	47	Mariposa	77	292	San Francisco	A332	905	Tehama	401	289
Del Norte	78	414	Mendocino	579	530	San Joaquin	2470	311	Trinity	93	366
El Dorado	568	456	Merced	1547	538	San Luis Obispo	1151	12	Tulare	2294	275
Fresno	4626	572	Modoc	184	851	San Mateo	4078	420	Tuolumne	135	47
Glenn	422	184	Mono	52	429	Santa Barbara	1878	860	Ventura	2062	386
Humboldt	657	527	Monterey	2194	538	Santa Clara	5336	341	Yolo	653	245
Imperial	1091	501	Napa	639	86	Santa Cruz	1431	494	Yuba	334	486
Inyo	147	598	Nevada	305	320	Shasta	684	528			
Kern	3427	60	Orange	5889	611	San Diego	Series 2 Book 1961, Page 183887				

(which provisions, identical in all counties, are printed on the reverse hereof) hereby are adopted and incorporated herein and made a part hereof as fully as though set forth herein at length; that he will observe and perform said provisions; and that the references to property, obligations, and parties in said provisions shall be construed to refer to the property, obligations, and parties set forth in this Deed of Trust.

The undersigned Trustor requests that a copy of any Notice of Default and of any Notice of Sale hereunder be mailed to him at his address hereinbefore set forth.

STATE OF CALIFORNIA,

COUNTY OF **Placer** } SS.

On **1 Jan 1980** before me, the undersigned, a Notary Public in and for said State, personally appeared **Bob Buyer, partner of the 1 Bargain Avenue partnership** ., known to me to be the person whose name **is** subscribed to the within instrument and acknowledged that **he** executed the same. WITNESS my hand and official seal.

Signature **Norah Notary**

Signature of Trustor

Bob Buyer, Partner

1 Bargain Avenue Partnership

(Seal)

Title Order No.

Escrow or Loan No.

SP123-78

(This area for official notarial seal)

To Protect the Security of This Deed of Trust, Trustor Agrees:

(1) To keep said property in good condition and repair; not to remove or demolish any building thereon; to complete or restore promptly and in good and workmanlike manner any building which may be constructed, damaged or destroyed thereon and to pay when due all claims for labor performed and materials furnished therefor; to comply with all laws affecting said property or requiring any alterations or improvements to be made thereon; not to commit or permit waste thereof; not to commit, suffer or permit any act upon said property in violation of law; to cultivate, irrigate, fertilize, fumigate, prune and do all other acts which from the character or use of said property may be reasonably necessary, the specific enumerations herein not excluding the general.

(2) To provide, maintain and deliver to Beneficiary fire insurance satisfactory to and with loss payable to Beneficiary. The amount collected under any fire or other insurance policy may be applied by Beneficiary upon indebtedness secured hereby and in such order as Beneficiary may determine, or at option of Beneficiary the entire amount so collected or any part thereof may be released to Trustor. Such application or release shall not cure or waive any default or notice of default hereunder or invalidate any act done pursuant to such notice.

(3) To appear in and defend any action or proceeding purporting to affect the security hereof or the rights or powers of Beneficiary or Trustee; and to pay all costs and expenses, including cost of evidence of title and attorney's fees in a reasonable sum, in any such action or proceeding in which Beneficiary or Trustee may appear, and in any suit brought by Beneficiary to foreclose this Deed.

(4) To pay: at least ten days before delinquency all taxes and assessments affecting said property, including assessments on appurtenant water stock; when due, all incumbrances, charges and liens, with interest, on said property or any part thereof; and all costs, fees and expenses of this Trust.

Should Trustor fail to make any payment or to do any act as herein provided, then Beneficiary or Trustee, but without obligation so to do and without notice to or demand upon Trustor and without releasing Trustor from any obligation hereof, may: make or do the same in such manner and to such extent as either may deem necessary to protect the security hereof, Beneficiary or Trustee being authorized to enter upon said property for such purposes; appear in and defend any action or proceeding purporting to affect the security hereof or the rights or powers of Beneficiary or Trustee; pay, purchase, contest or compromise any incumbrance, charge or lien which in the judgment of either appears to be prior or superior hereto; and, in exercising any such powers, pay necessary expenses, employ counsel and pay his reasonable fees.

(5) To pay immediately and without demand all sums so expended by Beneficiary or Trustee, with interest from date of expenditure at the amount allowed by law in effect at the date hereof, and to pay for any statement provided for by law in effect at the date hereof regarding the obligation secured hereby any amount demanded by the Beneficiary not to exceed the maximum allowed by law at the time when said statement is demanded.

(6) That any award of damages in connection with any condemnation for public use of or injury to said property or any part thereof is hereby assigned and shall be paid to Beneficiary who may apply or release such moneys received by him in the same manner and with the same effect as above provided for disposition of proceeds of fire or other insurance.

(7) That by accepting payment of any sum secured hereby after its due date, Beneficiary does not waive his right either to require prompt payment when due of all other sums so secured or to declare default for failure so to pay.

(8) That at any time or from time to time, without liability therefor and without notice, upon written request of Beneficiary and presentation of this Deed and said note for endorsement, and without affecting the personal liability of any person for payment of the indebtedness secured hereby, Trustee may: reconvey any part of said property; consent to the making of any map or plat thereof; join in granting any easement thereon; or join in any extension agreement or any agreement subordinating the lien or charge hereof.

(9) That upon written request of Beneficiary stating that all sums secured hereby have been paid, and upon surrender of this Deed and said note to Trustee for cancellation and retention and upon payment of its fees, Trustee shall reconvey, without warranty, the property then held hereunder. The recitals in such reconveyance of any matters or facts shall be conclusive proof of the truthfulness thereof. The grantee in such reconveyance may be described as "the person or persons legally entitled thereto." Five years after issuance of such full reconveyance, Trustee may destroy said note and this Deed (unless directed in such request to retain them).

(10) That as additional security, Trustor hereby gives to and confers upon Beneficiary the right, power and authority, during the continuance of these Trusts, to collect the rents, issues and profits of said property, reserving unto Trustor the right, prior to any default by Trustor in payment of any indebtedness secured hereby or in performance of any agreement hereunder, to collect and retain such rents, issues and profits as they become due and payable. Upon any such default, Beneficiary may at any time without notice, either in person, by agent, or by a receiver to be appointed by a court, and without regard to the adequacy of any security for the indebtedness hereby secured, enter upon and take possession of said property or any part thereof, in his own name sue for or otherwise collect such rents and profits, including those past due and unpaid, and apply the same, less costs and expenses of operation and collection, including reasonable attorney's fees, upon any indebtedness secured hereby, and in such order as Beneficiary may determine. The entering upon and taking possession of said property, the collection of such rents, issues and profits and the application thereof as aforesaid, shall not cure or waive any default or notice of default hereunder or invalidate any act done pursuant to such notice.

(11) That upon default by Trustor in payment of any indebtedness secured hereby or in performance of any agreement hereunder, Beneficiary may declare all sums secured hereby immediately due and payable by delivery to Trustee of written declaration of default and demand for sale and of written notice of default and of election to cause to be sold said property, which notice Trustee shall cause to be filed for record. Beneficiary also shall deposit with Trustee this Deed, said note and all documents evidencing expenditures secured hereby.

After the lapse of such time as may then be required by law following the recordation of said notice of default, and notice of sale having been given as then required by law, Trustee, without demand on Trustor, shall sell said property at the time and place fixed by it in said notice of sale, either as a whole or in separate parcels, and in such order as it may determine, at public auction to the highest bidder for cash in lawful money of the United States, payable at time of sale. Trustee may postpone sale of all or any portion of said property by public announcement at such time and place of sale, and from time to time thereafter may postpone such sale by public announcement at the time fixed by the preceding postponement. Trustee shall deliver to such purchaser its deed conveying the property so sold, but without any covenant or warranty, express or implied. The recitals in such deed of any matters or facts shall be conclusive proof of the truthfulness thereof. Any person, including Trustor, Trustee, or Beneficiary as hereinafter defined, may purchase at such sale.

After deducting all costs, fees and expenses of Trustee and of this Trust, including cost of evidence of title in connection with sale, Trustee shall apply the proceeds of sale to payment of: all sums expended under the terms hereof, not then repaid, with accrued interest at the amount allowed by law in effect at the date hereof; all other sums then secured hereby; and the remainder, if any, to the person or persons legally entitled thereto.

(12) Beneficiary, or any successor in ownership of any indebtedness secured hereby, may from time to time, by instrument in writing, substitute a successor or successors to any Trustee named herein or acting hereunder, which instrument, executed by the Beneficiary and duly acknowledged and recorded in the office of the recorder of the county or counties where said property is situated, shall be conclusive proof of proper substitution of such successor Trustee or Trustees, who shall, without conveyance from the Trustee predecessor, succeed to all its title, estate, rights, powers and duties. Said instrument must contain the name of the original Trustor, Trustee and Beneficiary hereunder, the book and page where this Deed is recorded and the name and address of the new Trustee.

(13) That this Deed applies to, inures to the benefit of, and binds all parties hereto, their heirs, legatees, devisees, administrators, executors, successors and assigns. The term Beneficiary shall mean the owner and holder, including pledgees, of the note secured hereby, whether or not named as Beneficiary herein. In this Deed, whenever the context so requires, the masculine gender includes the feminine and/or neuter, and the singular number includes the plural.

(14) That Trustee accepts this Trust when this Deed, duly executed and acknowledged, is made a public record as provided by law. Trustee is not obligated to notify any party hereto of pending sale under any other Deed of Trust or of any action or proceeding in which Trustor, Beneficiary or Trustee shall be a party unless brought by Trustee.

REQUEST FOR FULL RECONVEYANCE

To be used only when note has been paid.

Dated_____

To St. Paul Title Company, Trustee:

The undersigned is the legal owner and holder of all indebtedness secured by the within Deed of Trust. All sums secured by said Deed of Trust have been fully paid and satisfied; and you are hereby requested and directed, on payment to you of any sums owing to you under the terms of said Deed of Trust, to cancel all evidences of indebtedness, secured by said Deed of Trust, delivered to you herewith together with said Deed of Trust, and to reconvey, without warranty, to the parties designated by the terms of said Deed of Trust, the estate now held by you under the same.

MAIL RECONVEYANCE TO:

_____   _____

_____   _____

_____   By _____

_____   By _____

Do not lose or destroy this Deed of Trust OR THE NOTE which it secures. Both must be delivered to the Trustee for cancellation before reconveyance will be made.

Short Form
Deed of Trust
WITH POWER OF SALE
AS TRUSTEE

ST. PAUL TITLE
COMPANY
AFFILIATE OF THE ST PAUL COMPANIES INC

COMPLETE STATEWIDE TITLE SERVICE

(Used with permission of St. Paul Title Company)

As you see, you will be able to make a dozen offers a day without putting up one dime. And there is no reason the seller should not accept a note instead of real money. The real money in most deals is going to be held by a broker or escrow company anyway. The seller doesn't get it. In those rare deals where you are forced to put up some real money, keep the deposit as low as possible. Like $100. I seldom make a deposit of more than $500 no matter how big the deal is.

Next: "Real Properties Situated In" Just fill in the address, city, town, county, and state. For example; 10 Bargain Avenue, Your Town, Your County, Your State. Then always describe the property, write down what it is. For instance, 'single family home', 'duplex', 'ten apartments' or whatever. Why? To guard against buying "illegal" units that were built without proper permits.

The next empty lines are for the terms and conditions. Of course, the best terms or conditions for a buyer are "An Interest Only Loan" at as low an interest rate as possible with no payments at all for as long as possible. The principal should be due in as far a distant future as the seller will consider. The terms are simply the best deal that you can negotiate. As a reasonable example; The seller will carry a $100,000 deed of trust for 10 years at 10% interest, payable interest only. If you think it is unusual to buy a $100,000 property with no money down and an interest only loan, be informed it is not unusual at all.

Brokers representing sellers do not like no money down deals but I have done it many times, even with agents in the deal. In fact, I bought one property recently for interest only, 10 years, 6% interest. Why? Because I gave the seller a higher price than he was asking for. As a result the seller was absolutely delighted to give me an interest rate 1/3 below the going market rate. Taxwise the deal worked out better for both of us. A high price and low interest rate gave me maximum depreciation. The seller had a tax deferred installment sale capital gain. He paid no tax at all on the sale.

Now, for "addendums"; That space gives you a chance to get a rebate for repairs. For instance, if you had obtained a commitment for an 80% institutional loan, you might want to have an addendum letter to promise that you will get a rebate to cover $10,000 in repairs needed on the property. Do you follow that? If you want a no money down deal, many times the lender, that is the institution willing to give you a first mortgage on the property, will lend you as much as 95% of the purchase price. But unless it's a government backed loan like FHA or VA , the lender generally will not want to give you a 100% loan. They want you to pay at least some down payment out of your own pocket. As a result of this attitude you might not want to advertise the fact that the source of your $10,000 down payment is a repair allowance you're getting from the seller.

What about personal property? You have always got to be careful. When you tour a property you're going to buy, there may be plants, chandeliers, carpets, or nice drapes that you hope to get as part of a package deal. But the seller doesn't feel they should be included. To avoid disputes, anything in the way of a fixture or a moveable object that you think should go with the property should be listed and attached to your offer in the form of an inventory. Then if the seller does not want to throw it in as part of the deal, argue and settle before rather than after the deal closes. There are often lawsuits or hard feelings on the subject of what was and what wasn't included. The general rule is that if personal property is not specifically mentioned in writing, it does not go with the deal. Rule? Settle what is included and what is not before the property changes hands. After property changes hands, possession is 99% of the law. Remember, refrigerators, appliances, drapes, furniture and detachable fixtures are typically removed by the seller and taken with him. Plants or bushes in the ground should stay, but potted plants or moveable window boxes can be taken out by the seller.

When you come to the next line about "Encumbrances," they are talking about mortgages or leins on the property -- like unpaid plumbing bills. All encumbrances should be paid by the seller, unless you plan to assume them and deduct the amounts due from the price.

Closing costs should also be paid for by the seller as far as I'm concerned (if you can get away with it as a buyer).

Once again, forget that the seller's broker tells you it's the "custom in the area" that buyers are supposed to pay for certain things like title insurance. Just put in "To be paid for by seller." If the seller accepts, you are home free. If the seller balks, it gives you something to negotiate about. Title Insurance in Northern California is generally paid for by the buyer. But that doesn't mean that you can't put in an X in the right place to suggest that it's going to be paid for by the seller. Not only that, if you check "to be paid for by the seller" and also insert the words "Binder rate," then you can sell or trade the property within 2 years, and get that title insurance premium back. Yes, you get the whole title insurance premium the prior seller paid even though it did not cost you a dime. We're talking about a tidy sum too. Title insurance costs around 1% of the property value. On a $100,000 property title insurance might be nearly $1,000.

Let me give you another little hint about the date chosen for closing. The closing date should be the day <u>after</u> rent is due. Let us say that you are talking about a building that is bringing in $1,200 a month. And you are doing a no money down deal. By closing the day after rent is scheduled to be collected you will actually get an extra $1,200 in cash at the closing. That's not only a no money down deal but a way to take out cash at the close. The reason it works out this way is that rent is typically paid a month in advance, but loan payments are paid a month late, i.e. Rent for January is due Jan 1st. The January loan payment is due February 1st.

Now what is the blank for "Deposit Increase?" Some sellers like to get their deposit increased after the happening of certain contingencies such as when the loan is approved. If you are a seller, a substantial deposit assures that your buyer is serious and that he is not stringing you along. But as a buyer I always write in there, "Not applicable." I've given the seller a $1,000 note and I do not want to come up with anything more until the deal closes. And as you saw in this particular deal, I'll probably get money back at the closing.

As to occupancy, check "Upon recordation of the deed." This doesn't mean you're personally going to occupy (for example) all four units of a rental property. It just means you are going to get the keys. On the closing date you are going to be entitled to take control and collect future rents, you'll also be responsible for repairs, taxes, etc. from the date of possession as stated on this agreement.

Last but not least, the most important thing on this form is what I call the ESCAPE CLAUSE. If you look over the provisions on the reverse side of the standard offer form, you will see several clauses about pest control.

Who pays for the so-called termite report? Generally, the buyer. But I always check off "Pest control inspection to be paid for by the seller." And then I check off number 4 which means the building is taken "as is," subject to my approving the termite report. This is innocuous looking but it is the most important clause in your whole purchase offer. It's your ESCAPE CLAUSE. You've agreed to buy the property "as is" but only after you've read the termite report. THE TERMITE REPORT SHOULD ALWAYS BE SUBJECT TO YOUR APPROVAL. Even if there is no termite damage at all (and that hardly ever happens), you can still say, "I don't approve the termite report." Perhaps you like termites. And you'd hoped there might be a few in the building. The fact that you don't approve the report lets you out of the deal completely. That's why this standard deposit agreement - the same one that every knowledgeable buyer in the business uses - is a one way street for the buyer. Once the seller accepts, the seller cannot get out of it. But for you it's just a piece of paper.

The seller has to sell you his property at the agreed upon price. But you can get out of buying it by simply not approving the termite report. How do you not approve a report? Well, you just attach it to a letter and you send it back to the seller (or his agent). In the letter you say, "The deal is off. I do not approve this termite report." That lets you out of the deal. So that's it. You are out of the deal. It's dead. Nothing else is going to happen.

Naturally, you will neither get rich nor make too many friends if you abort all your deals. But isn't it comforting to know how to draw up an offer so that you can't possibly lose anything? When you make a Bill Greene style offer in a typical real estate deal, there's no risk. The point is you can't get hurt financially by simultaneously making a lot of low offers. There's no money of yours at risk. There's nothing valuable of yours that the seller could keep. You've given him a note that's payable only if you close the deal. If a seller accepts your offer, you get what amounts to a free option on the property for the closing period which is whatever is stated in your offer. It's usually 30, 60 or 90 days. If you were going to buy an option on a hundred thousand dollars worth of stock for 90 days, you'd have to pay big money for it. But when you make an offer on $100,000 worth of real property you've got 30 to 90 days to resell your contract for $110,000 to someone else. The "option" you obtained was free of cost.

You could make $10,000 or more by merely assigning the deal to someone else. In stocks, you can never guarantee yourself against loss. But in a no money down real estate deal or during the period from acceptance of your offer until the close, as I've shown you, there's no possibility you'd lose anything. In the real estate business we call that "no downside risk and unlimited upside potential."

A very good thing that happens once you start owning real estate is that you'll never have to pay Federal or State income taxes again. You'll never pay income taxes! Once you have acquired a substantial amount of real estate, overflow depreciation and creative accounting will not only shelter all your future income but you'll be able to get a loss carry back for the last three years. Your depreciation losses will so far exceed your income that you can think about how to earn money in other ways. Some marginal projects might look better to you because you won't have to pay any taxes on the additional income or profits. By refinancing your properties every year you'll wallow in unlimited tax free cash to spend.

The big question that people who think they're smart always ask me is "If it's so good, why doesn't everybody do it?" The fact of the matter is, that about 60% of the population of the United States does do it. And although 60% of U.S. families owns real estate, most heads of household are timid souls. Property owners in general usually own only the home they live in and maybe one other property. A mere 5% -- that's of course over 10 million people -- own several investment properties. Wouldn't you like to be a member of that 5% group that owns several properties? It's a big club. There are 10 million bigtime property owners out there. You should be one of them! Or perhaps you'd rather be a member of the 35% of the United States population which doesn't own any real estate at all and are for all practical purposes economically unfree. They are wage-slaves or welfare cases. For the most part, they choose to be "victims" of the system rather than masters. For them, things are going to get worse in the coming years. The taxpayer's rebellion will reduce the dole to less than subsistence. Workers will have to work more hours or become minor league capitalists to preserve their present standard of living.

I think making the choice to be rich is pretty easy. Getting started in real estate involves nothing more than getting off your fanny and beginning to look at properties. Once you feel comfortable, start to make offers. Get an education. Don't be afraid to take good courses like the Bill Greene Tycoon Class. Learn how to make offers, how to negotiate, how to look at properties. Learn everything you'll need to know about Real Estate. But even if you do nothing more than read this book you'll have learned the most important secret. You have to get out there and hustle. Nothing will come to you if you stay locked in the bedroom. Yet there are plenty of deals for those who look. There never was and never will be a shortage of promising deals. If you know that basic secret, you are in a position to start your own program today.

There are no convenient excuses for a real estate tycoon. The nature of the business makes it impossible to blame anything but your own laziness for lack of financial success. No one discriminates against property owners on account of sex, color, social class, educational background, religion, or handicaps. Some sellers may not like you. But if I sense that someone does not want to deal with me for reasons of personal prejudice, I simply send in a friendly ringer: If a black seller does not want to deal with me because I'm white, you can be sure I'm not going to court and wait five years till my civil rights case comes up. I simply send in a black friend to negotiate on my behalf. He closes the deal for me, transfers title to me, and I owe him one.

In getting loans, minority group members and females actually have a slight edge over garden variety white protestant males. The reason is that the Feds have launched a program to make lenders give preference to borrowers in these heretofor disadvantaged groups. The main problem for the lender is finding reasonably qualified minority or female borrowers.

The only way to be a loser in real estate is to think of yourself as a loser and to sit at home doing nothing but watching the boob-tube. If you get out there and use the tricks of the trade in this book you'll make your million in one, two or possibly three years. If you do everything wrong, you'll still make it in five years.

There is more to learn - the fine points - tricks of the trade. They can make or save you an _extra_ million or three during the next few years. It's cheaper to learn about mistakes to avoid from someone like me than to make my most costly mistakes all over again yourself. Finish this book, look at properties, read the recommended books in my list. Take good courses and seminars - particularly the Bill Greene Tycoon Class - when they come to your town.

If you could read and relate to this chapter, you've got what it takes to be a Tycoon.

You mean that with this book and nothing else I could own that building, for no money down?

Bill Greene:

Yes! Yes! Yes!

DEPRECIATION

QUESTION: PLEASE EXPLAIN DEPRECIATION?

Depreciation is an abstract concept that can put you in a position where you never have to pay another cent in income taxes. You might even be able to get a refund of taxes you have paid for the past three years. This is how it works.

The IRS allows you to deduct a portion of the value of a building, car, or other property owned and used by you in business over what they call its "useful life." What the IRS feels is the useful life, and what, in reality, is the actual useful life may be totally different. But you have to play by their rules. Any IRS office will give you suggested depreciation schedules on items of interest to real estate tycoons. Drapes, carpets and furniture in rental units would have a useful life of about three years. A brand new "tilt-up" concrete wall warehouse would be assigned by the IRS a useful life of as much as fifty years. Everything else is in between. Depreciation on property is determined largely by the type of building materials used, and the type of use anticipated. Thus, assuming a warehouse building cost $50,000 you could deduct from your income $1,000 per year for fifty years as a "reserve for depreciation."

Even though you did not lose or spend $1,000, if you claim the $1,000 depreciation for accounting purposes in figuring your income tax, you would be treated exactly as if you spent $1,000 cash per year on repairs, or any other expense that could be deducted from income. If your warehouse was subjected to unusual wear and tear, you could claim a shorter useful life. The IRS ignores the reality that our 10% per year inflation is probably increasing the value of your warehouse by at least 10% per year.

For a different example, assume that you were able to buy a wooden rental* house and rent it out. Say you assign $25,000 of the price to the land value and $50,000 to the building. Further assume you were able to borrow $75,000 to make the purchase. An older wooden house would have a useful life of say ten years and this useful life of 10 years divided into the structure's cost of $50,000 would allow you to get a depreciation deduction of $5,000 per year, even though you didn't put up a dime of your own money for the purchase of the property. Assuming you earned $5,000 per year at your regular job for the next ten years, you'd pay no income tax because each year you would have a $5,000 depreciation "loss" to offset against your $5,000 of earned income. You are never allowed to depreciate land because the IRS feels its useful life is infinite.

There are lots of technical variations, but I hope this explains basic depreciation.

*Footnote: You can't take depreciation on a home used soley as a personal residence. But if you have room-mates who pay rent, or if you use your home for business purposes, you can depreciate that portion of your residence used "soley" for business purposes or for the production of income.

GET YOURSELF ORGANIZED

If your goal was not to make a million, but to climb Mount Everest, your preparations would not be limited to putting on tennis shoes and buying an Air India ticket to the base camp, would it? You would prepare carefully. You would learn all about climbing, and Everest in particular. You'd get your personal affairs in order, make sure of your financing, spend a few years on smaller peaks, getting yourself into shape mentally and physically. After all that, with tried and tested gear, you'd make the climb. Mountain climbers tell me that when you make it to the top, the feeling of exhilaration and freedom is unequalled by anything. Maybe that's true, but to me, once you get to the top of a mountain there is nothing to do but come down again.

The freedom that means something to me is financial freedom - - and attaining it is a lot easier and less risky than climbing mountains. Don't get me wrong: this exhilarating financial freedom requires the same planning and preliminary testing as climbing Mount Everest.

America today is "Answerland." Everybody has answers to what we want in life. Encounter group! Primal Scream! The spiritual path of Yoga and Brown Bread...but to me, working on my inner life was not an answer. I wanted to be financially independent, and two years after starting my real estate career, I made it to the top.

115

I don't have The Answer, but one thing is certain -- this book is not designed to make you feel better between your two ears. This is no head trip. I'm telling you how to get out in the Real World and work effectively. If you follow my program, the rewards are great. You can make $30,000 or more, on one deal! With a lot of effort you might be able to do it once or twice a week. And if you can do that for a year or two, outmaneuvering petty bureaucrats and outwitting the tax man, you will be a millionaire. Within two years! Now, that may not be The Answer. But being rich is a comfy solution to a lot of problems.

Making a million, getting ahead, achieving independence - whatever you call it - can be done by anyone. Sometimes people create their own mental barriers that make success harder to achieve.

Some barriers are more binding. Like being married, for instance. I've found that making money is easier if you are single and can move with opportunities. That goes for men and women. Getting tied down, particularly if your spouse doesn't share your vision, gets in the way. Children can absorb money like a sponge and make it even harder. If you have ever marvelled at those terrific success stories of the penniless immigrants who made it big in a foreign land without even knowing the lingo - - like Onassis - - and you wondered what they had going for them. Well, they had one big advantage, they were single. Don't be in any rush to get hitched.

Now if you've already got a spouse and hungry kids, that doesn't mean you have to give up. Certainly not. The fact is that most tycoons do make it while being married. Some even had their kids early in life. Of course because there are more married people than singles, it is likely that you'll have more married tycoons than single ones.

So hold off on having those kids until your tycoon career begins to blossom. If you already have children, don't despair. Let them earn their keep as soon as possible. Even a three-year-old can put on postage stamps, seal envelopes, sharpen pencils and help around the office. What's more, they love it. Had your daddy put you to work when you were three, you wouldn't have to be reading this book now. You'd have had your million and your financial freedom by the time you were 21.

However, if you are planning to tie the knot, here are a few things to look for. Get a spouse who has a career and will be busy pursuing his or her interests while you go about yours.

FRANK THE FAMILY MAN

Years ago when I started my first business tracking down missing heirs to estates, most of the people I hired were duds. But a year or so into the business, Frank answered an ad and started working for me. He was intelligent, motivated, and hard working. He made about $10,000 a year before he met me and this rapidly doubled. I suggested he invest his $20,000 a year income in real estate to build up a nest egg. But Frank had 9 kids and even when he doubled his income once again (which he did the following year), orthodontists, music lessons, athletic gear and other family expenses absorbed all his extra income like a sponge.

Now, I'm sure Frank enjoys his family. He spends all his money and spare time with them. But Frank's timing was off. In my opinion, he should have made his million first, and had his nine kids later. A big family may be fun, but it certainly limits your freedom of choice.

IF YOU WANT TO BE RICH - -
DON'T GET MARRIED! DON'T HAVE KIDS!

Second choice is a spouse who leaves you alone during working hours, doesn't give you any opposition and who will not be a consumer and spend all your capital -- the quiet traditional type mafia-spouse who doesn't get in the way or ask too many questions. The worst spouse is a neurotic nut who keeps you worrying all the time, can do nothing but spend your money and disparages every project you work on. The one-word solution to that type of marriage is -- DIVORCE!

In some communities local prejudices can be a real barrier to financial success. If you have unusual sexual preferences, skin color, religion or politics not acceptable in your community, I have another one-word solution for that -- MOVE!

OVERCOMING HANG-UPS

Many people create barriers to success with imaginary handicaps. They blame their loser-status in life on irrelevant things. My friend Anna, for instance, felt she was unattractive. Before becoming successful or even trying, she just had to have a nose job. If the nose job did her any good, it was 99% psychological. A big nose won't have any effect on your business effectiveness.

One of the world's greatest orators, Winston Churchill, couldn't speak very well when he was a boy. He lisped. Another person with a similar affliction was Demosthenes the Greek, who practiced speaking with stones in his mouth until he overcame his handicap and who, like Winston Churchill, became one of the greatest orators of his age. My personal acquaintances include a friend from high school who had polio. Yet he went on to become a great American golfer. I myself was never a very good student in high school. I barely passed English composition in college. But you're reading my book, aren't you?

Instead of dwelling on faults or defects, just get on with your plans. Don't cop out. You'll find over and over again that people who had more serious problems than yours, were able to overcome them. If you have something wrong with you don't use it as an excuse - ACT - do something about it. Or do something in spite of it.

PSYCHOLOGICALLY INCAPABLE OF SUCCESS

My high school friend Cory was good looking, talented in sports and music and was voted "Most Likely to Succeed". He had the sort of personality that everyone likes. Women were crazy about him even in high school. I cultivated him because he was everything I was not. He was far more popular and talented. At parties he was the best dancer. He had a smooth line for the ladies and a snappy retort to make everyone laugh.

He was always the colorful one, while in a social situation I was nervous and never had much to say. We started out in the Army together. He came out tops on the Leadership tests and was soon an Officer. I stayed at the lowest possible level and was never considered a very good soldier. After the Army, he moved in with a stunning New York fashion model and together they moved out west, where he built magnificent houseboats. Life Magazine even did a picture story on his creations. But Cory never cared about money. He spent it as fast as he made it - one of his endearing qualities, people said.

During all these years, however, I was living a nonflamboyant life. When I started to get rich I tried to do business with my old friend Cory. At one point he invented a process for making artistic stained glass windows out of plastic resin. I found a builder who placed a big order with Cory. But Cory failed to deliver. Another time we were in a real estate deal together. But when the time came to sign the papers, Cory was off waterskiing and he never showed up. Cory had talent, people liked him, but he never followed through on a deal. Eventually creditors were following him. I invited Cory and his lady friend over to my place for an occasional free meal. I knew times were rough for him. Once, a few sterling silver knickknacks were missing. I found them in a pawn shop and learned that Cory had pledged them. By that time we were in our late thirties. Not kids anymore. Cory was still charming and a good talker. But for reasons I will never understand, Cory seemed intent on putting barriers between himself and success. Even from me, his only substantial friend in the business community, Cory cut himself off by stealing a few dollars worth of nothings.

Maybe Cory had it too easy. Maybe the girls who aren't so pretty or the guys with crooked buck teeth are the ones who will make it as tycoons. They have to show a world that does not accept them, just how good they are.

Maybe that's why top capitalists are often members of minority groups, or are seldom selected in school as "Most Likely to Succeed". That's my theory anyway.

THE MANANA SYNDROME

What is the Main Reason that enthusiastic, healthy, capable men and women never make it? THEY NEVER START. Or, having prepared Step One of a plan, they piddle away time until the 'long run' arrives. And in the 'long run' we are all dead. Making money is like being an athlete. You have to organize and develop good habits, and keep at it. Once you start to become a champion, work even harder! Have you ever known exactly what you had to do, but just couldn't bring yourself to do it? You did something else to waste time, like cleaning up the house, going to a movie or sleeping. You just didn't feel like working because you weren't properly inspired. So you procrastinated.

Then, first thing you know other things came up - busy work, social obligations, a TV program you couldn't miss. The Manana Syndrome has hit you. Without something to snap you out of it, it could be terminal. You suddenly realize that there are so many other things to do, that you dread even starting the main project.

So you waste time with trivia. You begin to feel 'too tired' to do anything. You wake up feeling guilty. You finally decide that you have to get organized, but first you must buy some vitamin pills and have a few drinks. Finally after piddling away the day 'getting in the mood', you belatedly start your project. But within a few hours you find yourself back in the old Manana rut.

Well, you are not alone. We all have the Manana Syndrome - this mental and physical paralysis that starts when we are in school and gets worse until we apply the following simple cure.

Remember the Popeye Cartoons when you were little? Popeye the Sailor Man always got himself into bad trouble, but one way or another, at the very highpoint of the story, he'd open a can of spinach. He munched. Then swallowed. And then the musical theme signalling the victory of Spinach over the Manana Syndrome came on loud and clear. Ra, tah, ra ta ra tah. Ra ta ta ta ra ta TAH. By the last ra ta, Popeye could do anything. His muscles swelled. He bent iron bars. And his enemies fell before his mighty onslaught.

Think of the Popeye song whenever you are procrastinating. Have a drink of carrot juice, a candy bar or your own spinach substitute.[1] Hum the theme song. After that, there is no excuse. Go to your list (of what you have to do) and do the first thing on it. Schedule exactly how much time you will need, but if you run over the time, keep at it until you are finished. If you are in the middle of a real estate deal and something goes wrong, keep at it. Don't take 'no' for an answer. Find a way around the problem. Go over it. Go around it; and if none of that works, try barreling right through it.

When hard work brings home a deal and good profit - - reward yourself! Have a good meal out or treat yourself to whatever turns you on. By psychologically conditioning yourself with small rewards for jobs well done, you will get as much of a charge out of your accomplishments as from the reward. An actor or performer gets more out of giving a good show and the applause it brings, than his paycheck. So it should be with the Tycoon. Pulling off the good deal is the thrill. Increased wealth is a secondary payoff.

So, go to it. Don't proscrastinate. Put the TV in a closet. Cancel your subscription to Playboy. Stop all reading that tends to make you think like a consumer instead of a producer. Go to it and start. 'Do it now' the voice will tell you. Why wait till Manana?

Now that you have seen some of the barriers people set up to stop themselves from becoming tycoons, how can you organize yourself for success?

EDUCATE YOURSELF. Read, not only the biographies mentioned earlier, but read all the real estate books you can find. If they give you one good idea, it could be worth thousands. Still, reading is not to replace action. Reading is for sitting on the toilet, getting yourself to sleep, riding on a bus or while waiting for someone. And there is more to read about than just real estate. Salesmanship, accounting, trade magazines for the apartment house owner, manager or builder. The public library in a big city will have more specialized magazines than you can dream about. There is a good reading list at the back of this book.

---

1 Play one of my inspirational cassette tapes! See back page for order form.

Having a creative accountant and a successful business-oriented lawyer on your team sure doesn't hurt !

Finally, take the most boring course in the world, ACCOUNTING ONE. I flunked it, but it was probably the most valuable course I ever took. Sometimes it is given other names, but always take the first basic course. Remember business is in many ways like a game. Accounting is the way you keep score. Without it you just don't know where you are. When you move to bigger deals, a property that looks great and sends goosebumps of ownership pride up your arms, would have given you rigor mortis if you could have understood the statements. Community college real estate courses are good too - - but not as helpful as a strong basic accounting course.

LEARN THE JARGON. Real Estate, like every other profession, has its own special vocabulary. Many of the new terms you will come across are explained in this book. Learn them. My Tycoon Home Study Course contains a complete glossary of words, expressions and abbreviations used in the trade.

STOP CONSUMING. Ben Franklin, one of the richest self-made men of the Colonial era had the right idea. Working in the print shop as a kid, he saw all the other printer's devils take several beer breaks a day. Ben drank water. He ran extra errands for extra pay. Within a few years, Ben had his own print shop. Then he started his own newspaper, while his contemporaries were still taking beer breaks. Ben Franklin was big on saving.

You can discover a whole new world if you apply,

THE FIVE PERCENT RULE

The 5% Rule is something to strive for, not to accomplish all at once. When I told a stewardess friend about it, she said I was absolutely crazy and she never wanted to see me again. But I explained to her that it was one of the most important early steps on the trial to Tycoondom. Here it is:

Determine what your gross income is. For example,
$1,000 per month.

Take 5%. That would be $50 per month. Plan to
spend no more than that on your living expenses and
taxes.

That leaves $950 to build your empire.

Find a way to channel that entire amount into investments
that will double, preferably in a month.

That is the goal. Now there are lots of ways to reach that goal. Let's take Sally, my stewardess friend.

Gross Income	$1,000
Income Taxes	300
Rent	250
Clothes	100
Car Payments	100
Food	100
Entertainment & Travel	200
Medical & Dental	50
Insurance & misc.	100
Total Expenses	$1,200
NET LOSS:	$ 200

Obviously this girl could never become a Tycoon. Her Christmas Bonus was the only way she got out of debt once a year. However, within two years of applying the 5% rule, she owned a thriving basket import business. Sally's tax free income grew to $70,000 per year. This is how she did it:

If she was going to live on 5% of her gross income, she decided that her gross income was much too small. She began looking for ways to increase that income. At one of her regular stopovers, Manila, there was a native basket weaver who sold rattan fruit baskets for 35¢. Sally brought back a gross, duty-free with her $100 allowance. She had no transportation costs because she was a "stew", and sold the baskets for $3.50 each. She picked up a few hundred extra every week that way. And that is where most other stews would have stopped.

Then the 5% Rule was brought into play. Instead of squandering the extra profit, it was all reinvested in more baskets. To get more capital, she eliminated her rent by (together with her boyfriend) offering to become manager of the apartment building they lived in. Presto, there was another $250 a month to go into the high-profit basket importing business.

She liked nice clothes and as manager of an apartment building she discovered the cast-off clothing of former tenants - the source I had been using for years. With a new twist, she began trading things that didn't fit her with other stews. Soon she was at the point where she never spent a dime on clothes. A combination of tenants' cast-offs and the trading of garments she couldn't use, kept her looking sharp.

Car payments. Sally discovered she could buy a Volkswagen for $1,000, drive it for five years and sell it for $1,000. Last year she bought a $10,000 BMW 3.0CS, expecting to do the same in another five years. Though you put up more in the first place, you can usually break even with a good German car. It has therefore always amazed me that people would buy a brand new American car and end up with nothing to show for their investment after four or five years. Just a rusted hunk-o-junk. There are several ways to eliminate car expenses. You might sell it and get along without one. Or have a part-time job which gives you a company car. At worst you can shop around for a used car at a good 'all cash' price where the car will hold its value if you take care of it.

Food, Entertainment and Travel. Sally didn't have to cut down much on these. As the basket business grew they were turned into deductible business related expenses which helped reduce her income tax by a third. (Purchasing a small rental property and gaining overflow depreciation got rid of the rest of her tax.)

If she keeps up the good work for a few more years, this stew will be a millionaire - - and real estate played only a small part in her story. She owes it all to the 5% Rule which started her thinking of ways to reduce expenses and invest the saved capital in money making ventures.

How could the 5% Rule work for you?

Perhaps you could eliminate much food expense by helping out as a bus boy, waiter or hostess during rush hours. The usual pay is a few dollars plus a free meal. If you can't eliminate an expense, the 5% Rule says "Find an alternate source of income" that gives you the same effect as if you had saved. In other words, make profitable use of your spare time.

Be creative! Be inventive! There are hundreds of ways to earn extra money if you put your mind to it. Remember: FIND A NEED AND FILL IT.

I once came across this money-making scheme which has to pull a high rank in ingenuity. This card was shoved in my Post Office mail box:

DEAR FELLOW BOX HOLDER:

I drag my bones down to the Post Office each
morning to check my box for mail.

So while I'm at it, why don't I look through your little window too? If I see that you have some mail, I will call you immediately.

This saves you (literally) dozens and dozens of time-wasting - sometimes fruitless - trips to the Post Office. So why not join the rest of the folks on my "call sheet" for a couple of weeks to see if you like it? Give me a call at 345-6789.

Yours in rain, sleet or snow,

Mr. J. FROST   P.O. Box XYZ   Chicago, Il.

Whether Mr. Frost had many takers I don't know. But at least he was trying.

Another way to success is to develop the traits of the successful. Assuming that you haven't quit your job or even made your first real estate offer, start revamping your image or changing it if necessary. Most important, create a reputation for extreme DEPENDABILITY. If you have an appointment at noon, don't arrive at two minutes past. Arrive early and stand there looking at your second hand. At precisely noon, ring the bell. If you have promised to return a book or a borrowed dollar on Monday morning, get it there at 9 AM. Be very punctual. Hold up your end of a bargain or transaction. Don't give excuses to anyone. Do what has to be done. Your reputation for being dependable, prompt and fanatical on meeting your obligations will be worth more than anything else as you move up in business. It works for the Swiss Bankers. It will work for you.

Finally, what is the best, most productive thing you can do to get yourself organized as a real estate tycoon? Eat, dream, live real estate. If you drive past a vacant lot, think of how you might improve and develop it. What would be its best use? When you see a junky or abandoned structure, figure out how you would remodel it and what would bring in the best rents. Stop your car at real estate offices and discuss your ideas with the local realtors. Get to know them all on a first name basis. Let them know that you are in the market for deals.

LET'S GET ORGANIZED!

The main difference between a Tycoon and the other 99% of the population involves three factors. The first is Ambition - and I covered ambition, motivation and persistence in the chapter, The Tycoon Mentality. The second element is having a workable, realistic plan. 'Realistic' means not spinning your wheels on projects that cannot produce a good profit. A nickel and dime business, like a neighborhood gift shop or hot dog stand simply won't make it. You must only expend energy on high potential projects or education experiences that will give you a very solid return for the hours and money invested. What's a good return? If you can't anticipate a venture making at least $10,000 profit after taxes in a year or less, don't bother. The third factor is your ability to put this plan into effect.

Your time and money must be organized in such a way that it is spent only on activities that will produce maximum financial reward. You will notice immediately a great torrent of required paper work. There are lots of records to keep, mainly for the Internal Revenue Service and other government agencies. If you don't get your paperwork organized at an early stage you will find yourself hopelessly buried in insoluble accounting problems. I know, because it has happened to me. Again, it will help you to enroll as soon as possible in a course of basic accounting. Don't take a specialized course like Real Estate Accounting because it's better to understand the overall basics first.

Remember, business is like any other game. You need a score card to know how your team is doing. The score card in business is your accounting record. Profits or losses are revealed only by good accounts. Because you may not have taken an accounting course yet, I will give you enough information here for you to set up a rudimentary accounting system today. However I still recommend that you take that accounting course at some future time.

If you hire a certified public accountant to do your tax returns, ask the same accountant or his staff to help you set up a system of keeping books and records. Then you can always know where you are and what the score is. How much do you owe people? When is it due? How much do your tenants owe you? You should be able to meet all your short term financial obligations out of the payments due to you from others. If you look at the books in the reading list (at the back of this book) you'll find that most of the real estate books on that list contain a chapter or two on accounting. Have a look at them. A particularly good basic book is Landlording by Leigh Robinson, sold in bookstores at about $13.00, or you can order it by mail from me. (See order form at back of book) It has a very good chapter on record keeping plus sample forms you can use to set up a basic system.

Here is an even more basic record keeping system:

A SIMPLE ACCOUNTING SYSTEM
(For Those Who Know Nothing About Accounting)

Let's assume you have just closed escrow on your purchase of of duplex at 1234 Anystreet, Yourtown, North Carolina.

The first thing I like to do is give each of my buildings a name. A good name can add charm to a property. Personally I like the exotic touch. But you can name anything you like. Buy an attractive little plaque and put it up on the property, for example:

> *CASA PARADISO*
> *APARTMENTS*
> *For information concerning this property:*
> *Phone 333-3333*

I don't like to use my personal name on a property, or give my home address, because I don't want just anyone dropping in. Yet I want anyone who is interested in buying or renting to have an easy time contacting me. That's why you should have an answering service or phone answering device 24 hours a day.

At the start I suggest having a separate bank account for each property. It makes life easier and at tax time, all you have to do is give your accountant the check register and let him figure things out from that. I·like to have each account at a different bank too. That keeps things well separated.

At the bank, ask for the checkbook and check register known as "The Executive" and if you have an assistant, spouse, secretary or other trust-

128

worthy person, put them on the signature card for the account in case you are away or out of commission. Have your checks printed:

> CASA PARADISO BLDG. ACCOUNT
>
> Your Box, Your town
>
> Your Name
>
> Your Phone
>
> Your Drivers License No.*

(*The reason for including your license number is that suppliers always ask you to write it on checks for purchases. This way it is already there)

This is the way your first few pages of checks and deposits will look:

CHECK NO.	DATE	CHECK ISSUED TO	IN PAYMENT OF	AMOUNT OF CHECK	√	DATE OF DEPOSIT	AMOUNT OF DEPOSIT	BALANCE
						BALANCE BROUGHT FORWARD →		1476.21
5074	6/23	Sam's Roofing Service	Repair leaks	375.45				1100.76
5075	6/26	Virginia Gordon	Cleaning	25.00				1075.76
5076	6/26	The Banner Daily News	Rental Ad	15.—				1061.01
Deposit	6/29	Security Deposit — Tessie Tenant					600.00	1661.01
Deposit	7/1	July Rent — Tessie Tenant					400.00	2061.01
5077	7/5	Howards Hardware	New locks + Keys	52.22				2113.23
5078	7/7	Sam's Home Improvements	Carport	1000.—				1113.23
5079	7/7	Citi-Power + Gas	Utilities	15.—				1098.23
5080	7/7	Allstate	(Insurance)	275.—				823.23
Deposit	7/7	Cash from Washing Machine					3.75	826.98
5081	8/1	Tax Collector	R.E. Taxes	876.—				
Deposit	8/5	Deposit from Bob Buyer					5000.00	

Naturally you must keep in mind that for income tax purposes, "repairs" in general are immediately tax deductible. They can be used to reduce or offset your taxable income in the year incurred. "Capital improvements" in contrast are not deductible and must be charged off over the remaining life of the building, or the life of the improvement (whichever is shorter). When in doubt, it is always better to have a "repair" than a "capital improvement" because there is more of a tax benefit. Assuming that the check register sample constituted your entire annual income and expense on Casa Paradiso, this is how the summary you would prepare for your accountant should look:

CASA PARADISO - ACCOUNTING SUMMARY

Repairs & Maintenance

Check #   5074 $ 375.00

Check #	5075	$ 25.00
	5077	52.00

Advertising
Check #	5076	$ 15.00

Capital Improvements
Check #	5078	$1000.00

Utilities
Check #	5079	$ 15.00

Insurance
Check #	5080	$ 275.00

Taxes
Check #	5081	$ 875.00

Cash Flow

Rents	$ 400.00	
Washing Machine	3.75	
Security Deposits	600.00 * [	Not taxable income
Deposit on Sale	5,000.00 * [	

I keep all of my fire insurance policies in a safety deposit box (in case of fire). All insurance against fire is in one file titled:

INSURANCE - FIRE & CASUALTY - Into this I put all fire, earthquake and other casualty policies. These are filed in alphabetical order by property so that once a month my secretary can review all policies and be sure that they are up-to-date and that the value insured for is the approximate replacement cost of the property. From time to time a mortgage lender will want to physically hold an original insurance policy. He has that right. However, to ensure the accuracy of your filing system, you must request a photocopy for each policy not in your files. Other insurance is broken down into several other categories:

INSURANCE - MOTOR VEHICLES (policies and correspondence)

INSURANCE - LIABILITY (policies and correspondence)

BILLING

As long as you only have one property, keeping expenses and income credited to the proper account is easy. But suppose you have twenty.

During a busy day you get a notice that "your insurance premium on account 2233445566 has not been paid and your policy will lapse in three days". Since it would take hours to find out which building the policy refers to, I use this simple trick. The address on each bill should refer to the property by name. In that way the notice on this particular bill would come addressed to:

Your name

Casa Paradiso

Your address

In my early days, when bills, tax statements, bank statements etc. came merely addressed to me, I had a devil of a time just allocating them to the proper parcel of real estate.

FILING SYSTEM

I suggest you purchase two matching standard letter-sized two drawer files. Not only will they be a convenient and semi-portable place for your records, but if you purchase a factory-second flush door as a desktop, you will have acquired an attractive typing table as well. Each property will have about four or five folders, for example:

CASA PARADISO - New Roof.

This file might contain your plans, building permits, contractors' bids, a copy of Notice of Non-responsibility for Liens and all else pertaining to this project. When the project is underway, it is kept in an upper drawer. When the new roof is completed and final inspection has been approved and all bills have been paid, it is filed below under "closed files".

CASA PARADISO - Tenants.

This might contain copies of ads, leases, photocopies of tenants' checks, so that if at any stage they don't pay up you can sue and know in which bank they are likely to have a checking account to grab.

CASA PARADISO - Financing.

This would have a copy of the note and trust deeds, showing how much was borrowed and a payment book or other computer print-out showing how much was paid on principal and how much interest is due each month.

CASA PARADISO - Original Purchase and Depreciation Schedules

This would contain a copy of original escrow statements, any side deals with the owner and a letter from a real estate broker setting forth the percentage of depreciation applicable to land, building and personal property   It would also contain your bill of sale on the personal property and estimated depreciation schedules for the next five years.

CASA PARADISO - Rents.

This file would include a list of all properties and a place to enter the rent as it comes in. I set the property address on the left; column two is security deposits; column three is scheduled rents with January, February, March, etc. marked out. Each month I enter the rent received. If there is a special note like, tenant got $25 off for painting or whatever, a note is made. If a tenant fails to pay - or is late - I mark a yellow circle around his name. If he gets too many circles I might take some action.

YOUR RECORD KEEPING SYSTEM SHOULD
ALSO INCLUDE THESE TIPS:

Small banks offer _free_ checking accounts if you have $100 to $300 minimum in the account. How do you get that first $300? Well, one way is from the security deposit from your tenant. The security deposit from a tenant will usually be a month's rent. (I personally prefer six weeks, but to each his own.) If you put this security deposit in your bank as a minimum deposit, then you should get the free account. If a tenant ever asks you for interest on his deposit, say that YOU don't get interest as the deposit is in a checking account. Therefore he isn't entitled to the interest either.

Open a separate account for each property you own. That way every expense and everything relating to a specific property can be assessed easily. If someone else is preparing your account books, this will make it easy for him to figure out what you took in and what was spent on each property.

If you have to pay in cash you can still accomplish the same thing. Keep a record in the checkbook itself of cash paid out. For example, always note the cash spent, its purpose and to whom it was paid, just as you would if the transaction had been by check.

When you get a check from a new tenant, have that person make it out to CASH. That way a tenant cannot stop payment on a check he has already given you. I know you like to trust people, but when you've been around real estate as long as I have, you'll find out a lot of tenants' checks turn out to be "duds". Never keep checks lying around. Cash them immediately.

If you are unsure about the signer, take it to the bank where it was drawn on and cash it there. That will save a couple of days' waiting. Sometimes checks go bad unintentionally. Tenants overdraw their account - had to buy their mother a present etc. What should you do? You should deposit all bad checks "for collection". That means any bad checks will not be returned to you, but will stay at the debtor's bank until that person deposits enough to cover it.

I find it a real bother to write out the same checks each month, i.e., the same mortgage payment to the same company month after month. Why not use post dated checks? If I buy a property and the seller carries the financing, I will write him twelve post dated checks, each dated January 1, February 1, and so on. Since banks rarely look at dates on checks. I write in bold letters over the top of the check: DO NOT CASH BEFORE... This will cause the banks to notice something special about the check.

Whenever possible I get post dated checks from my tenants too. That way I don't have to chase them for payment. I have them pinned to the bulletin board and simply pull them off when the payments are due.

Another way to handle things automatically through a checking account is by something called "transmatic". This works when you have an institutional mortgage holder, like if you owe Philadelphia Savings money. Sometimes you forget to write them a check, thereby incurring a substantial late charge. The transmatic plan automatically withdraws a mortgage payment from a checking or savings account. Savings and Loans and most banks will provide this service for you at no extra cost. It saves a lot of time.

If you have a contract of sale and you don't want the lender to know that you have acquired property, this must be handled differently. Supposing the lender is Dell Savings & Loan. You go along with Sam Seller and you, Bob Buyer, open up a joint account with Sam. You tell Dell to automatically withdraw all mortgage payments from that savings account. Then, all you, Bob Buyer have to do is to make regular payments into that savings account, which can also be arranged automatically. The loan department will never know it is anyone other than Sam Seller paying the loan.

Next, a very helpful step in any potential tycoon's career: Join your local association of property owners. In many parts of California there is a local California Apartment Association. Most counties or towns will have their own associations, such as the Irvine Income Property Owners' Association. If you consult a phone book under "Clubs and Associations" or ask around, you will find the appropriate group in your area. Join it. These associations probably cost as little as $10 to $20 a year for dues. Besides the obvious advantage of associating with people of similar economic interests, these associations recommend many helpful publications which are cheap or free. They make deals with merchants who will give members big discounts on carpets, drapes, washers and dryers or whatever you need. These associations also take an interest in laws and regulations that are pending both statewide and local. Their opposition to rent control, for instance is the only bulwark standing between you as a property owner and the fuzzy thinking leftists who would like to take all your property away and smother the free enterprise system.

Therefore, one of your first steps in getting organized is to join your local organization like the Association of (Income) Property Owners. If your business is single family homes perhaps you'll also want to join the local association of home owners. This group would have a name like the Forest Park Improvement Association. You'll make friends there and if you have problems it is nice to have experienced people to help you out, who are familiar with the local public officials. They'll be your co-members. There is a spirit of comraderie in these associations and additionally these property owner groups often sponsor low cost educational forums and seminars. These courses will help you be more effective in buying, selling, managing and trading up your properties. They also set up tax write off junkets and conventions in exotic places like Pismo Beach, maybe even Hawaii.

To summarize, borrow all the real estate books from the public library you can find. Acquire paperbacks if you can afford them - they'll be cheap - mostly under $10. All books and lectures should be studied if you feel they will be of value to you. Take an accounting course. Join your local Association of property owners. Get on my mailing list - newsletters, Tycoon Classes.

Here is how to plan your time! First, it's a good idea to list all the things you want to do on a big sheet of paper. Then rearrange the list in order of priority, putting a Number 1 next to the things of great importance, and so on down the list. Each specific project on the list should be related to your general plans and goals in life. If your main goal is financial independence, one of your first steps is to get an education, both formal and in the real world before you jump into a deal.

Get your education in real estate by going to classes or reading books. Most important by far, however, is get out and look at the real estate deals available in your community. When you start out, the first thing to do is circle ads with magic markers or clip ads from local newspapers. You organize them, to spend   time, perhaps all weekend, looking at properties. Later on priorities may change from looking at new deals to digesting the ones you have. Once you get into owning a few properties, you'll be making needed repairs and improvements or you'll make changes in tenants as appropriate. You should never get up in the morning without going over a plan for what you will accomplish that day and that week. Do not spin your wheels doing things unrelated to your major goals in life. It's so easy to get side tracked into other diversions. Remember, you have a goal, and that goal is to achieve financial independence in the shortest possible time. Every minute counts and you must do only those things that relate directly to your goal.

That doesn't mean cutting out all pleasure. You must give yourself some treats now and then. But try to arrange going to the Bijou, or what-ever else turns you on as a reward for accomplishing a high priority activity. In other words, if you have ten or fifteen things in the Number 1 Category to accomplish, do not go to a movie or take time off until you have done those things. Robert Redford can wait. You can't. Then treat yourself to a night out. Psychologically it is very helpful to look forward to the reward you promise yourself for closing a deal or doing something important.

I have also found it most essential to get a diary or appointment book with a separate big page for every date. That way I can put down in detail what I want to accomplish each day. At 7 A.M. I have to do one thing, at 7:30 another, and at 8 A.M. still another. Time from now on should be closely scheduled. Your days chould be filled up with properties to look at, books to read, people to call, etc. Don't get discouraged if you don't accomplish everything you map out to do on a given day. I always seem to schedule twice as much as I can accomplish and I am usually a little bit behind. I would rather have the feeling that I'm behind than that I have nothing to do.

People sometimes ask me "Are you really happy?" Frankly, the only unhappy people I have ever met (outside of the terminally ill) are people who are bored. Often these are rich people with too much leisure time. Just as often, however, they are working people who get home from work and the only thing they can think of doing is to watch television. These days, in our affluent society, even the poor folks have too much leisure time.

HAPPINESS IS HAVING A GOAL AND WORKING TOWARDS IT.

MANY PEOPLE SPEND MONEY ON SHRINKS INSTEAD OF DOING SOMETHING PRODUCTIVE WHICH WOULD MAKE THEM HAPPY.
THE SHRINK GETS HAPPY AND RICH. BUT DOES THE PATIENT? NOT USUALLY.

In business you may have to devote almost every waking hour to your work if you are going to be extremely successful. You will have to cut out all time-wasters and people who don't have a direct bearing upon your main activity -- people who might lead you off in wasteful directions. If you are lucky enough to find a boyfriend or girlfriend who shares your interests, they could be a very good influence on you and help you reach your financial objectives. Every race horse has a pace setter. Unfortunately in my life and most of my friends' lives, it is very difficult, if not impossible to find such a person; someone you like to be with, like to make love with and also find thinking the way you do about acquiring a real estate fortune. If you have such a partner, you are in an ideal situation. Chain that person to your wrist! You might even consider marriage!

Making such friends, both for myself and participants is another aim of my courses for graduates of the Tycoon class. Why not place an ad in your local newspaper and find a group of property owners to share experiences and work together on trades. If you are married and have a spouse who is interested in working with you, you might want to join another couple on projects. If your spouse does not share your interest, perhaps you can find another married individual with whom you can work.

To keep problems at a minimum, your partner should be of the same sex. On the whole, romance and real estate don't mix. The clinch should be in the deal, not in hanky-panky with your partner. You are out to make money, not whoopie. Real estate deals I have made with compatible partners have been more satisfying and more enjoyable than those I have done alone. It is simply more fun to share your high and low moments with someone else.

So where do you find a compatible partner? Often through ads in the paper. Or you might meet people selling their property or buying yours. At real estate seminars like my Tycoon Class or through groups you join or organize on your own. If you make your desires and interests known, like minded individuals are guaranteed to come your way.

You can no longer be a consumer. You should never spend your time and money on fashion clothes. They will have very little impact on your business success and will only waste your time and money. There was once a book published, called Dressing for Success. As if dressing made any difference! A few years ago, a friend and I both used to dress in patchy blue jeans and frayed shirts. We thought about putting out a parody of this book, in which we would be visiting our banker in raggedy jeans. Then, in the same raggedy jeans, we would be looking at property, closing deals, etc. I am convinced that bankers, sellers and everyone else is more interested in what you have to offer than in the name of your tailor. So don't kill a lot of time worrying about how you look. Just stay neat, clean and presentable. Again: Put your TV in the closet. They don't call it the "Boob Tube" for nothing! If you just have to watch the American Band Stand Reunion, then schedule it in. But watch nothing else. TV is a prime time killer. The same thing is true to a lesser degree, of the radio. Instead of listening to music, have a cassette player in your car. Then, when you're driving you can slip a cassette educational course into your player and spend the time learning as well as driving. It just so happens I put out a good set of them.

You might also, while you are driving and learning, try flossing your teeth. You can floss with one hand, if you use a plastic holder. I give you this helpful hint because most people lose their teeth by the time they are 50. Not decay - it's the result of gum disease. Nobody wants to buy real estate from a toothless wonder. Flossing with a little plastic holder will keep the gums healthy and your mouth smelling fresher. It will prevent you from wasting time and money on dental work when you could be out looking for property.

I didn't bring up flossing your teeth to be funny. In fact, being healthy is a tycoon's biggest concern. If you do not work at maintaining a healthy body, all the money in the world can't buy you a new one. Luckily, property ownership means that you can get plenty of exercise by working on your properties. Don't be afraid of strenuous physical activity! Others would have to go to an exercise club or whip themselves into a frenzy playing tennis. All this healthy work, like shingling, stonework, painting, and land-scaping, is also probably saving you $50 an hour. Improvements and sweat equal appreciation in the value of your real estate. I much prefer painting a building to playing golf. The paint job may bring me an extra $100 in rents, $10,000 in increased net worth. In the meantime, I am keeping fit.

In the next few years you may want to leave your job. But take that action only after accumulating enough wealth and cash flow to live comfort-ably. When you leave your job, you will lose your group medical plan. So why not join a group like Kaiser Plan in California. I am sure there is one in your area. With Kaiser you pay a relatively small amount (like $30 a month) for full medical coverage. Unlike medical insurance, where you have to select your own specialist who may turn out to be incompetent, Kaiser will refer you to their own staff specialist. Having paid the basic $30 a month, any extra treatment like x-rays is only $1 or $2. This minimum charge is probably designed to keep the hypochondriacs at bay. Kaiser also has complicated instrument and diagnostic gear that no sole practitioner can afford. Hospitals charge hundreds of dollars for the same tests. Unfortunately, at Kaiser you do have to wait days or weeks for service and the level of service is generally average to mediocre. Still, it is cheap and provides a reasonably satisfactory level of service, which I was not able to obtain consistently from private or small groups of practitioners. But you may also be able to trade something for medical services. I have found many doctors, particularly the younger ones, open to barter. Like getting a break on rent, in exchange for molar work. So always offer a trade, whenever possible. It conserves cash and has obvious tax advantages for all concerned.

One of the most important steps before buying your first property is: Use the HUNDRED HOUSE RULE.

Here is what happened to me on

THE BAYVIEW: This was a gorgeous home with a most magnificent view of the San Francisco skyline and all of San Francisco Bay. It was one of the first homes I looked at. Because it was worth about $150,000 at the time, I considered it way out of my league and figured there was no way I could make money on it. It was a very attractive redwood and glass house. Apart from the pink trim, which screamed to me for a coat of Barcelona Brown, there was nothing wrong with the place.

Yet after I had completed my Hundred House look, it was still on the market and the price had been reduced to $125,000. I was told it had been vacant for a year or more. I smelled a problem. Inquiring of the neighbors, I learned that, a year earlier a beautiful young girl had her throat slashed, reputedly by a Mafia Don, who had caught her in the arms of another man. The man had been strung up in the kitchen in a very unpleasant way. It appeared that the hoodlum had purchased the house for his girlfriend, but after the "incident" had taken off for parts unknown. The heirs of the girl had been notified that they owned the property, but they, wanting nothing to do with the situation, merely told a local lawyer to sell the place for the best possible price and just send them a check. The lawyer had the property appraised ($150,000) and listed it with a broker. From time to time offers were made --mostly by people who were new to the area and who had not heard the murder story. When they heard the tale, they generally backed out of the deal, figuring that the house had bad "Kharma". By the time I returned for a closer inspection to the house six months later, the neighbors had even embellished the tale. The girl, it turned out, had been a belly dancer who often did exotic things like stripping to the nude on moonlit nights. According to the neighbors, the ghost of the slain girl was doing her striptease every time there was a full moon. The story was retold and found its way to the papers. Nobody in town would buy the property.

My reaction was a little different than most. I figured if I owned a haunted house with a full moon show of that calibre going on, it would sure beat going to a Drive-In. The property had been listed with several brokers and all their listings had now expired. Even the local brokers didn't want to be bothered showing what they regarded as an unsaleable property. I asked more questions and ordered a "title report". I learned from the title report that a private loan on the property amounting to $75,000 was in default by several months. It appeared that the people who originally owned the property would get it back in a foreclosure for $75,000, less than half of what it was worth. The owner of the mortgage turned out to be a widow living in Carmel, California, about 200 miles south.

I drove down to see her. The information I got might have upset most people, but for me it represented an unusual opportunity. She told me that she would under no circumstances take back the property even if she had the legal right. In a foreclosure, if no one bids the amount of the mortgage, the mortgage holder gets the property. If the mortgage holder does not want the property, a person who comes to the sale and bids 3¢ (or anything) gets it. I told her that if she didn't bid for the property it was likely to go for a song, and that I would personally bid $10,000.

I asked her why she didn't just take over the property and rent it out for the $1,000 per month it should rent for. She broke into hysterical tears, but when she had regained a measure of composure told me:

"My husband committed suicide in that house in the bathroom four years ago, just two weeks after we moved in. He shot himself in the mouth with a shotgun. It wasn't pretty. The house was vacant for a long time. Two weeks after Mr. Moravia and his beautiful young wife bought the place from us -- well, you know what happened. I don't want to go near the place."

I gulped. But thought to myself, "What the heck..." So I offered the lady a deal whereby I would take over the mortgage and tax payments of $600 per month. She agreed that I should bid the full amount of the mortgage at the foreclosure and she would extend the loan for five years. Assuming there were no other bidders at the sale, I would have made my first "no money down deal".

Feeling I wanted to be sure of my ownership, I placed a long distance call to the heirs of the dead girl. They were resigned to the fact that the house would be taken from them in a foreclosure, and had no interest in doing anything about it. To be sure that there would be no surprises with an outside bidder going against me at the sale, I offered the heirs $300 for a "quit claim" deed. They accepted at once, since that was $300 more than they had expected to get. I became the owner and holder of legal title.

With the permission of the lady who held the loan on the property, I called off the foreclosure sale and moved into the house. I never even thought about the two week curse, until fifteen days after I moved in - I got a lot of calls from the mortgage lady and neighbors asking if I was OK. I was of course, and in the two years I lived in the house, never had an unhappy moment.

The view was great. I watched big ocean liners pass under the Golden Gate Bridge, past Alcatraz and under Bay Bridge. The house itself was laid out as a duplex and the smaller unit was rented by me to another bachelor who was in the wholesale fine wine business. I got $375 a month, plus fifty dollars in wine for the lower unit. My cash outlay every month for loan and taxes was six hundred dollars.

$600

375 Rent for lower unit

––––––

$225 Net outlay

The place I was occupying had to be worth at least $600 per month rent. It had three bedrooms, two big bathrooms and a super modern kitchen, etc. In fact it was a little too big for me, though with all that wine to drink every month I kept it pretty full with parties three times a week. In due course I painted it, put in some rosewood panelling, expanded the size of the living room and took in a girl roommate. She paid $275 per month which more than covered utilities and kept snacks in the refrigerater. She was good company too, though to keep the relationship businesslike I made another rule which I have always followed: NEVER SLEEP WITH YOUR TENANTS. We were very good friends, and when she was down she could rely on me for a shoulder to cry on. But most of the time our relationship was quite formal and correct. It worked out well, for over a year.

The net result of my first deal, including the roommate's contributions, was that I got a free place to live in, all the good wine that my friends could drink, utilities paid for, free food, usually cooked by my girl roommate, and good company. Not only that, when I went to see my accountant at income tax time, he told me I had a slight tax loss or write off from the depreciation I was allowed on the property. [See the section on depreciation.]

In two years, the property I bought for $75,000 with nothing down, was sold for $275,000. By trading up, a maneuver which is covered later in this book, I got $200,000 cash, tax free. Part of that $200,000 profit was due to the devaluation of the dollar, or inflation. But don't forget, the property was worth $150,000 when I bought it, so as soon as the ink had dried on my purchase contract, I was $75,000 richer. Without any inflation or increase in the general price of property, I would have made $75,000 just as soon as I had changed the image of the house from a deserted, deadly haunted place to a bachelor pad of fun and parties. As it turned out, my first buy had been at the start of a real estate boom in California. But even without a boom this deal would have been a winner.

That's why you must get yourself organized and look at 100 deals. I'm sure you will find several of your own winners.

THE TYCOON'S CREDO

A tycoon is:

1. ORGANIZED

   I will schedule a program of my activities and objectives and stick to it the entire day.

2. DEDICATED

   I will do at least one thing I should have done, but have been putting off.

3. CONFIDENT

   I will feel as good as possible and achieve a sense of well being by meditating fifteen minutes every day.

4. APPRECIATIVE

   I will tell my family, friends and business associates "I like you" and mean it.

5. OPTIMISTIC

   I will not dwell on past failures but will think positively about the present.

6. EDUCATED

   I will read something to improve my mind each day, and will keep away from non-productive and time consuming people and activities.

7. THRIFTY

   I will not be a consumer or a taxpayer any more than is absolutely necessary.

8. SOCIABLE

   I will be charming and agreeable to everyone and speak badly of no one.

9. ALERT

   I will be open to new ideas, experiences and people who might teach me something new, and I will not let myself fall into a rut or routine.

10. DEPENDABLE

    I will meet all my business and social obligations punctually.

Finding Super Deals

Did you ever hear of Father Flanagan, the founder of Boys' Town? He is famous for the quote "There's no such thing as a bad boy". Well, here is Bill Greene's variation on the same theme: I say "There's no sucn thing as a bad real estate deal!" Every deal, every property, is potentially "good" or profitable, but sometimes (read "sometimes" as "usually") the PRICE is TOO HIGH. Yet, bought right, and properly leveraged with good loans, any property could be an excellent deal. This is why, once you know the market, you should make an offer on virtually every property you look at. Much of this book is concerned with what sort of offers to make. Here we will deal with the process of ferreting out all the deals on the local market. More importantly, you'll learn to flush out deals that are not on the market, but can be yours exclusively.

Making big money in real estate is as easy as falling off a log. But if I told you to fall off a log this minute, you'd have a problem. First you'd have to find a log. Downtown, in some cities that would be difficult. Then you'd have to find a lake or a stream. The third step, getting the log into the water - would involve a bit of work. Finally, the hardest thing of all, you'd have to stand up on the floating log. After all that, falling off is easy.

Making money in real estate is just as easy as falling off a log. But

MAKING MONEY IS AS EASY AS FALLING
OFF A LOG. GETTING <u>ON</u> THE LOG
IS THE BIGGEST PROBLEM.

the problems in getting on are similar. First you must <u>find</u> suitable property.
It might not be available in your neighborhood, or even in your city.   Then
you've got to negotiate for it, arrange financing and close the deal. Finally
you must get the property in proper running order. Once all that is done,
you'll make nothing but money. Finding the right property, negotiating
the deal, and staying on top of it is the hardest part.

Obviously you are nowhere until you find your first property. IF YOU
DON'T LOOK YOU'LL NEVER FIND ANYTHING! Let me show you <u>how</u> to
look for good deals and how to recognize a bargain when you see it.

How can you find or create that elusive first "good deal?" Do you
think that if you sit in your living room and watch television, some salesman
will come to the door and present you a super deal with a red ribbon on it?
And all you'll have to do is write out a check and wait for the profits to
roll in? Unfortunately, any deal presented to you by a salesman with a
smooth, memorized presentation and four-color brochure isn't worth beans.
You'll have to get off your fanny and as a preliminary step you must educate
yourself to the point where you can recognize or create a good deal when you
see a promising situation. Educating yourself is easy. It costs nothing but
a little time and shouldn't take more than four to six weeks. You simply
learn and apply the:

HUNDRED HOUSE RULE

Look at a minimum of one hundred properties for sale. If you are
interested in single family houses, look at one hundred houses. Or you
can look at 100 small apartment houses, 100 warehouses or 100 motels. Look
at whatever type of property you would feel comfortable owning and managing.
I suggest that you concentrate your attention on run-down or "problem"
properties of one to four units for starters. Compare "problem" properties
with well-managed, clean, income properties that command high rents and
Top Dollar asking prices. Try to figure out the difference between the
"good" and "bad" properties. Ask yourself, "How could I improve this
particular sick property? How might I cure the problems to make the
building worth more rent? What would my changes mean ultimately in terms
of market value?"

Remember, until you have actually gone through 100 properties, both physically and on paper, it's all just six weeks of looking. Mere mental exercise. You do not make any offers. You just ask questions. It's an educational time only. Don't let anyone "sell" you anything. During your Hundred House period, explore different neighborhoods. Visit nearby towns and communities. Observe where the growth areas are. By growth I mean new construction and upgrading. Which areas seem to be declining in popularity? Are undesirable elements like bums or porno-massage-pinball parlours moving into the nearby shopping areas? Where are the trendy young professionals shopping? How much remodelling is going on? Check out different types of property. Be alert for special situations.

WATCH OUT FOR SPECIAL LOCAL FACTORS AFFECTING VALUE

Even though you may be preliminarily interested in buying small apartment units, don't be afraid to look at property containing stores on the lower floors and apartments upstairs. This is called a "mixed use" in real estate. Look at homes, duplexes, apartment buildings, stores, offices, manufacturing buildings and warehouses. Notice which seem to be the best value for money. Where do you get the most square footage per dollar? Compare prices for comparable properties in fashionable neighborhoods with prices in up-and-coming areas. Try to notice patterns of change. Consider the possibilities of converting abandoned warehouses into offices or apartments, apartments to offices, or remodelling any type of property for alternate uses. Discuss your ideas with real estate agents, contractors, sellers and other people already in the business of owning, managing or remodelling. Look at other developers' successful projects. What makes them work? Look at failed projects, places with a lot of vacancies or into foreclosure. What mistakes can they help you avoid?

To ascertain the prevailing rents in an area, spend time posing as a prospective tenant. Seek to rent various types of property. If landlords are anxious to give concessions like paying your moving expenses and giving three months' free rent, obviously the rental market must be soft. True rents are often not the same as the scheduled rents. Scheduled rents are what sellers try to make you believe they can get for their property.

How do you find 100 properties to look at? The traditional method is simply read ads in the local papers. Probably one-third to one-half of all real estate deals are initiated through newspaper ads. With a magic marker, circle ads for interesting properties. Call. Make appointments with the owners or agent handling the deal. Don't waste time. Arrange your schedule so there is order and flow to your viewing. In other words look at all properties on the north side of town in the morning and on the south side in the afternoon. Stay organized! Don't spend time driving and going back and forth unnecessarily. Use time efficiently. Ask a lot of questions.

What's the local real estate market been like over the past twenty years? Are there more people anxious to sell than there are buyers - or visa versa? How long does it take for fairly priced deals to sell? Where are the schools and churches? Does the town have a master plan? Is there any urban renewal or condemnation activity in store?

Are there special grants-in-aid or subsidized government loans available for owners in the area because it is considered historical or otherwise worth preserving? Is a freeway going through? What new developments are going in? If expensive new apartments are planned for the area, it could be possible that the higher rents scheduled for the new projects will make the older units by comparison more attractive to prospective tenants. A new shopping center or rapid transit stop could make all properties in an area more convenient and therefore more valuable. Has there been any local agitation for rent control? If so, run in the other direction. Rent controls spell devastation to the area, both physically and economically.

What improvements made by other real estate operators are most profitable? Perhaps installing a lot of skylights, modern kitchens and exterior shingles make the difference between a $60,000 and a $100,000 property in some areas. It is up to you to ascertain the costs of value adding improvements. Call up general contractors. Have them stop over at a property that you are "considering". Let them give you their estimates and suggestions on restoration, remodelling, conversions or needed repairs. You may see indications that $10,000 in work could give you $30,000 in added value. In many instances merely cleaning up and painting could turn a lemon of a property into a juicy grapefruit. Can you do the work yourself? Being your own contractor, carpenter and painter can save at least two-thirds on most projects.

The most important thing is, that by looking at a hundred or a large number of deals on the market and considering all the possibilities, your creative mental juices will start circulating. You will begin to have original ideas on where to buy, how to make profitable improvements and how to best take advantage of the existing situation.

Why did I choose the Hundred House Rule instead of the Fifty House Rule? Is there any magic in the number "100"? Of course not! If you feel comfortable making your first serious offer after looking at 63 properties, do it. If you don't feel you know the market after carefully examining 100 deals, then look at 200. Can you look at too many deals? Yes! As in the search for a spouse, it is impossible to find perfection. The perfect real estate deal doesn't exist either. You can look forever and you'll never find perfection. There's always work to be done, and no guarantees.

Once you are familiar with every property on the local market, you have to take that giant step. Make an offer on the best deal available. You must get into the game and do as well as you can. If you wait for perfection in a lover, you'll die a virgin. In real estate there are plenty of virgins who have been "just looking" for forty years.

If everything locally is so high priced that you would rather be unencumbered, it could be a good time to take a trip and see what sort of opportunities exist in Vermont, Hawaii or wherever attracts you. Before you begin your career as a real estate tycoon, it may well be the opportune moment to move to an area you have always wanted to live in. Real estate investments, at least in the beginning years, will tie you down to a given locality. So you might as well acquire those first properties in a climate you are happy to be in. To make it big in real estate you will probably have to put some roots down in a community for at least a few years.

Earlier, I said that up to 50% of all real estate deals are initiated by ads in the paper. If you are thinking, you might have asked yourself, "Perhaps the other half of deals are initiated in some other, possibly better way?" Right you were! Most of the best deals are never placed on the market or advertised. In my experience, looking at properties with an average real estate agent or responding to ads has been a wonderful way of getting an education; that is, doing the Hundred House bit. But once familiar with the market, I quickly discovered better ways of ferreting out super deals.

GET A REAL ESTATE BROKER WHO WILL DO YOU SOME GOOD. When you visit real estate offices in response to an ad or just walk in off the street, casually ask whoever you are dealing with "Who is the most successful broker in the office?" The agent on duty or "floor person" will probably point out a busy looking individual on the telephone with three people waiting to see him. Don't call him or waste his time during your Hundred House period because he will rapidly size you up as a "looker", not a buyer and won't have anything to do with you after that. But keep his name and number on a 3 x 5 card for future reference. Once you have clearly in mind the type of property you want, and the prices and terms you are interested in, call this broker. Also call any and every other top notch broker at every other major firm in your area. Give him your requirements and explain that you are ready, willing and able to acquire large amounts of property. Any top notch broker is already very familiar with the tycoon principles because he and all his heavy duty clients already use the techniques.

As a top producer, your new agent will have many clients who are interested in trading out of properties as they move up to bigger and better deals. These properties will be available out of trades to buyers who can make quick decisions. Many of these deals will never be listed for public sale because the American tax laws penalize the owners (by making them "dealers") if the property is advertised. Thus they are "available" but not on the public market for sale. You as a buyer will find out about them by attending local trading sessions for professionals in real estate, or getting to know the brokers who specialize in representing the wheeler dealers. These brokers will invariably be the "top producers" in every busy office. They have no time for amateurs, novices or lookers. They will be among the 5% of brokers who earn 90% of the commissions in an area.

Don't waste their time! Just remember that the best deals are often not advertised, but are called in the trade "pocket listings". Probably because the seller is in the pocket of the broker and the broker keeps the listing in his pocket. He shows it only to his favorite investor clients. The broker does not share the listing (and the potential commission) with the other brokers because he will earn a full (usually 6%) commission on the deal by representing <u>both</u> the seller and you as the buyer. If the broker knows exactly what you want, he will only call if a deal pretty close to your requirements materializes. The advantage of dealing with a top producer is that he does not waste your time showing you unsuitable properties.

I have several brokers who only call me once or twice a year. When they do call, I know there will be a deal because they know exactly what I want: Low up front cash requirement, potential for improving the income stream and pots of money to be made in the ultimate resale or trade up.

The most successful brokers are successful for very good reasons. They know the market and they do not float around wasting time with sellers who want outrageous prices, or who change their minds. They have no use for "buyers" who are only lookers or clients who will try to chisel down or circumvent their commissions. Good brokers will do their best to solve any problems as they come up: they persuade lenders to loan during tight money periods. They convince title companies to waive objections. A successful broker cajoles building departments to approve permits or zoning if these are a contingency. If necessary to close a deal, a good broker is usually flexible about carrying back all or part of their commission in the form of a note. For this they normally ask for and get the buyer's agreement to resell through him.

GOOD BROKERS ALWAYS HAVE POCKET LISTINGS!

A good broker is worth his weight in gold. The only problem is that as few as one in fifty of the real estate agents in the business are any good. But the good ones are knowledgeable of the current wrinkles in the tax laws and all current trends in the local market. They probably earn well over $100,000 per year in commissions by handling in excess of two or three million per year in sales. If you are clear about what you want, they will let you know of good deals from time to time. You must be ready to move fast. If they call you at 8 AM, be ready to meet them at the property at 8:15 and be ready to make an offer by 8:30. The best real estate deals are always snapped up on the day they are offered.

Naturally you are in no position to recognize, much less make such a deal, until you know the market: the best way to know the market quickly is to use the HUNDRED HOUSE RULE. Once you have looked at 100 properties, make low offers, or no money down offers on every deal you look at from then on. Remember there is no such thing as a bad real estate deal! At the right price or with good terms, any deal can help make your million.

How about other ways of finding super deals? Going back to the ads, before we pass on to other methods, look particularly for ads that say "for sale by owner". Normally owners have an exaggerated idea of what their property is worth. Often they start out asking well over market prices. But owners will sometimes accept terms that brokers would convince them to turn down. Also, many sellers are what I call "non-money motivated". So if you can deal directly with a seller rather than through an agent, you may find that your seller has things other than money in mind when he begins to negotiate with you. A seller represented by a real estate agent generally acts more rationally. In my comments on negotiating, coming right up, I'll give you several hints on dealing directly with sellers. There are definitely different and more creative techniques you can exploit in direct negotiations.

Another type of ad, which I call the HOT TIP AD is where it says something like "Owner will take 29% down". That statement, appearing in many ads, tells you that the seller is willing to carry all the financing on the property. The seller found out that if he takes 29% OR LESS as a cash down payment he will get certain tax benefits. He wants an installment sale. The tip off that is important to you is that the seller is mentally prepared to lend you the money to buy his property. He will "carry the paper". To you as a buyer this means that there will be no need for you to qualify for a bank loan. You only have to convince the seller that you are reliable, namely that you will make the required monthly payments to him on the mortgage he has carried back.

It may be possible for you to convince a seller advertising "29% down" to carry back a 100% loan. For those skeptics who say "it can't be done" I say, don't knock it if you have not tried it! Over half of my own deals have been no money down deals, with the sellers carrying the entire loan. There may be many good tax reasons why a seller is willing to do this, and

I've discussed many of them in my chapter NO MONEY DOWN DEALS. Here I just stress that where you see a "for sale by owner" ad you can occasionally get property at a super price. More often, you can negotiate creative loans that are very advantageous for you. Where you see "29% down" in ads it always means that the seller is willing to carry the financing. If you are just starting out or are overextended, or if for some reason you find it difficult to borrow from financial institutions, "29% down" means that you do not have to look too good on paper and you can usually make the deal with a lot less than 29% down. You only have to charm the seller, who seldom requests or requires a financial statement.

Whenever you meet a seller or an agent through a newspaper ad, whether the deal advertised works out for you or not, never fail to ask if they have any other properties now or coming up in the near future that you could look at. Many a property advertised in the paper has been totally unattractive to me. But the owner had another deal around the corner or up his sleeve and I bought the other property. Every owner or agent you meet is a contact. And in real estate (as in any other business) it is having contacts who want to deal with you that is important. A GOOD CONTACT IN THE BUSINESS IS BETTER THAN ANY ONE DEAL.

If someone in business appears to be exceptionally LUCKY time after time, you will find that his or her "luck" is always OTHER PEOPLE. You'll often be presented with a deal or opportunity as a result of knowing someone who knows you are a serious, reliable buyer. Or they simply want to do you a favor. You'll be able to utilize that opportunity or take that deal because you have other contacts to help you do it. In real estate your contacts will range from sellers, to handymen and construction people. There will also be potential tenants and financial backers and a whole gamut of acquaintances who can supply the pieces to make a deal work. In your Hundred House period you will not only be getting an education, but just as important, you will be cultivating a wide range of potentially useful contacts in the business.

Your preparation or training period should be complete within two months. Thoroughly familiar with the local market, you should at that point, be able to do what I call a "second gear appraisal": You hear of a property for sale. You drive by in second gear. If you have done your Hundred House Homework, you should be able to look at any building from the outside. Within a 5% margin of error, you can estimate the asking price, and the price it will actually sell for. Try it a few times. If you are way off, go back to the drawing boards -- or rather, the ads, and keep looking and asking questions.

Once you can make "successful second gear appraisals", you have arrived! You are as good as the so called professionals in the area, and you should have full confidence in yourself. If you know the market, you can't make many mistakes.

Now that you are educated and are ready to become a serious shopper and buyer, let's go on to the ways that "insiders", people who really know their way around, get the very best deals.

Multiple Listing Book: "Multiple" is a monthly or weekly picture book put out as a cooperative effort by all the real estate agents in a given community, listing the unsold inventory of properties. Generally the MLB is the last place to look for good deals because after an owner has tried to sell property on his own and it didn't move, he gives it to an agent. The agent shows it to all of his favored investor clients. They don't take the deal because it is overpriced. He advertises, but still no takers. The agent shares it with other agents in his office. None of the other agents want the stinker of a deal, nor do their clients. After exposure to several hundred buyers, the broker decides to share his commission; to put it in the Cooperative Multiple Listing Service. That is his last resort. The broker proclaims to the community "I couldn't move this turkey to any of my own clients, so I'll pay half of my 6% commission to any other real estate agent who can find a sucker to take it." Obviously the best deals never get into the Multiple Listing Service. The best deals are the pocket listings or the deals that never get listed at all.

Can you ever get a good deal out of Multiple? Of course you can. There are at least two ways I have gotten super deals out of Multiple. The first involves having a real estate agent who is willing to go to the printer or publisher and get the first galleys of the Multiple Listing Service Book just as they come off the press.

Here's how an occasional winner gets on Multiple. Picture this: Little old, incompetent broker, doesn't know the market, has no clients, is in real estate only to have a one man office to get away from the wife and play cards with his cronies. This bloke hits it lucky and a listing comes into his office at a price well below market value. Not recognizing the good deal for what it is, nor having any clients to show it to, he puts it into Multiple. When it is published, the broker is immediately deluged with dozens of full price offers. Legally the seller is obligated to sell at the first full price offer by virtue of the contract with the Multiple Listing Service. He thinks the broker did a swell job by bringing in so many offers. The seller doesn't realize that his agent made a terrible blunder by listing too low. But the point is, you have   to be the first offer. In a decent sized community, there may be one or two sleepers a week coming out in Multiple. To take advantage of them you have to get the sheets early!

GETTING MULTIPLE LISTINGS BEFORE THE INK IS DRY

Getting to those rare underpriced offerings before the crowd is one way to get good deals out of Multiple. Being first is the best way. However, being last is another way: Every listing in Multiple carries an expiration date printed right above the photograph of the listed house. If you call the listed owner a few days before the expiration date and ascertain that the property is not sold, you can deduce several useful bits of information. These can be used to draft an offer cleverly post-dated to be accepted one day after the expiration date. If the asking price was $50,000 you know the seller was willing to pay out $3,000 for the standard 6% commission. He doesn't have to pay the broker commission after the listing expires. There was probably a factor in the asking price for negotiation: at least 10%. So an offer of $40,000 to $43,000 net would likely be accepted. But since the property didn't sell in 3 to 6 months, the owner may be more than a little discouraged. He may be desperate to unload. That could mean he's willing to carry secondary financing or to lower the price drastically.

Therefore, to often get a good deal out of Multiple, all you do is call the owner of an expiring listing a few days before it expires and feel him out. If the owner intends to relist the property (as most do) ask him to specifically exclude any deal with you from any new listing agreement he signs. That way there will be no commission payable on a sale eventually concluded with you, even if the property is listed with another agent. Once the earlier listing expires you have a clear shot at the seller, can sit down with him and present an offer for say $30,000. You may be able to walk away from the closing with cash in hand. Who knows what sort of a deal you can make? It is all in the negotiating. And in real estate negotiating you can offer anything. A dejected seller may accept whatever you offer.

I once bought a property this way. The asking price was $50,000. I offered $18,000 cash. To my surprise, this offer was immediately accepted. I bought with an unsecured bank loan. In a few months I repaid the unsecured loan because I had obtained a $25,000 long term bank loan. Within three years I sold the property for $88,000. Why did I get the property so cheap? There was a divorce going on. The wife wanted to keep the house as long as possible, so she refused to sign a listing unless it was over priced at $50,000. She figured that pricing it out of the market would enable her to live in it longer. The property was actually worth closer to $30,000. Six months passed. The husband moved out and didn't make payments. The wife later moved out and the mortgage people had about $16,000 past due.

The place was a "yuck house". It was dirty, the yard was full of weeds and it smelled of cat pee. The lenders from Upright Savings & Loan

THE "YUCK" HOUSE

told the wife she'd better take the first offer that came along over $16,000 or they'd take over the property and she'd get nothing. Mr. and Mrs. Yuck could have sold at $30,000 and split an equity of $14,000 but the wife was happy to have screwed her husband out of his half of a $14,000 equity and he was equally pleased that she didn't get any money in the divorce. There were no assets besides the house. It was your typical American divorce - - both sides were vindictive and angry. They let their assets go to hell and to their lawyers. But there's always a budding tycoon around to pick up the broken pieces. In the right place at the right time, with the right offer. There are dozens of deals like this being made every day. For you to get your share, you just have to be there, looking and making offers.

If you drive through almost any neighborhood you'll see "for sale", "for rent" or "open house" signs on property. For me it's as regular a habit as breathing to come to a screeching halt, knock on the door and talk to the owner or the agent handling the deal. Every enquiry gives you more information on market prices, rents asked, etc. Just as important, it will create an ever widening circle of contacts. Never fail to ask the Magic Question "What else do you have for sale or rent?" It will lead to other deals, further information and more contacts. Never stop asking questions! If it's a rental sign, ask the owner "Did you ever consider selling this place so you wouldn't have to go through the bother of renting it?" If it's a "for sale" sign and the deal is obviously not for you, ask "What have other properties in this area sold for recently?" "What is currently on the market? Are any of your neighbors thinking of selling or moving?"

One of my best deals resulted from going up to a door to read a tiny calling card with the cryptic message "For information on this place, call – phone number". Hardly the way to get maximum exposure for the seller, but it permitted me to negotiate an excellent deal with a seller who didn't want to be bothered with hoards of lookers. He figured that anyone who took the time to climb twenty stairs to read his little card would have to be a serious buyer.

Real estate is traded in what the economists call a very imperfect market. Every property is unique and every buyer and seller has peculiarities or motivations. You can regularly buy properties at well below their market value if:

1. You know the market.
2. You can learn of special situations through your network of contacts.

AUCTIONS - PROBATES - CONSERVATORSHIPS

PARTITION SUITS - FORECLOSURES - TAX SALES

All of the above come under my general heading of distress sales. If you are looking for bargain basement prices, distress sales is where you'll find them. You learn about these situations in several ways. In most communities, banks, savings and loan associations, trust companies, the Public Administrator, Auction houses and even the IRS will put you on their free mailing list. Most County Courthouses have bulletin boards where all probate estates, trustees' sales (foreclosures) must, by law, be posted. They must also be advertised in a newspaper of "general circulation". In every community there is an obscure legal paper that almost nobody reads. It will have a name like the Law Bulletin or Legal Advertiser. It's the favored place for publishing notices of these sales. Also you could simply go to the local courthouse regularly to check their bulletin boards where the same notices are posted. Check the postings and read the newspapers containing legal notices for those pertaining to real estate. If you call the law firm mentioned in an ad or posted notice you will get the details of appraised value, location and problems and decide whether you want to bid on the deal. Obviously you must always go and inspect the property physically.

There are technical rules for each type of sale and before bidding you must ascertain whether you must have "all cash" with you at the auction in the form of a cashier's check, or just a deposit. Sometimes a cash deposit (such as 10% in probates) will do. When only a deposit is needed, the closing can generally be scheduled for 30 or 60 days after the successful bid is accepted and confirmed. At that point you need to pay out the rest of the cash.

The main problem with distress or estate property is that it is generally impossible to get a seller to help with the financing by carrying back a loan for part of the purchase price. The nature of distress or probate property is that the seller needs all cash in order to pay his own debts or make distribution to the heirs. Thus until you have a line of unsecured credit, it is necessary to bid real money to take advantage of the generally lower than market prices for distress property.

Usually there is no room for creative negotiations with trustees or estate administrators who merely put property up for the best all-cash bid in a public auction type sale. Yet you should be on the lookout for special situations. From time to time the property is such a dog that no bidders materialize at the sale. Or, the best bid for a substantial property is so low, it is unacceptable. In those cases, (often occurring in a half finished construction project or vandalized building) it may be possible to get a very cheap price at least an option or a large mortgage from the estate. You can then control the property without significant investment.

When you get property cheap, it is very cheap! At a delinquent property tax auction, I once bought a half acre in San Anselmo, California for $10. At the time similar sized lots were selling for $30,000! Why was this one so cheap? For starters it was landlocked - - that is there was no access to it from any road. No road could be built because most of the surrounding properties had homes on them and all the adjacent owners refused to give an easement to pass over their land. Equally significant, at least half of my lot was under a creek in a community that did not permit construction on underwater lots. Other people at the auction thought it was worthless, so I bid the minimum. For $10, I figured, how wrong could I go?

I didn't go too far wrong, because two years later I sold that lot for $10,000. I did it by picking up an adjacent parcel at a fair price.   Combining two sub-standard parcels, I created one excellent creek-side apartment building site. The two sites together had proper square footage and enough above-water land to get a building permit. Moral to this story: If you watch all the published and posted legal notices and check them out carefully, all sorts of opportunities will come your way.

The annual delinquent real estate tax sales and public land dispositions produce all sorts of weird slivers and parcels that nobody seems to be interested in. They can be picked up for peanuts. I generally bid the minimum ($10) on all of them, figuring that if worse comes to worse, I can grow a weed garden or use them in a trade (see: NO MONEY DOWN DEALS). What usually happens is that the owner of an adjoining property will pay me at least one hundred times my ten buck investment. In the story I told you I made a return of one thousand times my investment. In the real estate business that sort of thing happens every day. Just keep your eyes and ears open, read the notices, attend and bid at the sales and then think creatively about what you can do with the property. It's as easy as falling off a log.

H.U.D. AUCTIONS, F.H.A., FORECLOSURES, GOVERNMENT DEALS

Another category of auctions will not be posted in the county courthouse. But you can get on the Federal government's mailing list or find out what sort of deals they have by keeping in touch with the local office of the Federal Government's Department of Housing & Urban Development, the

Federal Housing Administration and your local Housing authority. There are myriads of Federal loan programs, subsidies, gimmicks and give-aways, the bill for which is all subsidized by the tax payer. To catch the gravy train and get your share, just call up the local numbers listed in the phone book. It would take another book of several volumes to go through all the government real estate programs. For our purposes, I just want to make you aware that if you are "low income", have a handicapped child or elderly person that you support, are blind, deprived or disadvantaged in any way, the government probably has a special give-away program just for you. For ordinary, unhandicapped folks, there are plenty of opportunities too.

For instance, when a government loan is foreclosed, the home or apartment building in question is often refurbished at government expense to high FHA standards, before it is put up for resale. The deal to the buyer often involves little or no money down with 40-year, 3% loans. The government always pays a full 6% commission to the broker who represents you, even if it's a no money down deal. If the broker is your wife or business partner, you can see that the family could close a deal and be net cash ahead sometimes.

On some deals, like low rent housing and historic area preservation, super fast depreciation (five years) and investment tax credits are allowed as additional tax incentives. On others, the financing can be at almost unbelievable terms. If these government subsidized deals are so good, why aren't more people into them? A lot of people are into them. Even me. But I don't like them. For one thing, the laws and complex regulations under which you must operate (as with all government programs) are almost incomprehensible. Profits are often limited by law to a lot less than you could make in the private sector. Rents may be controlled at arbitrarily low levels. The resale of property may be limited or restricted. And if you wittingly or unwittingly violate the law, the Feds play very rough and might give you a two year paid vacation in San Quentin prison. As always, the main problem in dealing with the government is that the paper work, red tape, regulations and time consumed in dealing with bureaucrats usually just isn't worth the prize. But many people do it and do just fine.

THE DIRTY WINDOW GAMBIT

Would you believe that looking for dirty windows could make you a fortune in real estate? It has certainly helped me. I don't mean your ordinary garden variety of dirty windows -- I mean really filthy, cracked or broken windows. They are usually found on a house or property that has a front yard full of weeds, peeling paint, signs of vandalism, graffiti or an abandoned looking car in the drive -- in short, abandoned or NEGLECTED property.

The owner of neglected property may be in a nursing home, the French Foreign Legion, or dead. He may have heirs thousands of miles away who'd love to get any offer to purchase a property they might not even know they own. In one case, I discovered that the owners of a derelict property were scattered heirs, all of whom, when contacted, wanted to sell. But one heir in Poland, Vladimir Dzerwinkovitch, didn't answer my letters, telegrams or phone calls. I figured if I could buy deeds for 3/4 of the property and take possession, there would have to be a way to get the other 1/4, whether the Polish heir wanted to sell or not. So I paid rather nominal sums, about $500 per deed, to three out of the four heirs. I recorded the deeds and went to the lawbooks. There were several ways to proceed. I had the choice of ignoring the interest of Vladimir for seven years after which, if I rented out the property and paid my real estate taxes, the property would be entirely mine by virtue of the laws of adverse possession. But that seemed risky. The missing heir might turn up in the sixth year. Also I'd be tied up for seven years. Another possibility was an immediate legal action against the Pole called a "Quiet Title" or "Partition Suit".

So I filed suit. This involved publishing a notice in the Law Bulletin that Vladimir's interest would be sold on a certain day at the request of myself as a tenant in common. The law has always given a remedy to partners who don't get along. In due course the property went up for public sale at my request. In this case, controlling three-quarters at the sale, I only had to put up cash representing one-quarter of my bid. Fortunately I was the only bidder at $10. The Polish heir, good old Vladimir, was credited with a deposit of $2.50 which I assume the County Treasurer is still holding for him.

If you had come to that auction, you might have bid me up to the $20,000 I was prepared to offer for the property. $20,000 wouldn't have been a bad

THINK CREATIVELY!

price either, because three years later it is on the market at $115,000. My
cost: $1,500 to the heirs, $2.50 to the recalcitrant heir, $375 in legal fees
and a lot of research, phone calls and running around.

An uncared for property is often an unwanted property. Someone
else's discards can make you a fortune. If a property isn't cared for physically it probably isn't being cared for financially either. I have a way of
finding those financially abandoned and unloved properties that is even more
efficient than cruising the streets looking for dirty windows. As mentioned
earlier, you should always watch the Courthouse Bulletin Boards for notices of foreclosure and the "Notice of Default" that is posted when a property owner doesn't meet his obligations under a trust deed or mortgage.

Someone who can't pay his mortgage is a good prospect for a buy-out. But suppose the property is free and clear. There is no mortgage to default on. How can you discover financially distressed owners of free and clear property? Simple. You go to the records of the County Tax Collector and compile a list of properties where the taxes have been delinquent for a year or more. You send the owners (their addresses can be found on the public records) a friendly letter noting that their tax is delinquent, suggesting that you would consider making them an attractive offer for their property. I have found that a mass mailing to this particular list of property owners brings almost a 25% positive response, and when things are slow it's one of my old faithful methods of stirring up a few good deals. If you go beyond a mere mailing and trace owners whose mail is returned as undeliverable, and telephone the rest, you'd get even more prospective deals.

While you are tediously going through the public records for owners of tax delinquent properties, I suggest that you also prepare a list of out-of-state owners. They as a group, are often anxious to sell and reinvest proceeds in their own area. In a letter explain to them the possiblity of their being able to trade their property, tax free (see chapter on Tax Free Trades), for equivalent property in their own area selected by themselves. You will find that 4% to 6% will have a high degree of interest in working out a deal with you.

PERSONAL CONTACTS

Last and most important are personal contacts! My local Fuller Brush Salesman makes about $10,000 a year selling hairbrushes and brooms door-to-door. He makes another half million a year trading real estate. He knows all the older people who plan on moving to Sunshine Retirement City. He's on a first name basis with all the pregnant women who will soon be pressuring their husbands to get them a bigger house. He is on top of job transfers, births, marriages, deaths, divorces and all the factors that cause people to make a change in their living or investment situations. His door-to-door selling job is literally worth half a million a year to him because it puts him in touch with everybody in the community.

You may not want to sell brushes, Shaklee vitamins or Avon cosmetics door-to-door - - but you should consider it. You must make and keep up your contacts some way. Other alternatives: Become a real estate agent and constantly solicit listings; political door-to-door canvassing is good. You could be on a payroll doing appraisals for local lenders. At the very least, you should join the local National Guard, Masons, Knights of Columbus, Rotarians or Jaycees so that you know lots of people. And lots of people must be made aware that you are interested in any real estate an owner wishes to sell before it is listed or advertised. Make a standing offer of a bottle of champagne for any such tip. Your friend gets at least a hundred dollars for any tip that results in a deal.

PUT A SMILE ON THEIR FACE

Many times, real estate agents, in the course of soliciting possible sellers for listings find that a seller is willing to sell, but does not want to sign a listing contract. The property owner tells the broker "Bring me an offer of X dollars and I'll sell". The broker is then in a bind. If he alerts a client to the deal without a listing, it may be difficult for him to collect his commission from the seller (who traditionally pays 6% of the sales price).

Brokers have been burned so often by this type of seller that they will usually not take any action to inform anyone of the deal without a written listing guaranteeing their commission. For every written listing, brokers may know of ten or fifteen possiblities of the type just mentioned. How can you take advantage of the situation and gain knowledge of them? Simple! Every broker you become friendly with should get the following offer from you: "Charlie, if you tip me off to a good deal, whether you have a listing or not, if I buy the property, there's $300 cash in it for you. And when I go to sell or trade, I'll put another smile on your face with another little bonus or a listing on the way out."

If you get a reputation for never trying to perform a commission-dectomy on brokers (that's where you cut out the broker's commission on deals that you close) but instead are known for always leaving these ladies and gentlement with a smile on their faces, your phone will ring constantly as your bird-dogs bring you more good deals that you can handle.

If you become a trustworthy wheeler-dealer, what happened to me last year will happen to you. Amos, a broker, woke me up at 6 a.m. with a phone call. In conspiratorial tones he said, "Greene, I've got a hot one for you."

"What is it?" I mumbled, half asleep.

"I want $4,000 - if you buy it."

"The deal was $300. I offered you a flat $300 for hot tips."

"But this is a real hot one. Take it or leave it!"

"O.K." I said. "I'll take it if: 1) I don't already know about it and 2) you get $4,000 only if I actually buy it."

I figured there was no harm in looking at the deal. Whatever price was set, I'd just mentally add $4,000 to the cost. If it was worth it, I'd take it.

"Done" said Amos. "I'll pick you up in half an hour."

Amos took me to a mansion I knew about. It had been on the market for years at $120,000. Very over priced.

"What's the story?" I said.

"The mortgage has been foreclosed and you can buy it at 10 AM for $30,000 from the Bank of America. I want $4,000 cash at the closing. There's a public sale scheduled but the time and place was given wrong in the papers. Only I know that the sale is on for this morning. You'll be the only bidder.

I almost didn't believe him, but as he had been a reliable source in the past, I toddled along with Amos to the Bank of America, picking up two cashier's checks as unsecured loans on the lower floor of the Bank. One check was for $30,000 and one for $4,000. Amos introduced me to the trust officer handling the deal, I made the only bid and handed $30,000 to the trust officer. At 10:02 I was given a trustee's deed to certify that I owned the property. It was easily worth $90,000. I slipped Amos his $4,000 on the way out.

The same day, I called a few of my own real estate investor friends and offered it to them at $64,000 "as is" all cash, quick close. A week later I sold the property at a $30,000 profit. I gave Amos another hundred dollar bill.

Amos had a smile on his face.

I had a smile on my face.

I made $30,000 in a week and I owe it all to knowing the market, having good contacts and a reputation for spreading smiles and sunshine wherever I go. NOW YOU DO IT!

BILL "TYCOON" GREENE, SPREADER OF SMILES AND SUNSHINE.

BILL GREENE MADE MILLIONS IN REAL ESTATE

YOU CAN TOO!

JUST FOLLOW HIS PROVEN METHODS...

and you will be financially independent in three years. Many of Bill's students have over $1,000,000 in property. Most of them started with NO MONEY. They all used Bill's techniques for investing in real estate.

> "Ninety percent of all millionaires became so through owning real estate. More money has been made in real estate than in all industrial investment combined."

These are the words of Andrew Carnegie -- one of the world's richest men! They were true 100 years ago and it is true today. Are you tired of hearing about all the money OTHER people make in real estate? Bill's methods teach YOU in detail, how to buy property for LITTLE or NO MONEY DOWN, how to shelter your outside income so you pay NO TAX, and how to run your properties to MAXIMIZE YOUR PROFIT.

It doesn't matter where you live, what you do, or how much money you have. YOU can acquire a real estate fortune using Bill's simple method. Bill Greene is a super successful real estate investor, attorney, businessman and nationally known author and lecturer. He is dedicated to the principles of American free enterprise and wants to show YOU how to acquire the money you want.

INCOME PROPERTY
INVESTMENT STRATEGY

Bill "Tycoon" Greene of Mill Valley, California is a spectacularly successful real estate investor who from 1973 to 1978 cashed in on the dramatic price rise in Marin. He felt this rise was caused by the ecologists' restriction of new housing by means of water and sewer bans. At the peak of the Marin boom he traded out and moved most of his investments to the Sacramento valley just in time to catch their greatest percentage value increase. After making several million in three years, Greene turned his interests towards the education of fellow investors. He joined the Libertarian Party which favors minimum government regulation and minimum taxation. Greene served with Paul Gann and Howard Jarvis and other Libertarian Thinkers on the Steering Committee for Proposition 13, which lowered California property taxes by over 50%. He is the author of *Two Years for Freedom*, a book on life, love and making money in real estate.

Greene's best ideas may be obtianed by calling 383-3229 or writing Box 408, Mill Valley, CA 94941.

Making Something Out Of Nothing In Real Estate

By JANE EVERT

Mill Valley millionaire Bill Green would like to help everyone make something out of nothing — in real estate.

Greene, financial mentor of "over a thousand" budding real estate tycoons, teaches a class that promises to help the masses take advantage of a Sacramento Valley real estate boom "the likes of which has not been seen before" and accumulate a tidy, tax-free fortune in the process.

"I teach people who have little or no money to start with how to acquire real estate and make money at it," says Greene, a 39-year-old self-made man

He claims that even someone who follows his program and does most things wrong can make a million dollars in five and a half years. For those wo do it right, it takes one to three.

"There always has been opportunity in real estate," he says. "And now there are new factors..."

Inland California, he says, is on the verge of a veritable Golden Age of real estate. And the locals can either sit back and watch it happen or be the first to take advantage of it.

Why the big real estate boom inland? Because, for one thing, the cost of housing in the coastal area is prohibitive for many home buyers, especially older people with fixed incomes, says Greene. An average two-bedroom tract house in Monterey or Mill Valley is going for $100,000 or more these days, he explains. And assessments keep rising too, forcing many homeowners to sell out and to search for greener, less expensive pastures.

And homeowners in colder climates are finding it increasingly difficult to keep up with their fuel bills. Hence a shift in population to the "Sun Belt" states where more congenial weather makes it "infinitely cheaper" to live, he points out.

Add in increased foreign investments in California and possible property tax aid from the proposed Jarvis-Gann Initiative and here we all are, sitting on another kind of gold mine.

Okay, the goose is about to lay the golden egg. So how does one go about getting a portion?

Naturally enough, Greene is not telling all his secrets (most of which are reserved for the paying customers.) But he is willing to part with a few free tips.

The first step is to buy a property for little or no money down. Greene suggests a lot of shopping around and some very selective buying.

The average person will buy an average house for, say, $50,000 at the standard 20 percent (or $10,000 in this case) down, he says. Due to inflation and increased cost of property due to required improvements and other factors, the value of the house probably will increase at least 10 per cent in a year, he says, and the owner will have made 50 percent (or $5,000) on his initial $10,000 investment.

But the house still would have increased in value and the owner have made the $5,000 even if he had put no money down, says Greene.

Use of the property for income purposes (renting part of all, raising chickens, whatever), he says, can pay the mortgage payments and allow the owner to take advantage of some substantial income tax breaks. Depreciation, deductible repairs and maintenance, interest, insurance, real estate tax, etc.

The owner also can borrow money on the increased value of the property, he adds.

"And why do it just once?" he asks. "In the first year of owning two or three properties you will not have to pay income tax."

An understanding of the tax law is a must, he says. And management and control, careful selection and creating an attractive environment are all just as important as being in the right place at the right time.

A prime rule is "never sell," he advises. "Refinance and trade up." And "never quit an income-producing job" while building that fortune.

A word of caution. People can and do lose money in real estate, Greene says. Real estate is a "very imperfect" market.

"The typical buyer does not look for a good deal," he explains. "He finds what he likes and he pays the price. You have to know how to negotiate a deal. You can't be swayed by your emotions —

Who qualifies for Greene's 14-hour weekend course? Just about anybody who can afford the price of admission —

For those not completely satisfied halfway through the weekend, the fee will be cheerfully refunded.

—Appeal-Democrat (Marysville-Yuba City, CA) Sat., April 1, 1978

But does his program work? He says success using his program depends on three assumptions:

1. That "you're not too smart." If you're too smart, you can't make it in real estate." Those who think too much lose time and miss valuable opportunities.

2. That "you're starting with little or no money." Rich people who haven't worked for their money tend to lose it,

3. That "government policies will not change drastically." In other words, as long as we don't have a revolution. As it is, Greene says, government inflationary policy is "too ingrained" for the economic picture to change drastically. "This is still basically a capitalistic system in which people can make millions."

But if he's so rich, why is he teaching this course?

Because, he says, he recognizes what he believes to be an unsettling "trend toward socialism" in this country and he wants to do his bit to stem the tide.

His fortune more than provides for his relatively simple tastes, he explains. So even though he could be making more money devoting his time to real estate deals rather than telling others how to go about it, he says, he wants to "help people to realize they can be independently wealthy in a short time."

BILL GREENE TYCOON CLAS

P. O. BOX 408
Mill Valley, Ca
94941

(415) 383 3229

Take The Tycoon Class AT HOME!

Now, at a fraction of the price of the "live" seminar, you can get eleven hours of cassette tape and all the study materials from the Bill Greene Tycoon Class for HOME STUDY. This Home Study Course includes all the major topics covered in the weekend class. It includes:

EIGHT CASSETTE TAPES (each covering more than the title indicates) attractively packaged in a book-like album

Think Like a Tycoon	Handling Tenants
Finding Super Deals	Pay No Taxes Ever Again, Legally!
Getting Organized	Advanced Tax Avoidance
No Money Down Deals	Trade Up Tax Free - 1031 Exchanges

THE TYCOON CLASS WORKBOOK, a fat, looseleaf reference manual you will refer to hundreds of times in your real estate dealings. Contains forms, vital tax information, negotiating tips and almost everything you need to know about investing in real estate. This is the new, updated 1979 edition.

LANDLORDING, by Leigh Robinson, a book so good that Bill wishes he had written it himself. It is fun, easy to read and contains all you need to know about handling tenants, managing property and keeping your books and records straight.

THE REALTY BLUEBOOK, the bible of real estate. No real estate agent leaves home without it. Not sold in stores, it was previously available only to professionals in the business. It contains forms, checklists, everything you need to know about the technical aspects of real estate.

TWO YEARS FOR FREEDOM, by Bill Greene, an epic on making money and avoiding taxes. It is 280 pages, profusely illustrated, helpful and humorous. This book should become a National Best Seller. Before the general public can buy it, it is available only to friends on our mailing list. If your order is recieved in the next 15 days you will get a PERSONALLY AUTOGRAPHED PREVIEW COPY that may be a collector's item once the book is nationally advertised.

The total cost of the Home Study Course is $180 plus $5 for UPS delivery. Many students felt the personal contact with dynamic and inspiring Bill Greene was an essential part of the Tycoon Class experience. But the written materials are exactly the same and the cost of the Home Study Course can be deducted, if you take the "live" course later.

Anyone who receives a Home Study Course and does not agree it's worth far more than its cost, can return it, undamaged, within two weeks for a full refund.

The next step is up to you. No salesman will follow up this letter and give you a sales pitch. The Tycoon Course will change your life drastically for the better, but you must give YOURSELF the push. YOU must get off your fanny and move! Get the Home Study Course on a no-risk trial basis.

* * * * * * * * * * * * * * * * * * *

THE MATERIALS IN THE HOME STUDY COURSE ARE AVAILABLE SEPARATELY, TOO!

SEE OUR PRICE LIST AND ORDER FORM.

PRICE LIST

COMPLETE HOME STUDY COURSE
Includes 8 cassette tapes, Tycoon Workbook, Landlording,
Realty Bluebook, Two Years For Freedom and UPS delivery............. $185

OR ORDER SEPARATELY

TWO YEARS FOR FREEDOM..................................... $ 16

THE REALTY BLUEBOOK..................................... $ 11

LANDLORDING..................................... $ 13

INDIVIDUAL CASSETTE TAPES..................................... $ 13

Think Like A Tycoon	Handling Tenants*
Finding Super Deals	Pay No Taxes Ever Again, Legally!
Getting Organized	Advanced Tax Avoidance
No Money Down Deals	Trade Up Tax Free - 1031 Exchanges

* Handling Tenants uses and refers to legal forms and documents in the Landlording
book, so you will need that text if you order this tape.

SPECIAL INTRODUCTORY TALK: "Buying Your First Investment Property" on cassette.
General summary of the Tycoon Class with detailed instruction on how to use the
standard offer form (included). This tape will be included as a gift to all those
who order the Home Study Course

THIS TAPE ALONE - SPECIAL .... $ 9

* * * * * * * ORDER FORM * * * * * * *

PLEASE SEND ME:

____COMPLETE HOME STUDY COURSE
    185 each.
____TWO YEARS FOR FREEDOM $16 each

____THE REALTY BLUEBOOK $11 each

____LANDLORDING $13 each

____BUYING YOUR FIRST INVESTMENT
    PROPERTY. $9 each
____INDIVIDUAL CASSETTES $13 each
    (designate titles desired)

_____

_____

_____

_____

NAME_____

ADDRESS_____

CITY/STATE/ZIP_____

Check enclosed _____ Charge me _____

Visa # _____

Mastercharge # _____

Expiration Date _____

TOTAL OF YOUR ORDER _____

TAX AND POSTAGE
(other than Home Study)
add $1 for each item _____

TOTAL ENCLOSED _____

PLEASE USE BILLING ADDRESS OF YOUR CARD WHEN CHARGING MERCHANDISE.

PHONE ORDERS ACCEPTED WITH CHARGE ORDERS AT (415) 383-3229   9 am to 4 pm.

X1179Y

NEGOTIATING TIPS & PLOYS

You have heard people say, "Never take NO for an answer." Sometimes you can get the answer you want, that is the YES answer, by merely asking the question right. When you are looking for property and you spot an owner working on his property, you <u>could</u> say to him in a negative way, "You probably <u>don't</u> want to sell your property right now, do you?" You've already given in your question, a suggestion of the answer. The logical answer is, "Yes, that's right. I don't want to sell my property." Why not think like a tycoon and ask the question in a positive way?

You could do it much more effectively this way: "If I can show you how to trade up for a much better property tax free without taking a dime out of your pocket, or paying a broker's commission would you be interested?" Of course, in the case of most sellers, their ears would perk up and they would be eager to know what you had in mind. And if you could show that fellow how to trade up, using Section 1031 of the Internal Revenue Code as explained in this book, he'd probably be willing to sell and move himself up to a bigger and better property.

Another way of posing a proposition positively is, for example, approaching a potential seller and saying to him, "If I can show you how to get much more rent money than you are getting now, would you be interested in listening to me?" Now, how many potential sellers would refuse to listen to your proposition? Even if they were not considering the sale of their property, you now have the opportunity to talk to them about installment sales or you could convince them that by selling their property to you and by acquiring a different, larger property in a tax free trade it will bring them in more rents and enhance their own financial position. Psychologically, it should be obvious that if a property owner asks you to outline a plan for how he could do better and you show him how to do it, he is in a way committed to dealing with you to implement the plan. But if you got a NO answer in the first place and tried to carry on a further conversation by explaining your plans, you might meet a wall of resistance.

When you are trying to get someone to interact with you, to work effectively with you or to make a deal with you, remember they are not generally interested in your needs. It's up to you to show them what you can do for them; where you can do it, when you can do it and how you can do it. How can they profit by dealing with you? What are the benefits to them? What are the risks they may want to avoid?

How can they protect themselves against loss? The tycoon anticipates needs, fears and all questions before negotiating.

It is true that you should seldom take "no" for an answer in a business relationship. But to get a "yes" you must structure your proposition so that the person you are dealing with has no choice, but in his best interest, to accept your offer. In other words, like the Godfather said, "Make 'em an offer they can't refuse."

The same approach can be used outside of real estate. If you're looking for a job and the employer says "I don't need you. My overhead is already too high. I can't afford another employee." Your answer will be, "That's true - I agree with you, I see your point BUT I will work for you for free for two weeks. If in two weeks I haven't made you far more than the salary I'll need, then you don't have to use me. Now, how can you refuse an offer like that? I'll work for you and make you profits of more than $1,000 a week and you don't have to pay me anything. And if I do work out for you, all I ask is that you pay me a part of what I make you." When you make your offers to people in such a way that it is difficult for them to refuse to deal with you. You'll find that if you perform you will always have success.

If the person from whom you want to buy a property has some objections to selling to you, treat those objections with respect. Never argue. Always agree with what they have to say and then add, BUT...and take it from there. For instance, if a person does not want to sell their property to you because the place they would buy with the proceeds would cost them considerably more in taxes, you can say: "The taxes on the next place will indeed be too high, but you can get enough extra income from the new raised rents you will be charging to more than cover those taxes.

Another pointer is that, after you have an agreement, to give you what you want, don't talk beyond the sale. Sometimes, once the person on the other side has done what you wanted, if you keep talking, he may have a change of heart. All you should do in a real estate deal once the person has agreed to sell is to both sign an informal written contract. It can be innocuously titled "memorandum." Remember that in real estate all contracts are meaningless unless they are in writing. After signing the "memorandum," and again after every closing, you should say something to encourage the seller that he did the right thing. One of my favorite remarks is, "Boy Mr. Seller, I certainly didn't intend to come up to your price of $100,000. I didn't think I'd have to go over $85,000. You did very well with me on this particular deal." In that way the seller's opinion that he got the best of you is confirmed. Give him that satisfaction!

Obviously if you had said at the closing "I was prepared to go to $110,000 on your deal. I'm sure glad you sold to me for $100,000," that would be the sort of uncalled for remark that would cause him to renege or speak ill of you for decades.

Regardless of the contract you may have with someone, remember a contract is only as good as the people who make it. If either side of the contract wants to get out of it, they can always do so. Once they do, all you have left is a law suit. In the process of negotiating, never lose your cool or give up, no matter how much of an idiot you are dealing with.

Sometimes the use of testimonials as to your character and reliability is very good. Rather than giving a reference to be used later, I found it very effective in negotiations to say to the person opposite me, "Look, Mr. Jones at the First National Bank has dealt with me successfully many times. I'm sure he will give me a good reference. I'd be happy to step out of the room while you call Mr. Jones for a reference on me."

That way, if you can supply the name of a person who is respected in the community, you may be able to close a deal that otherwise would have been impossible, because the seller in question thought you were some sort of a flake. Developing good references and using the name of someone well respected in the community like the local banker, is particularly useful to younger tycoons, who perhaps at the age of twenty to twenty-six might not be taken seriously by older sellers of substantial property. Don't appear too wealthy, bright, slick or money hungry. Being sincere, understanding, helpful, and interested in the other person's problems is your best negotiating stance.

THE MAGIC QUESTION

Once you have made a bit of money, in spite of valiant attempts to keep a low profile, word of your prosperity will leak out. Then inventors, promoters and con-men of all shapes, colors and sizes will convincingly offer to triple your money. The deals touted will be wonderfully entertaining. But don't part with a dime unless you want to lose it! Listen to their stories. Let them wine and dine you. But remember, there are more than the two choices most people make when approached by a pie-in-the-sky salesman. Obviously you could say a firm "No thank you and goodbye." Or, you might be a fool, take the deal offered and lose your shirt. Here's a third alternative that has made me a little richer, several times. Not to mention psychological rewards! There is nothing quite as satisfying as out-conning a confidence man. When a hot-shot salesperson departs from my home leaving <u>his</u> money behind, a warm glow radiates from me for days! Here's how you can take the money of fast talking salespeople.

Ask the MAGIC QUESTION: "If this deal is so good, why don't you keep it all for yourself?"

The answer will always be: "I would if I could, but I just don't have the money."

Here is where you turn the tables. You say: "Instead of investing in your deal, Mr. Conniver, I'll LEND you the money in return for half of the profits you just promised me. That way you, Mr. Conniver, can multiply my borrowed money and keep half of the gains for yourself without putting up a cent. You will take the risk of course, but as you've told me...'It's a sure thing'. All I want is some security pledged plus your personal note and a postdated check due six months from now." You should casually throw out some bait with the comment, "If and when this deal works out, I will probably invest lots more money on similar deals."

Why should you offer to make a loan to every promoter and why must you always ask for security?

Most promoters, inventors and syndicate fund raisers will be personally broke and totally worthless to you. They will (if you let them) take your hard earned cash. Usually you will never see any of it again. Sometimes the MAGIC QUESTION will give you the opportunity to create a profit for yourself. If the conniver in our example has any assets at all, and if he really believes in his scheme, then one time out of a hundred you both will make a profit. But whatever happens, even if his deal goes sour, YOU'LL come out smiling.

First: Find out what assets the con-artist has control of. Car? House? Listed stocks? Perhaps his wife has a diamond engagement ring. Maybe he has a fine oriental carpet or a Picasso. Anything of value will serve your purposes. My favorite security is a deed or trust deed on real estate. A home is good if conniver's "equity" over his mortgage or the net value involved is a least triple the amount of money he wants from you.

Second: After establishing that old super-salesman has an object worth $15,000, you can offer to lend, or rather "invest" one-third of that value -- say $5,000.

Third: The sample contract on the following page is one that you might use to close a deal.

You might properly comment that these contracts were the strangest loan package you ever saw. It looked more like you bought a car at a bargain price, and got a 50% interest in a risky venture thrown in as a gift. Actually, you DID buy a car, diamond, house or whatever at a bargain price. Conniver will probably lose it to you as well as losing HIS shirt on the actual deal he was trying to sell you. He will not be able to raise the cash to exercise his option in 95% of all cases, and you will end up with his property at a bargain price. In my experience, as a result of this type of

AGREEMENT

1. For the sum of $5,000 Mr. U (that's you) has purchased from Mr. Conniver one 300 SL Mercedes Benz Gull Wing Serial No. 12345, 1959 Model. (Note: You should comply with all local sale formalities. You take physical possession of the car and the title documents.)

2. It is further agreed that if, for any reason, Mr. Conniver wishes to repurchase said vehicle within six months he may do so, at a price of $7,000. (Note: The value of the property being triple what you are paying, is $15,000. Thus the buy-back price should always be about 50% of market value.)

Dated: _____   Signed: _____

                                              _____

Subscribed and Sworn to
Before Me:

   NANCY NOTARY

Notary Public in and for the State of California
My commission expires 1982.

At the signing, as part of the deal Conniver must give you a check for $7,000 dated six months ahead. You also execute this 'Side Deal'.

AGREEMENT

For a valuable consideration, plus time and effort invested by John U in connection with (describe venture in detail), Sam Conniver of 123 Ace Lane, Yourtown, does hereby agree to give John U a 50% interest in the gross profits and sales price of said (invention, restaurant, massage parlor, etc.) with profits or losses to be distributed and fully accounted for monthly. Conniver is to be the general partner or active participant in this venture, and John U is to be a silent investor without personal liability. John U is to have access to the books and records of the business al all times.

Dated:_____   Signed: _____

                                              _____

Subscribed and Sworn to
Before me:

   NANCY NOTARY

Notary Public in and for the State of California
My commission expires 1982

deal, I have ended up with many goodies.

Once I got a nice sports car at a bargain price from an operator who was going to triple "our" money in three months. His scheme was to open a chain of massage parlors in Alaska to service the boys working on the Alaska Pipe Line. For one reason or another, as I predicted, it didn't work out. In a different deal I got a $50,000 house for $33,000 cash when I bought it from a self-proclaimed wheeler dealer for $3,000 over his mortgage of $30,000.

In the first case, I was told that Alaska had the best cops money could buy, but they didn't stay bought and unexpectedly shut down the rub-down emporiums. In the second situation, the big profit was supposed to be made by buying silver coins at near their face value from a "secret source" and reselling immediately at their "collector value" of triple the cost. But instead of buying silver coins, the wheeler dealer (without informing me of his alternate plan) bought a plane load of Colombian marijuana and other similar items. The dope was hijacked in Mexico (of course!). In this case, however, the dealer "saved" enough Cocaine to offer me two pounds in lieu of the $3,000 needed to repurchase the house. Terrific! I politely refused his offer (as I suggest you should do in any deal involving illegal substances). Not that I have any great moral feelings against Cocaine. I personally believe it should be legal to drink Draino or do anything else your heart desires. But life is just too short for me to traffic in anything illegal unless survival depended on it.

To sum up this MAGIC QUESTION bit: If and when some person comes to you with a Red Ribbon Deal where all you do is hand over your money to get a fabulous, absolutely safe, super-return in a short time, remember: 99 times out of a hundred, you will loose every penny that you put up. The loss can result from incompetence, dishonesty, and most often an ill-advised, illegal venture. The person trying to sell you a deal often does not own the proverbial pot to pee in, but sometimes he does have assets. In those cases there is often an opportunity for YOU to make a risk-free profit. It will work out well for you in those comparatively few instances where:

1. The promoter believes in the project
2. He or she has assets or,

3. Where a con-man with assets wants to get you involved and is willing to give you a handsome phoney profit on your first venture hoping to sucker you in more heavily without security on the next deal.

Don't be a sucker. The sting (loss) will come at a time when you are holding no security. Grab the first profit and run!

To repeat, even if you make out like a bandit on your first deal -- DO NOT ASSUME THAT YOU CAN HAVE A REPEAT PERFORMANCE without the same security agreement.

Can you trust anyone?

I used to say you can't trust anyone except a major Swiss Banker. Then in 1977 my Swiss Banker, manager of Swiss Bank Corporation's Chiasso (Switzerland) branch was found to have diverted almost one billion dollars into personal and disastrous speculations. He went to the pokey. Today I have NO EXCEPTIONS. Don't trust anyone!

HOW TO AVOID LENDING MONEY -- ALWAYS ASSUME
THAT ONE OR MORE OF THE FOLLOWING WILL HAPPEN:

A. The person pushing the deal is involved in something illegal and soon will be in jail.

B. Within ten minutes of getting your money, your new partner or debtor will:

    a. Be abandoned by a lover. He'll decide life isn't worth living and will split the scene (with your cash) for Brazil. Or perhaps he'll go to an even more celestial region by jumping from the top of a skyscraper.

    b. His mother, father, sister, brother, spouse, and children will simultaneously be afflicted by terminal leukemia or other fatal disease. Meeting their medical bills will become far more important than returning your money.

    c. He will turn into a certified lunatic, have an accident that will make him an incoherent vegetable.

    d. He will be murdered or fatally injured.

    e. A person that HE trusted with the investment will be a thief, disappearing not only with your money, but with his alleged life savings, those of his widowed mother, and so on.

    f. The business deal that was so highly touted in the initial meeting just '....didn't work out'.

After hearing those stories in at least fifty deals, I vowed to never again invest in a Red Ribbon Deal or lend out money.

A basic rule to remember in dealing with other people is:

IF ANYTHING CAN POSSIBLY GO WRONG, IT WILL !

Assume that all of the above (and more) will really happen in every deal, loan or investment. Protect yourself in advance. With a little bit of luck, you'll do a lot better than I did, particularly if you meet an inventor.

The most dangerous person you'll ever meet in your business career is not a robber, murderer or even a representative of the I.R.S. The most dangerous person you'll have the misfortune to encounter will be an INVENTOR. Once an inventor has you believing in his new product or process, your entire fortune and all your prospects will go down the tubes. The time demanded of you to promote the invention and attract other investors will become an endless treadmill; your money will go into a bottomless pit !

I want to repress all memories of the time I became involved with the inventor of a solar panel. The small scale prototype was convincing: It produced usable heat-energy in arctic climates with only a few hours of sunlight per week. The cost was a fraction of the cost of a conventional heating plant. Once installed, fuel and operating costs were almost nil. Because of Federal Income Tax Credits and a financing package available to the buyer, any user of these panels would actually MAKE MONEY from day one. Nothing could possibly go wrong. Wealthy Arabs had already been after the patents for $3 Million, but the inventor didn't want them shelving his project in order to sell the world more of their oil. That was his story anyway...

It seemed like the opportunity of a lifetime. The inventor's projections showed that my $10,000 investment would return a million a year. Of course once production began, there were a few "minor bugs" to be worked out. Three more $10,000 contributions were required -- each one to "turn the corner." To my sorrow, the corner never was turned -- and probably never would be turned. I kissed my $40,000 goodbye.

What went wrong ? In my case, the invention in large size just never worked nearly as well as the doll house sized prototype. But with your inventor friend, it might be anything. See "How to Avoid Lending Money" a few pages back. Those are a few of the things that can go wrong.

Dealing with a product that works is tough enough, but backing an unproven item -- a new invention -- will give you what I got from my solar panel: A lot of useless hot air.

DuPont or IBM can afford research and development. They can afford a dead loss on 99 out of 100 ideas because of the one product that makes it big. You are not in that league. Don't be a pioneer !

A sound rule to follow:

IF SOMEONE WANTS YOUR MONEY (INVENTOR OR OTHERWISE), ASK THE "MAGIC QUESTION." IF YOU CAN'T BE PLACED IN A 100% SECURED POSITION, RUN LIKE HELL IN THE OPPOSITE DIRECTION !

The sad truth is that most inventions, like most movies, most oil wells, most real estate syndicates, most new products, and most commodity options never make the novice investor a dime.

The only "sure thing" in an investment is probably in your back yard. Let's move from the exotic to the mundane. I'll show you how to buy the house next door without investing or risking anything of significance.

BUYING PROPERTY WITHOUT MONEY

In a "No Money-Down Deal" you acquire property without putting up any of your own money. The first type of No Money Down Deal is an option. People don't tend to think of options as a way of getting property for no money down, but it certainly is a way of doing just that. Using options to get control of real-estate is one of the least risky and most profitable ways to deal in real-estate.

An option is the right to buy a given piece of property for a set period of time - say 6 months or 5 years, at a fixed price. Any item, whether it's real estate or personal property or stock, could be the subject of an option. Every option has a definite time period. It gives you the right to buy a specific property in the future for a certain time period, for a certain price, both clearly stated in the contract.

You could, for instance, get control of a $100,000 property for $100 (or even one Dollar!) and tie it up for a year. During that year, if you are able to sell the parcel to a third party for $150,000, you could make $50,000 on your investment. Results will often be that spectacular! So, options are a method of 100% financing you should be familiar with.

Let me give you another example of how to use an option to make big money: Supposing you are about to become a tenant in a three-flat apartment building in Oakland. At the time that you move in, the property is worth about $70,000. In the process of negotiating with the landlord for a two year lease, you say to the landlord "I would like the right to buy this property during the term of my lease for the price of $70,000". The landlord may be willing to give you that right, or he may say "No, I'd only sell for $80,000". He may charge you $1 for the option, $100 or $1,000. Often the price of the option will be deductible from the price of the property. However, it won't be unless you provide in the contract that the amount paid for the option is to be applied against the purchase price.

In a more typical landlord/tenant option, you the tenant might lease a single family home for a period of two years at $400 a month rent. During these two years the landlord might agree by writing on the lease that you have the right to buy that home for $40,000. The consideration (there always has to be a consideration for any contract) is the fact that you are leasing it and paying rent. You don't really need to pay an extra $1 to the landlord to have the right to buy the property in that two year period. But I always pay at least $1 for an option. That way, if you default on the lease by missing a rent payment or moving early the option is still good.

How do you get a lease option? You simply ask for one. Tell the landlord you would like to buy his property. Ask "What would you sell it for?". Merely by asking any potential seller for an option, you may get one. Perhaps the seller is willing to sell to you for $40,000 but at the moment you are not able to qualify for a loan, or you don't have quite enough money for the down payment. Then you ask your seller if he will give you a few months to raise the down payment or arrange for the mortgage. Very often the owner of a property will be willing to give someone a six month option in this type of situation. That gives you time to get your deal together and the details of the option are only limited by your (and the landlord's) imagination.

In many cases where an option is negotiated, the rent charged is the fair rent, and the entire fair rent is deductible from a reasonable option price if it is exercised during the first year. That sort of option is a very good deal for the tenant. The landlord may want to raise your rent as consideration for the option. But he may also give you credit for the extra rent off the option price. You could counter by asking for a cumulative monthly credit. There's no limit to the ways of working out an option contract.

When you get an option contract from a landlord it is very important that you have it notarized and recorded with the County Recorder of Deeds. Why? Because recording protects you against the seller's change of heart.

Let's say you have an option to buy a property for $40,000 and during the course of the next year the landlord simply forgot about it. It slipped his mind, perhaps because he got a better offer from an outsider of maybe $50,000; totally forgetting about your option to buy the property for $40,000. If you didn't have your option contract notarized and recorded, the new buyer would own the property free and clear. You might have a claim against the landlord and you would certainly have a good lawsuit. But you want to avoid lawsuits, and if you've had that option contract recorded, a new buyer would only be able to get control of the property by buying you out.

Now, suppose you have an option on a property at $40,000. You've been lucky. It's gone up in value to $100,000. That sort of thing isn't as unusual as you may think. Especially if it was a commercial property and you also had the lease. You may have had a long-term lease, perhaps for five years. During a three to five year period a price rise from $40,000 to $100,000 isn't unusual at all. Still, you may exercise this wonderful option to buy a $100,000 property for $40,000 even if you do not have $40,000. At this point you have several choices. You could let the option expire. That would not do you any good. You would not own the property and the landlord would regain full rights. (An option must be exercised before it expires!) In this case you would have lost $60,000. That is your potential profit: $60,000. Therefore I don't recommend this choice.

Or, you could go to the seller and say "Mr. Seller, let's take out a loan to refinance your property. Now that it's worth $100,000 you won't have any problem getting a loan for $50,000 on it. Then I will take over the property and assume your new loan."

The Seller would say "Why should I do that? What's in it for me? You have the right to buy my property at $40,000. If you want it you can have it. But why should I borrow for you and sign a note for $50,000?"

You will have to make it worth the seller's while. You may want to offer him $5,000 extra for his property. And if your seller got a $50,000 loan under these circumstances, it would be in your favor too. You could

walk away with an extra $5,000 cash at the close. All you do is assume
the seller's new loan of $50,000 and make all payments on it thereafter.
Result? You bought property with $45,000 that the seller borrowed. To
get your seller to cooperate with you, you will of course have to convince
him that you are a reliable person and won't default on the loan.

If you have an option and the property has gone up in value above
your option price, the more common thing to do is to put up a "For Sale"
sign and sell it to a third party. Perhaps you are lucky enough to find
a buyer at $100,000. Then $40,000 goes to the landlord and you make
$60,000 on the deal. All that profit is your return on the price of the option.

You may ask, "Is it legal? It seems too good to be true." The answer
is yes, because that's what an option is all about! You do not have to own
the property to sell it if you have an option. An option is transferrable
during the entire time-period of the option. So you could sell the property
to someone else, or you could just sell the option.

An option contract is very simple. Here's how to prepare one:
Take a blank sheet of paper and title it OPTION CONTRACT.

OPTION CONTRACT

I, LARRY LANDLORD, for the sum of $1 (or other agreed sum) hereby sell
to TOM TENANT an option to purchase my four-plex at 44 Montgomery Street,
San Francisco, California for a full price of $40,000 from this date until
January 1st, 1985.

Terms: All cash to seller.

_____

LARRY LANDLORD   Date

_____

Accepted, TOM TENANT   Date

(It is very important that the option contract is dated, and on the same
date acknowledged before a notary public or a witness. After acknowledgement take the option to the County Recorder and record it. It will cost you
$3 and will be the best $3 you have ever spent.)

Some people will tell you that, as the buyer, you don't have to sign the option contract. This is true. However, I always recommend that you do sign it. This indicates that you and the landlord (option seller) had a "meeting of the minds" so to speak and that you both knew exactly what you were doing. Larry Landlord, your seller on the other hand must sign it. If he or she is married, the spouse must also sign it. The option contract might be enforceable without a spouse's signature, but it could get you into court. The most important thing about court is to avoid it at all costs. Once the contract is recorded with the county no one else can buy the property without being on notice of your interest in it.

One of the first deals in my career involved the use of a kind of option. One of the hundred houses I had looked at during my self education period was a little summer hiker's cabin in the woods. To some, it was a "Yuck" house because the floors tilted at a 10° angle, the heavy redwood plank walls were of single thickness with cracks and knot-holes to let in plenty of wind and rain. The fixtures and fittings were "early American Pioneer" and had been put in about 1895. But the cottage had charm. The lot was an acre on a sunny hillside in an area which had become the setting for many a wealthy San Francisco family's mountain hide-away. The average price for an old summer home was $75,000.

Here was a charming little, unlivable cabin for sale at an asking price of $25,000. It was livable perhaps if your name was Thoreau, but I imagined that it would be pretty difficult to rent. I made enquiries about the property with neighbors and real estate agents. It seemed there had been a few offers near to the asking price, but all were dependent upon 80% financing. Unfortunately no bank or savings and loan would lend anything unless the buyer came up with architect's plans to put in a new foundation, expand the house from one tiny bedroom to a more conventional three bedrooms, put in a garage and spend about $50,000. Since a ready built home in the area could be had for $75,000 I was told that no one wanted to tackle a major construction project and what might be worse-- all the paperwork of getting building permits, environmental impact reports and other red tape. So the house sat vacant.

As you should know by now, when a property has been on the market for a long period of time, the owner is usually amenable to "unusual" offers that would initially have been rejected. My first step was to talk to a local lender.

"Would you lend me anything on the place if I put in a foundation, straightened up the floors and made the place barely livable, and was able to sell it for $34,000?" The banker said, "Because of its unusually good location we'd go 50%" That was the banker talk meaning a loan of $17,000 could be obtained.

I knew I could put the place into shape for $3,000 with my lightning technique in a weekend. I didn't expect the building inspector would catch me. No permits to be applied for. My next step was to contact the owner. This was my offer, with a personal check for $300 attached.

OFFER TO PURCHASE REAL ESTATE

The undersigned, William Greene, hereby offers to purchase
the house at 10 Redwood Lane, Mill Valley, further identified
as Assessor's Parcel No. 4545 for a full price of $16,000, all
cash to seller.

The sum of $300 is attached herewith and may be cashed by
seller upon acceptance of this offer. Upon acceptance, possession of the property shall go to buyer in order that buyer
may put in a foundation and otherwise improve said property
in order to qualify for a bank loan which will enable him to
complete the purchase within 6 months.

In the event that the balance is not fully paid to the seller
for any reason within 6 months, the seller shall have the right
to repossess the property, retain any improvements made by
the buyer and keep the buyer's $300 deposit.

                              (signed)

                              William Greene

ACCEPTED

_____

Sam Seller
(Note:
A STANDARD NOTARY PUBLIC ACKNOWLEDGEMENT IS REQUIRED IN
ALL CONTRACTS REGARDING THE SALE OF REAL PROPERTY.)

My offer was much lower than the asking price. But it was a direct principal to principal offer. Without the usual 6% commission, it was equivalent of $1,000 more than an offer through a real estate broker. I stressed this point to him. Furthermore I explained to him what he already knew. The property had been on the market for 6 months and people poor enough to want to live in, and fix up a house of its nature didn't have $16,000 cash. They couldn't qualify for a loan, and even if someone qualified for a loan, banks wouldn't lend on that particular property without a fortune being spent on a foundation and improvements.

My plan, was to buy for $16,000 - with only $300 down. I would improve the property by working on it myself and spending about $3,000. I was going to get those costs and more by taking out an $8,000 Home Improvement Loan on the place where I lived. After I completed the improvements, my plan was to get my promised loan of $17,000, rent the place out for $275 per month and have enough rent coming in to pay off both the $17,000 first loan on the property and the $8,000 Home Improvement Loan on my own place. Here is how the Cash Flow would have worked:

CASH OUTFLOW		CASH INFLOW	
$300	For downpayment	$ 8,000	Home Improvement Loan
$3,000	For improvements	$17,000	First Loan
$16,000	Price of House		
$1,000	Closing costs, reserve		
$20,300	TOTAL	$25,000	TOTAL

Yes, within 6 months I would end up with almost $5,000 in my pocket; the loans would all be paid back by the tenant; I would own the property, be cash ahead, and get tax benefits that would shelter other income.

That was the plan, but something even better was to happen as a fluke: I put up a little card inside a front window so that it could be seen from the outside. (If you post notices outside, someone is sure to pull them off.) The card said:

FOR INFORMATION REGARDING
THE SALE OR RENTAL OF THIS PROPERTY
CONTACT W. GREENE, OWNER. Phone 777-7777

(Why make it hard for people who might want to make you an offer you can't refuse?)

Here is what happened: The old owner signed my contract on a Thursday morning. I posted the sign at about noon. At 3 o'clock I got a call from Helen, a real estate lady I had dated occasionally and knew pretty well.

"I heard you've got an option on Redwood Lane for $16,000." She made me a firm offer. "I'll take it over from you for a thousand profit. I'll give you $1,300 today for your option."

I explained to my friend Helen that I would like to deal with her, but that I had a plan for fixing up the property and hoped to sell it for around $34,000. I hoped to make a profit of more like $15,000.

She told me that I was crazy, that it wasn't worth it. Helen then got abusive. She said "I've had my eye on the property for over six months and now you've stolen it from me." She said she was getting all set to offer $17,500 all cash to the seller, and I would be the meanest, cruellest man alive if I didn't sell to her. She threatened to never speak to me again if I didn't sell to her at once. Now Real Estate Helen was no dummy. She was into house speculation two years before I was, and I felt if she was willing to offer $17,500 real money in cash, I must have pulled off a coup by getting it for $16,000 on a "no money down deal".

I told Helen to cut the hysterics, that I hadn't even known she was interested, consequently I didn't steal her property, and that if she was getting all set to make an offer, she should have made the offer instead of keeping it a secret. Helen slammed the phone down and has been bad mouthing me in real estate circles ever since.

In any event, as soon as Helen hung up on me, someone else called. He had seen my card on the property and he also had been planning to make an offer when the owner was more desperate. He too was planning to offer $17,500. I told him that I had a firm contract to buy the place at $16,000, had received an offer of $17,300 a few minutes earlier and had turned it down without hesitation because I hoped to sell the property for $34,000 as soon as I had fixed it up. This chap then said he'd offer $18,500, all cash. I said, "I will consider it and call you back."

An hour later, another, even higher offer came in. I wondered why all these offers had been hiding in the woodwork, and when I later asked, the answer was that people were timid about "insulting the seller" by offering so much below the asking price of $25,000. But once they heard that I tied the property up for $16,000 they felt very good about offering me a quick profit. Thus my advice to budding tycoons is:

NEVER BE AFRAID TO MAKE A LOW OFFER.

FORGET YOUR PSYCHOLOGICAL PROBLEMS, JUST MAKE
THE OFFER.

THE SELLER MAY BE DELIGHTED THAT SOMEONE WANTS
HIS PROPERTY.

IF HE REFUSES, WHAT DID YOU LOSE?

Getting back to our tale, the property I had bought at $16,000 was absolutely the lowest priced home in town. The house next in line, offered on the multiple listing service was $35,000. Thus, every buyer searching for a cheap house had seen Redwood Lane, but everybody waited till my deal went through and then got interested.

I had the hottest property in town. In the next three days I got a dozen more calls and eventually sold my contract for a $5,000 profit. The lady who bought it from me (at an effective price to her, of $21,000 cash) didn't do a thing to the property, rented it for $200 a month and three years later sold it for $34,000.

As for me - I had invested $300 and gotten back $5,300 in a few days. I had never made that much return in such a short space of time in stocks, commissions or anything. At that point I was hooked on real estate.

Another method of getting property for no money down is with 100% loans. A few years ago I came across some charming old cabins in the country. They were very rustic, surrounded by redwood trees near a stream, but very run down. I had heard that the owner, a retired gentleman of about 70, had told neighbors, "I'm really tired of fixing up that place and running after the tenants for rent. There's always something wrong. I'm working all my days repairing things and I would sure like to sell." I knew that on this particular property, lenders would not give a conventional loan because they were run-down sixty year old cabins. Lenders and bankers generally don't like charm. Only tenants do.

So I went to the seller. We talked and I did the most important thing that you as a buyer should always do. I quickly found out what the seller wanted. I simply asked, "What are your plans if you sell this place? What do you want to do?" Basically he wanted to move to a retirement community up North and have a comfortable extra income in addition to his pension. That was his real need. By telling him about my career and engaging in friendly conversations during the course of a number of visits, I won his confidence. I let him know I wasn't a flake, that I had some other property and was regular in my mortgage payments. He soon realized that I was a dependable person. He felt that if we did negotiate a deal and he gave me a mortgage, he could rest secure that in his golden years, he could depend on a check coming in from me every month.

At first he hemmed and hawed about chasing me for late payments. I countered with: "Look, I'm prepared to give you post dated checks for 5 years on these mortgage payments. As you know it's a criminal offense to pass a bum check, so I will give you whatever mortgage we agree upon in the form of post dated checks. You will have a big stack of them and be very secure that they will be paid on time. When you get near the end of your stack of checks, I'll give you another stack of checks. That way you'll always be at least a year ahead." That offer seemed to turn him on.

Then we had to negotiate price. We had established that the present rents from the property were about $750 a month. (For the sake of this example, lets' assume that this was NET, after expenses.) So I said to him, "Look, would you like to get exactly what you're making now in the form of loan payments? "I'll give you that $750 a month without you having to do any repairs - no work, no vacancy problems, no chasing tenants for rent. In other words, you'll be getting exactly what you're getting now, without any work for the rest of your life. That's my offer."

"Great," he said "but for how long do I get that $750 a month?"

I said "Look, you're 70 years old now - how does 10 years sound?"

The owner said "I might be around in 10 years, in fact I hope to be a-round in 30." In the end we compromised at 20 years.

Then we went to the Blue Book*, checked the amortization tables and

*See Reading List at end of this book.

190

looked for the figure $750 and 20 years. That came out to a 7½% loan on $93,000, fully amortized or paid off over 20 years. Basically that's how we set the price - with the help of the Blue Book. We agreed on a dollar amount - $93,000 - and 20 years. My seller got exactly what he wanted - $750 trouble-free net cash every month. I became the proud owner of the Dipsea Cabins.

Why was I willing to give him exactly what he was getting in rent with the buildings in such rough shape? Because I knew, if I improved the cabins just a little, I could raise those rents up from $750 a month and almost from the very beginning have a little profit each month for myself.

Three years later, I still own the Dipsea Cabins. The monthly net is now $1,750. I am making $1,000 a month net cash flow out of the building I bought for no money down, and at the same time I'm paying off the loan. In 17 years more I'll own the property free and clear - and think what the rents will be then!

The seller is well pleased. He's up in his Sonoma County retirement home getting $750 a month. He feels secure with my post dated checks. He is secure. He sold to me for no money down - gave me a 100% loan - yet he couldn't be any happier. We're good friends. I talk to him on the phone about every 6 months.

As mentioned, I bought the Dipsea Cabins in rough shape. During the last few years I built up what I call sweat equity. In other words I went out there personally on weekends. I took out rotten boards, I put in some sun decks, I added ivy, I took good care of the place; did all needed repairs and painting. The place is in much better shape now.

Three months ago I put it on the market for $250,000. The loan was $93,000. I put no money down, I've been taking $1,000 a month for almost a year and have been getting a nice tax loss because of the depreciation the IRS gives me. When I walk away from that deal for $250,000 I'll have over $150,000 as my profit. Where else can you make $150,000 in a year without any investment? Only in real estate! Of course I will never sell it. I would always trade up to a bigger and better deal using my $150,000 equity as a down payment on a $1 or $2 million property.

Now, going back to those original purchase negotiations, supposing the

the same seller liked everything I proposed but said "Bill, I just have to get some cash out of the closing. Can't you come up with some cash? I would like to get at least $40,000 up front to buy my new retirement home free and clear." If I had a fairly good credit standing I could have gone to the bank with the seller and probably have borrowed $40,000 on a first loan. Then I'd have made arrangements with the seller to give me a $60,000 second loan. So I would get the net effect of a No Money Down deal, except that I would owe one loan payment each month to a Savings and Loan and one loan payment to the seller. That's how to deal with the situation when the seller wants money up front.

Here is another variation. Let's assume your credit is bad. Until now you have been a slow payer or a non payer. You don't have a good reputation and lenders would consider you a bad risk. (Incidentally, CHANGE YOUR WAYS - if you want to make it in real estate you must develop a good reputation for meeting your obligations.) Here's a little gimmick you can use to get the seller the cash he wants. I could have said, "Before we make the deal, Mr. Seller, you get the property refinanced." In other words, get the seller to go to a banker, preferably one he has a relationship with and get whatever loan they will give. Here, we're talking about a $93,000 property. Even when money is tight and things aren't so good, you can always get a 20% loan or a 30 or 40% loan. It's the 80% or 90% that you don't get when money is tight or the property is run down.

So the seller could have gone to his friendly Savings & Loan to say he wanted some cash just before he sold to you. He could then have refinanced the property using his credit and not yours. In that case you might want to be a co-signer. But if your credit was really bad you wouldn't want the bank to know your name. You could then take over the property from the seller on a Contract Of Sale. A contract of sale, which I will talk more about later, is where the seller retains legal title. In every other way it is a sale. You collect rents; you take all the deductions.

The secret of 100% financing or 120% financing is finding someone who will carry the loan. Most often it will be the seller who carries the entire loan, but sometimes a bank or Savings & Loan will make a first loan, and the seller will carry the second. Sometimes outside lenders will be brought in. But the key to making a No Money Down Deal is a 100% loan.

Supposing you found an owner who has a building which he wants $100,000 for. You are going to get an $80,000 loan from a lender, but you don't have $20,000 for the down payment. You give the owner a $20,000 second loan on properties you already own. Obviously this suggestion can only apply to people who already own property. In other words you could create a lien on your own home or other property you already own shortly before the closing. The seller would give you his check for $20,000. You give him an IOU or note for $20,000 secured by property you already own. Then you use his own check as the down payment on the new place.

Everything in this world is negotiable. The seller might say something like, "I don't really want to take a second mortgage on your home as a down payment. I want $10,000 cash. I don't care how you do it." A lot of sellers just don't want to do fancy deals. You can show him that at the closing he would be getting $80,000 cash from the bank. But the seller may still not want to lend you the $20,000 for the down payment.

Here's one way to get him "all cash". You will need the seller's co-operation. You give the seller the second on your property, as in the last example. Only, this time you raise it to $25,000. You tell him the truth - There is a big market out there for second mortgages. People are trading second mortgages at a discount all the time. All you have to do is look in the Sunday newspaper or the phone book to get a long list of people who are actively in the second mortgage business. I would say without any doubt that you could always sell a relatively short term $25,000 note for at least $20,000. Generally a 10% or 20% discount is what you'll run into in discounting second mortgage paper. - So you tell your seller he'll get his $80,000 from the Savings & Loan and he'll get his $20,000 out of that second mortgage. I always personally guarantee that my $25,000 second mortgage can be sold at a discount to a third person.

Many small loan or finance companies will issue a written commitment to purchase the second loan in our example for $20,000 cash. So there should be no reason why you shouldn't be able to raise that $20,000 by creating a new $25,000 second mortgage on property you already own before the deal closes. As mentioned there are plenty of people out there dealing in second mortgages, and like real estate, it is a very big field in itself. There are a surprising number of older people who don't want to deal with rental property, but they love wheeling and dealing in second mortgages at discounts. An ad in the paper might bring them in. Once you get involved in the market, you'll get familiar with it. So, if you put an ad in your local paper saying "second mortgage, $25,000, 10% interest, two years, well secured. Will sell for $20,000." You'll gets lots and lots of calls.

Of course it would be much more convenient and cheaper for you if your seller takes the $20,000 note at face value as the down payment. But if he doesn't, you can always raise the value and discount it to a third party to come up with the $20,000 that you need.

There is another problem that can arise. The seller may say to you "Look, I know and love the property I'm selling to you. I'm prepared to take a second loan on <u>that</u> property, but I don't want a second on your own home or any other property of yours that I don't know anything about." You would go along with that. There is no problem for you and this offer without more, gives you a No Money Down Deal. But the problem is the lender. The bank or savings and loan who's making an 80% first loan will not finance a No Money Down Deal if they know about it. They seem to feel that people who don't have anything invested will walk away from deals to leave the bank holding an empty bag.

I think the lenders are dead wrong in this attitude. If I were a banker I would rather hold a first loan in a situation where there is a second loan held by a wealthy seller. Why? Because the holder of a big second will pick up the property and make the payments on the first loan if the owner goes under and the first goes into default. If the seller doesn't keep up payments he loses the money that is due him on the second mortgage.

In the case of the seller who wants a second on the property he is selling you, here is how to handle the deal. You issue him the note and trust deed as in our previous example. The security is property you already own. You write on it: "This trust deed is transferrable at seller's option to the property on Oak Lane at any time after thirty days."

So we solved the problem of getting the $20,000 cash down payment you needed to buy the $100,000 property - you got that $20,000 by creating a a note and trust deed on property you already own. As before you have to own property already in order to make this deal. Now the seller has never seen your home, but he does know and love his own place. He's willing to take a second loan on that, but you can't give him a second loan simultaneously because the bank that's making the first loan won't let the deal go through if you do it that way. They just don't want to make loans on No Money Down Deals--at least in California. They might do it in Las Vegas or Reno where I hear the bankers are real swingers. But in California they won't. You start out by creating a note or trust deed on your own property or home. That's legal. The bank won't object to that.

You make this deal with the seller: A month after closing he is to transfer security for the note from your home to his. That means he releases your home, and has the same note secured by a trust deed on the place he's selling you. If you do that maneuver anytime after the closing of the new property, it will work out. You get the lien released from your old property and it is placed against the new property you have just bought.

A title company will show you exactly how to handle the technicalities of releasing one property and putting a loan against the other property. A good title company will always help a customer out on any paperwork problems without charge.

The most usual and traditional way of getting a No Money Down Deal happens to be illegal. It is fraud and I am not suggesting that you use that method. Why? Because there are always legal ways of doing almost anything you want to do. The fraud that goes on between a lot of professional real estate owners and bankers is that a buyer and seller meet and agree that the price for a certain property is $80,000. The buyer will pay $80,000 to the seller and the seller will sell for $80,000, but they make side agreements; to tell the bank that the price is $100,000. So on paper they draw up a phoney deal showing the price as $100,000 subject to getting an 80% first loan. The closing comes along. A non-existent $20,000 changes hands, the bank lends $80,000 and as you can see, the bank has financed the deal 100%.

Things like this are done every day, but I STRESS that you shouldn't do it that way. It is very simple, but it is also fraudulent. Though you probably wouldn't get caught on such a deal - it's called "pumping" or inflating the price. You could get into big trouble if there was financial difficulty and you couldn't pay off the loan. In most Western States there is no liability on purchase money loans on property. That is, in a legitimate deal where you borrow money to buy property, if things go sour, you can walk away from that deal with NO PERSONAL LIABILITY. The lender cannot come after your other personal assets to satisfy that debt. They can only take over the property given as security. But when there has been fraud, they can proceed against you personally. Thus if a lender discovers that you made a fraudulent deal and got 100% financing by giving him a false statement, he might grab your other assets and try to send you to jail. I don't think the risks are worth doing a fraudulent deal. Particularly since you don't have to take any risk. There is a way of doing exactly the same thing, legally.

Suppose you are negotiating for a property. The seller is asking for $100,000. You have a feeling he'll take $80,000. So you say to the seller "Look, I'll take your property for $100,000" and his eyes will widen because he was expecting you to offer a lot less than that. "Yes, I'm going to give you $80,000 cash but part of the deal is that I want you to buy from me my antique Wedgewood coffee set for $20,000." He says "What are you talking about? I don't want a coffee set." Then you tell him "I have these antique cups, an empty lot, or paintings, or an oriental rug (something that should be of value to somebody but that isn't necessarily of value to you) . You tell the seller that it's part of the deal, that you are going to use your antique cup as a down payment and that we will establish the price of the cup at $20,000. "You want me to buy your turkey of a building for $100,000, so you've got to buy my turkey of a coffee cup set for $20,000."

The seller will think about it, and perhaps realize that you are offering him the $80,000 he really wants for his property. This is what lawyers call an "arm's-length-deal". If he takes it he will give you a check or receipt for your coffee cup set for $20,000. Or he may give you a receipt saying that he has received $20,000 outside of escrow as down payment on his property at Oak Lane. Now you go to the bank and show them the price of $100,000 and ask for an $80,000 loan. That will be legal because the price really *is* $100,000, and it was negotiated at arm's length.

It just so happened that you used personal property in trade as all or part of the down payment. Your lawyer might raise an eyebrow at this, but I know that old hands in the real estate game do it all the time. Their favorite trading vehicle is an empty lot, or some odd shaped parcel of land they picked up for a song at a tax sale. Like an art work, these parcels are difficult if not impossible to value. On your first trade deal of this type you should confer with an experienced real estate lawyer or agent and get an outside opinion on how to handle the paperwork. Escrow officers who have been around for a few years are always very helpful, and they don't charge a fee for advice if you get title insurance through their office.

There is another variation on the No Money Down theme that I picked up on by accident. A few years back I bought a place with the standard 20% cash down, financed with an 80% institutional first loan. Naturally the $20,000 had been borrowed unsecured, but that's another story. In this deal, when the seller moved out his possessions and I took over, I was shocked to discover that the floors looked like Lake Michigan on a windy day. That is to say they were seriously warped. The waves in the floors had been caused by annual floods. But, the strategic placement of oriental rugs and furnishings had totally concealed this condition during my inspection of the place.

I wrote the seller immediately upon discovering the damage: "Dear Mr. Seller, I am giving you a choice of taking back your building, El Warpo, or sending me $25,000 immediately as an allowance for repairs. I have just found out that you intentionally concealed material faults in the property including severely warped floors and a faulty drainage system which promises to flood the place each spring. If I do not hear from you in 24 hours, I will retain counsel and bring an action against you for rescission of contract."

In real life you never settle anything with one letter, but to make a long story short, eventually I got $22,500 out of the gyp-artist seller. Later I did part of the repairs myself. I never spent anywhere near the $22,500 I received. After building a $1,000 concrete spillway to prevent future flooding, I was happy to keep the wavy floors, cover them with thick-pad carpeting, and kid around with future tenants that they had been put in at great cost by Mr. Wavy Gravy, a rock star. But the net result of the deal was that I picked up over $21,000 tax free on the deal. Why was it tax free? Because recoveries of damage claims in lawsuits are tax free, by definition. Now doesn't that give you a lot of ideas?

You might have a similar situation sort of prearranged, like this: A sale is agreed upon at $100,000 but you make up a long list of expensive repairs that the seller is to take care of before the closing. You both value this work at $20,000. At the closing of the deal guess what? The seller has not gotten around to doing the repairs he agreed to do. I can't see any legal reason that without telling the institutional lender a thing he simply rebates $20,000 to you. I have been to many a real closing--even one where the bank knew of the rebate--and they let the deal go through, assuming that the buyer would use the money to make the repairs. A more sophisticated bank would have held back $20,000 of the loan pending completion of the repairs.

If you made a deal with a seller that he was going to give you a rebate for repairs -- and it was informally understood that the reason for this was just to get the lender to come up with more money -- and if the rebate arrangement is not disclosed -- then you are beginning to get into the gray area. But this situation is not the blatant fraud of establishing fictional contracts and a phoney sales price for the bank, and keeping the real deal in a separate secret contract. Just as in tax matters, the substance of a deal can be one thing -- but the form in which it is done, the "appearances" can make one transaction legal, while a slight variation is fraud.

It is best in my opinion, to never wave red flags in front of lenders. They like simple, easy to understand contracts and never want to wade through a lot of side deals. You should therefore consider making minimal disclosure so that the lender can't later claim he wasn't put on notice that some repairs were to be done. I would suggest something innocuous like a clause in the deposit receipt: "Seller agrees to put the property into first class shape before delivery to buyer." The private rebate agreement (the clarification of this clause) then spells out what first class shape means, exactly what repairs are contemplated, and provides that the seller is going to pay the buyer $20,000 if he fails to deliver the property in first class shape.

The way you can handle a No Money Down Deal is limited only by your imagination. There are millions of ways of doing it since every real estate deal is different. Getting money back at a closing -- that is actually getting cash out of a deal at the start -- is accomplished by more aggressive use of exactly the same methods. The most important thing for you to realize is that it can be done, it is being done every day and that you can do it. Get your mind working in the right direction! Soon you will control a highly leveraged real estate empire having acquired it in exactly the same manner as countless other successful magnates or tycoons.

Getting off your fanny and overcoming inertia is all you have to do. You now have the knowledge!

To summarize:

A No Money Down Deal is any acquisition of property where you don't put up significant sums of your own money. I would put in this category a deal where you buy property for all cash with an unsecured loan, and shortly after the close arrange for a combination of first, second and possibly third loans to arrive at the point where you have none of your own money in the deal. Many deals require several steps until you get your money out by refinancing; others require little or no cash to begin with. Let's look at them in the order I regard as most preferable to the buyer:

A) Seller gives buyer option to purchase at a reasonable price for a lengthly period of time. The contract provides that buyer gets possession at a low rent during the option period.

B) Outright sale with seller carrying back a loan for the entire purchase price. Often sellers will insist that this be done with a contract of sale by which the seller retains title as security for buyer's meeting his obligations.

C) Sale with seller taking as downpayment the buyer's personal or secured note -- or a legitimate investment property in trade. The balance of financing (usually 70-95%) comes from a lending institution.

D) Down payment borrowed from an outside lender by seller who refinances property. Buyer assumes loan and seller carries balance.

E) Down payment borrowed by buyer from outside lender either as an unsecured note or secured by the property buyer already owns.

F) Property is 100% (or more) financed by an institutional lender. The most common ways of obtaining such a loan are:

    1. Outright fraud in manufacturing phoney documents establishing

a higher than actual sale price. This emphatically not recommended though it goes on in perhaps 20% of all commercial deals.

2. Over-valuation of property or odd-ball assets used to put together a trade.

3. Rebate for repairs from the seller or other imaginative schemes to transfer part of purchase price back to buyer at or shortly after closing.

4. Drastically increasing value of property by some action taken by buyer between time of contract and closing as for example, favorable rezoning, lot split, or issuance of building permits; evicting undersirable tenants or establishing new and favorable leases; subdividing; establishing higher and better use for property. Item 4 is preferred by me.

G) Property bought with substantial down payment (or all cash) and this cash is recouped shortly after purchase by refinancing.

Why should you try to make No Money Down Deals? The answer is that it is possible to acquire a large number of properties having a high dollar value in a relatively short time. In the West, the laws of many states make purchase money loans "non-recourse". That means if the deal goes sour you can walk away from it. There is no downside risk. No one can claim your other assets. In Eastern states, the same risk-free status can be obtained using land trusts, straw men, corporations and other legal entities to insulate the buyer from personal liability. If inflation continues, as it probably will, you can become a millionaire in one year or less. All you have to do is buy a lot of property and sit back and wait. Your debts will become insignificant, rents will go up, and your equity will soon be a million or more.

NICE GUYS FINISH LAST!

Let's take this scenario: Assume a temporary dip in real estate prices. Mr. Nice Guy believed his friendly banker's advice that it is more conservative to buy one fourplex with a large downpayment than to "speculate" in several fourplexes with the same amount of money.

So Mr. Nice Guy buys a $100,000 fourplex with a $30,000 downpayment, taking out a $70,000 loan with the Friendly Bank. He didn't even consider the possibility of a "no money down" deal. As it happens, Mr. Nice Guy bought at the top of a period of escalating prices, just before a local rent control law, economic adversity or other problems forced him to roll back his rents slightly. To make matters worse, Mr. Nice Guy lost his job. The combination of circumstances causes him to be unable to meet his mortgage payments of $700 per month. Mr. Nice Guy can barely squeeze together $400 per month, leaving him $300 short each month.

At the same time, Miss Tycoon who also had $30,00 cash to start with, decided to buy six fourplexes. She told a little white lie to the Friendly Bank and five other banks, and (see NO MONEY DOWN DEALS) was able to acquire six small apartment buildings, each for $100,000 and each with a $95,000 loan. Miss Tycoon was hit with exactly the same temporary crisis, viz. rent controls and the loss of her job, and like Mr. Nice Guy is barely able (under the new rent control laws) to come up with $400 per month on each loan, even though in her case, $950 per month is due on each loan.

Real estate price levels have dropped drastically, and the buildings can be liquidated quickly in a slumping market for about $70,000 to "all cash" buyers.

THIS IS WHAT WOULD HAPPEN IN THE REAL WORLD:

The friendly banker would assess the situation. Money is tight. The bank, like everyone else needs money to keep afloat. "Where to get it?" asks the friendly banker.

He sees on Miss Tycoon's deal that if the bank foreclosed it would get a $70,000 duplex and be able to realize $70,000 cash, but that would mean writing off a $95,000 loan and taking a $25,000 loss on the books. Under these circumstances, a banker would be very friendly to Miss Tycoon and offer to take lower payments of interest only until the local economy recovered. That way the bank wouldn't take a loss. Nobody likes to take losses, especially bankers who might lose their jobs if the stockholders objected to their having made too high a loan relative to the security involved.

But Mr. Nice Guy has a different situation: The bank can foreclose, sell the property and get $70,000 cash. They take no loss whatsoever. Thus there is no reason at all to be friendly to Mr. Nice Guy. This is what happens in the real world. The bank "works with" the tycoons and forecloses on the "nice guy". A year or two later, when the market recovers, and duplexes can be sold for $120,000 each, here is what happens:

Mr. Nice Guy was wiped out. He started with $30,000 but is now out of the game. He has lost his $30,000; and his credit is lousy because he must now admit on new loan application that he went through a foreclosure.

Miss Tycoon sell or trades up her six buildings for a handsome profit of $120,000 (6 x $20,000). The bankers love her because she had "staying power" and helped them ride through a difficult period by sticking with her properties. She did not cause them any litigation or losses. On her $30,000 investment she made a 400% profit. Everybody loves a winner!

THINK ABOUT THE MORAL OF THIS STORY. WRITE IT HERE:

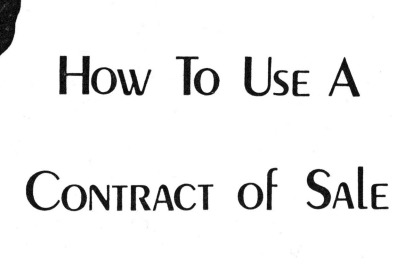

How To Use A
Contract of Sale

Until recently a CONTRACT OF SALE, sometimes called a land contract, was not popular in the Western States. It was and still can be dangerous for both buyer and seller. But it became very popular in California after the 1974 case of Tucker versus Lassen Savings & Loan Association knocked out the "due on sale" clause. This decision by the California Supreme Court, made virtually every loan in the state assumable - - <u>if</u> the deal was drawn as a contract of sale. The position of almost all banks and Savings & Loan institutions in California today is that today they will not "call" a loan if the seller who was the original borrower transfers the property by contract of sale, retaining title to the property as security for the payment of the debts secured by the property.

Let's look at an example that will make it clear, when a contract of sale can be used to your advantage:

In 1976 Sam decided to buy Blackacre, a home, apartment building, or whatever. The price was $100,000 and Upright Savings & Loan lent Sam $80,000 of his purchase money for 30 years at 8% interest. Upright insisted on a clause in the loan agreement that said if Sam should sell Blackacre, the balance due on the $80,000 note will come due then and there.

This is the "due on sale" clause that gives
property owners trouble. All lenders want a due on
sale clause because it forces a new buyer to apply
for a new loan. That in turn, means that the lender,
Upright, can get another set of appraisal fees, points,
prepayment penalties and a higher interest rate, if
rates have gone up.

In 1979, three years later, Sam wants to sell. Sam
and Bob Buyer make a deal where Bob offers to pay
Sam $125,000 for his property, contingent upon a new
80% loan at Upright. Upright turns down Bob's application for a new loan, but agrees to let Bob assume
the old loan of $80,000 if the interest rate is raised to
11% and if Bob pays a loan assumption fee and costs
amounting to $4,000. Bob figures the extra 3% in the
interest amounts to about $200 per month and the extra
$20,000 cash required (because Upright would only
lend $80,000, not the $100,000 requested) makes the
deal very unattractive to Bob. Bob goes back to
Sam and says "Tear up my offer. The deal is off."

However, Sam has another idea. He will make Bob
an offer he cannot refuse. He says, "Bob Buyer, you
were willing to pay me $25,000 cash down. You were
going to pay at least $3,000 in closing costs, and were
probably willing to pay 10% interest on the $100,000
debt. I, Sam Seller, will make it all possible with a
contract of sale on even better terms.

Sam explains that under the rule of Tucker vs.
Lassen, "ownership" of the property can be transfer-
red by a piece of paper known as a contract of sale,
but title on the public records stays in the name of
Sam Seller until the fulfillment of certain conditions.
Those conditions are usually payment in full of any debt
to Sam Seller, and the payment of the debt to Upright
Savings and Loan.

THE MAIN PURPOSE OF A CONTRACT OF SALE
IS TO ALLOW A BUYER OF REAL ESTATE TO ASSUME
EXISTING FINANCING ON PROPERTY WITHOUT THE
PAYMENT OF FEES OR HIGHER INTEREST RATES
WHICH MAY BE PREVAILING IN THE MARKET PLACE.
THE CONTRACT OF SALE ALSO SETS FORTH THE
OBLIGATIONS OF THE BUYER TO THE SELLER.

THE DANGER OF A CONTRACT OF SALE TO THE
SELLER IS THAT IF THE BUYER DOES NOT PERFORM,
THE SELLER'S ONLY REMEDY TO ENFORCE THE
CONTRACT MAY BE IN A COURT OF LAW. IT COULD
TAKE YEARS AND COST A BUNDLE. IN CONTRAST,
THE PROCEDURE FOR FORECLOSING ON A STANDARD
DEED OF TRUST IS SPEEDY (ABOUT 90 DAYS),
FAMILIAR, AND DOES NOT INVOLVE THE LAW COURTS.

THE DANGER OF A CONTRACT OF SALE TO THE
BUYER, IS THAT IF THE SELLER DIES, GETS A JUDGE-
MENT AGAINST HIM OR GOES BANKRUPT, THE BUYER
MAY HAVE EXTREME DIFFICULTY IN GETTING CLEAR
TITLE TO THE PROPERTY. THE SELLER WILL BE IN-
CAPABLE OF DELIVERING A VALID DEED ONCE HE IS
DEAD.

Bearing all these risks in mind, the buyer and seller may still want to
enter into a Contract of Sale. From the seller's point of view the risk of
getting into a lawsuit is not great if he is dealing with a buyer of good reputation for meeting financial obligations. Additionally, the seller in our
example is going to get all his original $20,000 investment money plus
$5,000 cash profit out of the deal. It is a lot easier psychologically for a
seller to take the risk that he may have to wait or sue for the balance of
his profits, than for "real money".

Also, certain safeguards can be incorporated in the contract. From the
buyer's point of view, if the seller is a responsible business man, it's unlikely he will go bankrupt. And if the seller is not too old, it is not likely
he will die before the property is resold or refinanced. In the event of
death or bankruptcy, while it may take time to get a deed out of a trustee

in bankruptcy or an Administrator of an estate, the main risk is one of delay and some legal costs. However, the contract buyer would normally not be in much danger of losing the property. In fact, death or bankruptcy of the original contract seller could offer a time of opportunity to settle the debt for something less than the value of the contract.

A serious problem I once had with a Contract of Sale wouldn't happen to you because its been solved with a provision I suggest you use in every Contract of Sale that you're involved with.

I was Bob Buyer. I bought a little office building for $125,000 under a contract of sale. For two years I made my payments to the lender, Upright Savings and Sam Seller, the gent who had sold to me on a no money down deal. Then I negotiated a resale with Tim Thirdparty. The price to Tim was $145,000. Tim got a $115,000 loan commitment from the Third National Bank and was to put the rest up in cash. All I needed to close the deal was Sam's deed transferring title to Tim Thirdparty. I called up Sam Seller to give him the good news that he was going to be paid in full, and to arrange to pick up Sam's deed. Phone disconnected! It turns out Sam had moved to Mexico. His last known address was in a little town where he had no phone.

Mail service in Mexico (to put it mildly) is undependable. Several telegrams brought no response. So I bought a $500 round trip ticket for our girl at the Title company. I told her to go down to Mexico and get Sam's deed. Two weeks later she comes back with a nice tan but no deed. Sam, she tells me, was out with his camper and would not be back for several months. This she had learned from neighbors. Tim Thirdparty's loan commitment ran out and the resale died. Months later when I was finally able to locate Sam and get his deed, I was obliged to sell to someone else at a lower price.

The problem of the "unavailable seller" has now been solved by a clause in my contracts of sale, providing that a <u>fully executed deed from the seller be deposited with a local title company</u>. The seller leaves instructions that if payment in full for him is deposited with the title company, they must release the deed to the buyer. Also I have the seller give a power of attorney to a dependable local lawyer "just in case."

When I made my first contract of sale deals, I looked and looked for a "standard form" but soon learned that there was no such thing. Each deal seemed to require a form that was tailor-made. And when I went to lawyers to prepare such a document the results were uniformly unsatisfactory. So for your benefit, here is a sample form I whipped together. It's a composite of the forms I used on my own deals. It should be tailored by you, your company, your lawyer and of course, the other party to the transaction to fit your needs.

CONTRACT OF SALE FOR LAND

(This sample agreement is provided as an example only and should not be used unless fully understood)

1. The parties to this agreement, made in duplicate on January 3rd 1979, are Sam Seller, a single man, 1234 Spring Street, Springfield, California 99922 (Phone (413) 334-4324), hereafter known as "Seller" and Bob Buyer and Mary Buyer, his wife of 555 Ligonberry Lane, Grapefruit Grove California 99922 (Phone (415) 331-9753) hereafter known as "Buyer" Buyers have agreed to hold the property and later to take title as joint tenants with full rights of survivorship and not as tenants in common.

2. The Seller has agreed to sell, and the buyer has agreed to buy in its present condition, without warranties, the following described property, commonly known as 1, 3 & 5 Blackacre Court, Springfield, California, said property being Assessor's Parcel Number 2248 and 2249 and further legally described as:

> Lots 429 and 430 of Higgins Manor, according
> to the official plan thereof filed in the office
> of the Recorder of Glen County California on
> November 10, 1967 in Book 5 of Maps as Map
> Number 328.

3. Buyer has this date paid seller cash in the amount of $25,000, receipt of which is acknowledged and has further agreed to pay the seller $200 or more per month at the above address of seller on the first day of every month starting Feb. 3, 1979 and continuing for a period of ten years until

Feb. 3, 1989 on which date the balance due on the principal amount as set forth below, shall be fully due and payable. Said sums were paid or agreed to be paid on a full purchase price of:

$125,000.00

ONE HUNDRED AND TWENTY-FIVE THOUSAND DOLLARS

Subject to:

$80,000.00	Note of Seller to Upright Savings and Loan payable at $600 per month, 8% interest, 30 year amortization, starting Feb. 3, 1979 which is ASSUMED BY BUYER
$20,000.00	Obligation of Buyer to Seller, payable $200 or more per month at 9% interest, Bal. all due ten years from date.
$25,000.00	Cash PAID

4. Seller agrees that when the $20,000 debt herein plus accrued interest has been paid, he will deliver a properly executed grant deed to the buyer. Simultaneously with the execution of this contract, Seller deposits with the Transatlantic Title Company (hereafter TTC) the promised deed, together with a copy of this contract, and instructions to TTC to deliver this deed on Seller's behalf to buyer upon showing (by cancelled checks, receipts and/or cash deposits with TTC) that Buyer has made or is making the required payment of the balance due to TTC. TTC is authorised to accept the balance due on my behalf, to release said deed and is held harmless by me for any errors in handling said transaction. Upon payment or proof of payment having been made, TTC is irrevocably instructed to deliver said deed to Bob Buyer or Mary Buyer, or their successors or assignees. Said deed is not to be delivered back to Seller except in the event of default by Buyer under paragraph 5.

5. Buyer agrees that as security for his performance herein, he has delivered to TTC as escrow agent, his quit claim deed to the property. TTC is irrevocably instructed to deliver said deed to Seller, his successors or assignees in the event of default by Buyer. Default herein shall consist of

not making a current payment as required herein on either the obligation to Seller or the underlying loan to Upright Savings & Loan, or being behind in payments totaling over $2400.

6. Possession of the premises shall be transferred to Buyer and proration of rents and expenses shall be as of January 3, 1979. Said prorations shall be prepared by TTC. All charges by TTC shall be paid by Seller.

7. Buyer agrees that in the event any installment of money due to Seller is paid more than ten days after the date due, he will pay Seller a 5% late charge. Seller will also pay any late charges imposed by Upright Savings & Loan together with extended coverage for fire and liability insurance premiums (fire coverage no less than $125,000) Seller will pay when due, all real-estate taxes, special assessments and all other of his obligations which are or might become a lein upon said property.

8. It is agreed that if Seller accepts payment from Buyer of less than the amounts due hereunder, said partial payment will in no way affect the rights of Seller under paragraph 5 herein or any other remedies available to Seller for default. It is expressly understood that in the event Buyer is more than $2,400 behind in any required payments herein, Seller shall have the right to receive Buyer's deed from TTC and to record said deed, and by doing so, to declare a forfeiture of this contract and of any rights Buyer might have in the premises. Buyer and Seller further agree that in the event of litigation over this contract, or default hereunder, the prevailing party shall recover, in addition to damages, all reasonable attorneys' fees expended. Provided however that in the event of a default in a required payment being the cause of litigation, Buyer shall have no right to recover his attorneys' fees as the party who by his default caused the litigation to begin.

9. The Buyer expressly agrees before the signing hereof to set up a savings account at Upright Savings & Loan as a joint account with Seller, and to deposit in said account the sum of $2,400, being 3 months of Buyer's debt obligations. Seller will keep passbook to said acount, and Buyer

agrees that he will at all times maintain a balance of at least $2,400 in this account. Upright Savings & Loan will be instructed to withdraw automatically when due the $600 monthly payment due Upright on its secured loan on Blackacre. Seller will withdraw his $200 monthly payment from the same account on the third day of each month. Any interest earned by said account shall accrue the benefit of Buyer. This agreement will be in default if the balance in said account falls below $1600 at any time.

10. Buyer may repay loan to Seller in full or in part at any time without penalty.

11. This agreement may be assigned one time by Buyer, but in the event of assignment, the buyer shall remain personally liable for all obligations of this contract.

12. The buyer agrees to make requests of institutional lenders for financing of said property upon written demand of seller and if a loan in excess of $99,000 is available at an interest rate of 11% or less, Buyer agrees to accept said loan and to use the proceeds received in excess of the Upright loan to retire the loan balance due Seller. As an inducement to Buyer to re-finance as soon as possible, Seller agrees to pay all points, closing costs or other charges in connection with such loan up to $4,000.00 during 1979, $3,000 in 1980 and $2,000 thereafter.

13. Buyer agrees to keep said property in a good state of repair, and to not make any structural changes without the written permission of Seller.

14. Seller shall, at his sole option have the right to make necessary repairs, to pay taxes or insurance premiums, or to take other such action as in his sole judgment may be required to protect his interest in said property, and to demand reimbursement therefore from Buyer, together with interest at 10% per annum.

15. In addition to Seller's other remedies herein, in the event of default by Buyer, Seller shall have the right, upon failure of Buyer to remedy the

default himself within five days after written notice, to thereafter be released from all obligations to Buyer. At Seller's sole option after default and five days notice, Seller may re-enter the premises, take legal possession of the premises without legal process, the Buyer becoming at once a tenant at will of Seller, with Buyer thereupon forfeiting as liquidated damages for the non-performance of this contract, any and all payments previously made by Buyer.   OR

Seller, at his sole option, upon default of Buyer and upon five days written notice to Buyer, may declare the entire balance due hereunder at once all due and payable, and may elect to treat this contract as if it were a note and mortgage or trust deed, and pass title to Buyer, and proceed to foreclose immediately in accordance with the laws of California, and have said property sold, with the proceeds applied to the payment of balances owing, including costs and attorneys fees; and Seller shall have judgment for any deficiency. In the event of foreclosure, Buyer agrees that, upon filing, all rents are assigned to Seller, that he will immediately vacate the premises, and that Seller shall be entitled to appointment of a receiver or to take possession of the property during any redemption period provided for by law.

16. It is agreed that time is the essence of this agreement.

17. In the event there are liens or encumbrances on the property at the present date, which have not been disclosed to Buyer, or if other liens or encumbrances shall become a lien due to acts or neglect of Seller, and suspend payments to Seller until such payment made shall equal any sums advanced as aforesaid. Said action by Buyer will not be considered a "default" by Buyer under this agreement.

18. Irrespective of arrangements made with TTC, Seller agrees to deliver upon demand to Buyer or his assigns any deed or other documents which may be required for the successful operation of the property or to pass title once all sums due Seller have been paid. Seller agrees to keep Seller's own lawyer, Jonathan P. Moneygrabber, 13 Lawyer's Tower, Sacto. Ca. informed at all times of Seller's whereabouts and by this document, Seller instructs J.P.M. to inform Buyer of Seller's whereabouts at any time upon

request. Seller also has deposited with J.P.M. a full power of attorney and has instructed J.P.M. to co-operate fully with Buyer in the signing of any deeds or other documents which might require the signature of the title holder during this contract of sale, in the event that Seller is indisposed or temporarily unavailable. J.P.M. is instructed to co-operate with Buyer in all matters requiring Seller's signature that do not prejudice Seller's interest in the property.

19. Buyer agrees to hold Seller harmless against all claims of the Upright S & L or any other claimant against Seller as title holder of the property, whether through negligence otherwise. To this end Buyer agrees to obtain and pay for Liability Insurance with a face amount of $1,000,000 or more in coverage from the XYZ Company, naming Bob Buyer and Sam Seller as the insured parties. Buyer will also keep said property insured against fire, flood, earthquake and vandalism to the extent of $130,000 and will provide seller with a copy of said policy.

20. This agreement constitutes the entire agreement of the parties and all prior negotiations, insofar as they are applicable, have been incorporated herein.

All parties to this agreement have signed hereunder:

_____   _____   _____   _____
Robert Buyer   Date   Sam Seller   Date

_____   _____   _____   _____
Mary Buyer   Date

State of California
County of Glenn

On this 3rd day of January 1979, before me, the undersigned, a Notary Public in and for said County and State personally appeared Robert Buyer, Mary Buyer and Sam Seller known to me to be the persons whose names are subscribed to the document and they acknowledged to me that they executed same.

—————————————
Lilly White
NOTARY PUBLIC

Jonathan P. Moneygrabber acknowledges receipt of copy of this agreement, and a power of attorney from Sam Seller.

—————————————
Jonathan P. Moneygrabber
ATTORNEY AT LAW

Transatlantic Title Company acknowledges receipt of a copy of this agreement, deeds from Buyer and Seller and instructions covering delivery of said deeds in the event of satisfaction of the debt herein in which case Seller's deed goes to Buyer, or default hereunder, in which case Buyer's deed goes to Seller. TTC acknowledges receipt of $122.50 from Seller as full payment for escrow fees in this matter, and $340 from Buyer for a title insurance binder on this property, and $300 from Buyer for recording the attached "Memorandum of Installment Contract for Purchase of Real Property."

—————————————
Eleanor Escrow
OFFICER for: TTC   Date

NOTE: It is unnecessary and generally unadvisable to record the actual installment contract. For maximum privacy and low profile, it is best to record a "Memorandum" which puts the world on notice of your interest in the property, without actually spelling out the nature of your interest.

EXAMPLE: MEMORANDUM OF CONTRACT FOR THE
                PURCHASE OF REAL PROPERTY

This memorandum is a notice of the following: By contract dated January 1, 1979, Sam Seller (Seller) has agreed to sell to Robert and Mary Buyer (Buyer) who have agreed to buy the real property located in Glen County California, more fully described as:

(Insert legal description)

All terms and conditions of said Contract of Sale for land are incorporated herein by reference.

Dated January 3, 1979

_____

Sam Seller

NOTARY'S ACKNOWLEDGEMENT

_____

Bob Buyer

(To be recorded with the
Recorder of Deeds)

_____

Mary Buyer

SPECIAL NOTE...As this book is readied for the printers in March, 1979, the California Supreme Court, in a September, 1978 case affecting California only (Wellenkamp vs. Bank of America) has decided in effect, that most "Due on Sale" clauses in California are void. This means that most institutional loans on real estate are assumable by subsequent purchasers, so long as the security of the lender is not impaired.
The effect of the Wellenkamp case is great for us as real estate buyers, and makes it possible to do "no money down" deals in a new way. Example: The seller wants $100,000 and is willing to carry back $20,000. Buyer does not qualify for an $80,000 loan. New technique after Wellenkamp: Seller refinances, gets $80,000 -- tax free refinancing proceeds -- then sells to buyer and trades up. Buyer can take title and doesn't have to go thru the complex contract of sale proceedure anymore. He can take title to the property, pay the old lender directly, and doesn't have to pretend to the lender that he is "not really" the owner to avoid the "due on sale" clause. No "points" or "assumption fees" to pay.
The Wellenkamp case eliminates the main reason for using a contract of sale in California -- but remember, this case applies ONLY to California chartered Savings and Loans or Banks -- not to private lenders, Federal or out of state Savings and Loans. The contract of sale will still be useful to avoid "due on sale" where those lenders are involved. Also, the Contract of Sale is still useful to sellers who recieve little or no downpayment, and for that reason are reluctant to give up title. In California, Transamerica Title and Stewart Title Company are now willing to insure the non-title or contract interest of contract purchasers. They are also willing to handle foreclosures for a contract seller as if they were "trustee's sales" if the escrow and Contract of Sale was done with them.
The Contract of Sale is also going to remain useful in deferred exchanges under Section 1031 of the Internal Revenue Code.

INSTALLMENT SALE

The installment sale is a TAX CONCEPT and should not be confused with the Contract of Sale. A Contract of Sale is a method of selling real estate where the seller retains title to the property sold. An installment sale is a method of selling property that gets favorable tax treatment. An installment sale can be by Contract of Sale, but doesn't have to be.

To get preferential tax treatment as an INSTALLMENT SALE, the seller of real estate or personal property must be paid in no less than two installments, payable over two or more tax years. Also, not more than 30% of the gross sales price can be paid to the seller (or any third person on the seller's behalf) in the year of sale. The preferential treatment is that in a qualified installment sale, the gain on sale is not taxed until it is actually received. Only a portion of each dollar received is treated as taxable gain; the remainder is treated as non-taxable return of basis.

It is always easier to understand with examples. Here is an example that should clearly show the difference to a seller in making his deal fit the installment sale requirements.

An Installment Sale Contract Giving
Maximum Tax Benefits to the Seller

I Sam Seller agree to sell to Bob Buyer, my property at 123 Sellers Street, Sellerstown, for a full price of $100,000. It is agreed that Buyer will assume the existing $70,000 loan on said property, and will make required payments on said loan at the rate of $800 per month. Further, Buyer will, at the closing of this deal on December 31, 1979 pay to Seller the sum of $29,999.99 and on January 2, 1980 the sum of 1¢.

/S/   Buyer

Seller

Under the above arrangement, we will assume that the property was bought many years ago for $10,000 of which $8,000 was attributed to building value and $2,000 was land value. We will assume that the building was fully depreciated many years ago, and was refinanced. If the seller sold for $30,000.01 "down" he would owe a capital gain tax on his <u>total</u> <u>profit</u>.

Cost	10,000
Less	
Depreciation	8,000
Basis	2,000
Selling Price:	100,000
Taxable Capital Gain	$ 98,000
State & Federal Tax =	$ 50,000 (Approximately)*

On an installment sale the gain is calculated only on the cash received at the closing. At the same rate, the tax would be 50% of $29,999.99, or about $15,000* for a tax savings of $35,000.

*The taxes on capital gains vary with each taxpayer, and depend upon how much income he has, how much capital gains he may have, and what state he lives in. The above approximations are for a wealthy taxpayer in a high tax state like California.

216

Managing Property & Problem Tenants

Once you become a landlord, your major challenge will be getting and keeping good tenants. You'll note I said "challenge" and not "problem" because, as in every aspect of your career, mental attitude is extremely significant. If you can meet the challenge of picking good tenants, you will preside over a smooth running operation. Rents will be mailed in on time. There will be a cordial tenant relations, low turnover, and a minimal vacancy factor.

When you buy your first rental property, existing tenants normally come with the building as part of the package. As soon as you take over management, adjust rents to market levels and evict undesirables immediately. Tenants expect it when ownership changes. If you procrastinate before introducing your new policies tenants will be more apt to argue or feel resentment.

What is an undesirable tenant? If you are already a landlord I don't have to tell you. If you are a novice, you'll discover that problem tenants come in two major categories:

A) Irresponsible Deadbeats

B) Inconsiderate Slobs

Often these qualities will be found combined in one tenant. When you inspect each apartment in a building you are about to purchase, the slobs will be easy to recognize. A slight mess doesn't worry me, but if I were

THE KIND OF TENANT YOU DON'T WANT

to describe the sort of visual and nasal experience you can expect now and then - sometimes even in middle-class buildings - I might scare you out of being a landlord at all. But suffice it to say that you'll definitely recognize a slob's style of living when you see it. You want them out at once, if not sooner.

The second category is the deadbeat - someone who won't pay their rent when due. They can't be detected by sight or smell, but during negotiations most sellers will be glad to give you a thumbnail sketch of their tenants. Some will be prompt payers, others late payers. But no-payers are the ones to get rid of. If your seller doesn't tell the truth, you'll know the deadbeats on the next rent due date. You want to reform the slow-pays with a rent discount arrangement like the one in my sample rental agreement.

Generally, tenants you want to get rid of will leave without court proceedings if you give them proper notice. Notices of various types are at the end of this chapter, with a suggested rental agreement. Buyers of this book may copy and use my forms.

Once your bad tenants are gone, you will begin to show the unit to new prospects. Don't ever show an apartment inhabited by a problem tenant until he is out and the place is cleaned, fumigated and repainted. If you show a pig-sty to a prospect, everyone except other slobs will be turned off. However, you may be able to develop rapport with another tenant in an identical apartment, and show that one. Obviously, a day of vacancy represents an irretrievable loss. Still, it's better to have a vacancy than to rent to a loser. A bad tenant could be so annoying to his neighbors that you could lose all your good tenants. And if you get a deadbeat/slob/fuzzy-thinking-leftist as your tenant, it will give you gray hair. Not only will he let the property run down and refuse to pay rent, but he will have legal-aid lawyers wear you out with frivolous legal proceedings that take up inordinate amounts of time, money and energy. You could even lose the building if Mr Deadbeat's rent was your only source of meeting the mortgage liabilities.

All of these problems can be avoided by careful tenant selection. Follow these suggestions, and you will seldom, if ever, have tenant problems or problem tenants.

Advertise appropriately in places likely to reach the market you seek. If you want gay tenants (who are usually pretty good) there are newspapers and publications read solely by that market. Local neighborhood papers are much cheaper and often more effective than the large metropolitan dailies. Your ad should be attractive and designed to weed out undesirables before they apply. Here's one of mine:

ROMANTIC CABIN IN THE WOODS $400/mo.
Fireplace, Deck, 2 Bdrms, 2 Baths.
Adults. No dogs. Tenants must be
employed w/good references.
Call 332-2345 from 6PM to 10PM

When the prospect calls, you should interview further to ascertain his desirability. On the phone if you detect a hostile attitude towards landlords or a tendency towards litigation it's best to suggest that he seek other accomodations. It is hard to reject a potentially bad tenant. But you must weed out problem tenants in order to have a successful real estate management program. Set up two specific times per week for all prospects to come at once to look at the property. There are several reasons for having all your prospects come at once. The first is that at least half of your phone prospects will not show up for their appointment. Thus, rather than wasting time going to and from the rental unit, if you set up a generally convenient time such as noon on Sunday for everyone, even if five out of ten are "no-shows," you will not have made five useless trips.

Psychologically, if there are several prospects at the same place, you create an atmosphere of competition for the rental. Hopefully at least one desirable prospect will feel it necessary to make a speedy decision rather than say, "I will think about it and call you back." If any prospect is interested in the property, have them fill out a rental application form. If you read over their application carefully it will help you weed out undesirables. Check the references! Call, not only the present landlord of the prospect, but also the predecessor landlord. The reason is that the present landlord may be so anxious to get rid of a loser that he will give him a wonderful send-off, even though he is the worst deadbeat or slob imaginable. The   prior landlord, on the other hand, has nothing to lose by telling the truth about your applicant. Always call the named employer and the bank of the prospect to ascertain his general level of responsibility and to verify the fact that he is employed and does have a bank account.

If you, as landlord, pay a surprise visit to the tenant at his own home, you can quickly determine whether his style of living is acceptable. You also discover, rather quickly, if the tenant has a large collection of dogs or disreputable friends camping in the living room. When a tenant who looks good has completed a rental application, I always ask if it's OK for me to accompany him back to his home. After a quick look you can determine whether he is suitable or not. That takes care of selecting qualified tenants. Next we'll cover money.

Never agree to hold a rental unit for a prospect without a substantial deposit, upfront. A substantial deposit to me is at least one month's rent,

DON'T MAKE THE MISTAKE OF ACCEPTING SEX OR DOPE IN LIEU OF RENT. NEVER GET SEXUALLY OR ILLEGALLY INVOLVED WITH YOUR TENANTS.

but preferably six weeks rent, my standard security deposit. Normally this sum will be paid in the form of a check. Until that check has cleared, the prospect should not get keys to the unit. The law is such that once you give a tenant possession of property, even if he gives you a bum check, you will have the problem of evicting him. That could take up to two months.

When you have obtained the proper deposit and have checked out your tenant thoroughly, there is still one step more: Go through the apartment with the prospect. Fill out an inventory and condition check list. I have found that most arguments with tenants occur in connection with the refund of their security deposit. The tenant leaves unclean areas, broken windows, or other damage. The invariable argument: "It was that way when I moved in." With a condition and inventory check list, signed by the tenant, you can refer to that document and quickly ascertain if the tenant is correct. You have a description of the property as it was in black and white. Reference to this document makes it possible to deduct the cost of any damage or clean-up from his security deposit without further discussion.

Now, for those who have a problem tenant in spite of all precautions: Money is the problem 95% of the time. But, sometimes you get a tenant who is breaking his rental agreement by doing something undesirable, like dealing heroin, or keeping 12 puppies that are poo-pooing on your new wall-to-wall carpeting. You want to get rid of a bad tenant, and you want him out as quickly as possible. First you consider "self help." Did you know that it's financially very risky to forcibly throw a tenant out without a court order? Nor can you go to the apartment, unscrew the doors and remove the windows. You can't shut off utilities. You can't harass the tenant. You can't pop in at any time you feel like it and you can't bother him unreasonably for the rent. You can't do any of that without risking being sued yourself for very substantial damages. So, stay away from that sort of self-help. But there is something you can do before going to court. You can visit your tenant - and you'd be surprised how often this works - appeal to his sense of fair play. Tell him that things aren't working out and you would like him to move out. Ask him how much time he needs. In many cases, a very reasonable approach works. The tenant agrees to move in a few days. You'd be surprised what you get by just asking politely.

222

Sometimes the tenant will tell you he doesn't have the money to move. If he's already behind in rent, maybe you'd be able to make a deal something like this. You say to him, "Look, I will pay for your moving. You just be out of here by 10 o'clock tomorrow morning and this $100 bill is yours. The place is to be left clean. You get moving money after I put a new lock on the door." That $100 bribe may be your best bet, rather than waiting the four to eight weeks it could take you to get a tenant evicted legally. During that time you'd lose more than $100 in rent, not to mention time and aggravation. So, the first thing to do when you have a

BE REASONABLE! BE RATIONAL!

WRONG!   RIGHT!

problem tenant is to talk to him - be reasonable, be rational. Appeal to whatever it is that you can appeal to in that tenant and try to talk him out. Also, keep your cool. It's only money. Don't get all emotional. Leave if an argument develops. Sometimes you can find a new place for your tenant by making a few phone calls yourself.

Now, let's assume that Plan 1 - talking - doesn't work. When you go to talk you should have with you the basic form that starts eviction proceedings. This is the "3 day notice to pay rent or quit the premises" found at the end of this chapter. You need to serve that on a tenant before you can file a lawsuit.

Now, let's assume just for the moment that your tenant isn't behind in rent but is breaking his rental agreement in some other way. Change the title of that form. Instead of 3 day notice to pay rent or quit the premises, you'd give a 3 day notice to quit the premises or "perform covenant." Then you write in the body of the notice what the tenant is doing that bothers you, like having a dog in violation of the lease.

There are certain things that you cannot object to. Every community has it's own rules. In San Francisco for example, you cannot kick out a tenant because he has a child. If a childless couple moved into an all adult complex in San Francisco and then had a child in the natural course of things, you could not tell them to get rid of the kid or move. In other cities you can. You can't kick anyone out, anywhere in the USA, because of race, creed, religious preference, or national origin. Nor can you discriminate against potential tenants for those reasons.

You can't do something that is called a "retaliatory eviction." For instance, a tenant has complained to the Building Department that you don't supply enough heat or that there are rats. You cannot get a tenant out through court proceedings just because he has made an official complaint against you. He has a legal right to complain to the Building or the Health Departments. You cannot evict him for this reason.

But, suppose that you want to get rid of a trouble maker - a bad egg - who is organizing a rent strike, calling you up with unjustified complaints every day and so on. Simply give him 30 days notice to move. Assume this tenant has made a complaint to the building department but you really want him out on general principles. For your day in court you'd better keep in mind only the <u>other</u> reasons you want him out (like he has a dog, or he's too noisy, or there have been tenant complaints about him.) In a 30 day notice you are <u>not</u> obliged to tell a tenant what it is that bothers you. In court or in your conversations don't even mention that he made a building department complaint or else the judge may accept his retaliation eviction defense. You don't need a reason to ask a tenant to move IF HE DOESN'T HAVE A LEASE. But if the court finds you have an improper reason for asking a tenant to move, that tenant can stay.

THIS RENTAL AGREEMENT IS BETWEEN *Mary Tenant* HEREAFTER TENANT(T) AND THE OWNERS OF
2 Hawthorn Dr., S.F. Ca. (Address of rental property) HEREAFTER LANDLORD (L), as represented by the agent whose signature appears below:
Received of T the sum of $*600.* as a security deposit, and $*300* as rent from *1/1* to *1/31/80*
Balance due $ *Ø* on or before _____.

This agreement establishes a month-to-month tenancy, however tenant may stay on premises without
any increase in rent for 12 months from the date hereof, at which time rent shall automatically
be increased by 6%, unless notice of other arrangements are given to tenant. Rent shall be
$*335.* per month, payable in advance, but T may take advantage of a discount and pay only
$*300.* if the following conditions are met A) Rent is actually received prior to the 1st day
of the month at
       *W.G.PROPERTIES, P.O.BOX 408, MILL VALLEY, CA. 94941 & B) All conditions of this agreement
are met by T. T agrees to pay the full rent on the first of the month, and a late charge of $5
per day for each day after the 3rd of the month, and $5 for each dishonored check. If more than
one prospective tenant has signed this rental agreement, all shall be responsible individually
for the total rent payments and all other provisions of this lease. T shall be responsible for
the payment of ALL utilities including water, PG&E, Cable, garbage and sewer charges if any.
There shall be no pets on the property except with the express written permission of L and if
any pets are brought upon the property without permission, T agrees to pay $300 per month for
the Pet even if the Pet is on the premises only one day or one part of the day. New locks or
security devices may be installed only if L is supplied with keys. L to have access at all
times for inspection, maintenance of the property, and showing to prospective purchasers and
tenants during daylight hours. The Security Deposit is NOT TO BE USED FOR LAST MONTH'S RENT
UNDER ANY CIRCUMSTANCES, AND IF IT IS, T AGREES TO PAY A DOUBLE LAST MONTH'S RENT. SECURITY
DEPOSIT WILL BE REFUNDED IN FULL 14 DAYS AFTER MOVE-OUT ONLY IF PREMISES ARE LEFT IN PRISTINE
CONDITION WITH WINDOWS WASHED, WALLS & CEILINGS REPAINTED IF MARRED, CARPETS SHAMPOOED, ALL
APPLIANCES AND FIXTURES SPARKLING CLEAN, ALL UTILITY BILLS PAID IN FULL, FLOORS CLEANED AND
WAXED, ALL DAMAGE REPAIRED, ALL WEEDS IN GARDEN PULLED, AND IF T MOVES BEFORE THE END OF ONE
YEAR, IT SHALL BE T'S RESPONSIBILITY TO EITHER GIVE 60 days notice of departure OR provide L
with an acceptable replacement tenant at a 10% increase in rent. T agrees that (s)he will be
the only persons living on the premises, and agree to pay $10 per day for any other persons
staying overnight on the property without written permission. T agrees that if he is given
3 day notice for non-payment of rent, he will vacate the premises within 3 days, and if he does
not, will thereafter be liable for, and will pay rent for the premises on a daily basis of
$30 per day; T also agrees that in the event it is necessary to goto Court to evict him, he
will pay L the sum of $250 for attorney's fees or for L's time and trouble if L acts as his
own attorney. L agrees to pay T, and T agrees to accept as maximum damages and attorney's fees,
the sum of $250 in the event T should prevail or L be guilty of wrongful eviction. If T is
absent from the premises for more than 3 consecutive days while rent is in default, T hereby
instructs L to consider the premises abandoned, and to dispose of any property left on the
premises as L sees fit, without liability to T. L shall not be liable to T for any damages or
injury to T, his guests, on this property. T is deemed to have exclusive control of the
premises and therefor T agrees to hold L harmless from any claim for damages no matter how or
to whom caused during the duration of this rental agreement or possession by T. L May retain
security deposit as liquidated damages if T fails to pay rent on time, or to keep the premises
in good condition. L's acceptance of any payment for less than the amouts due hereunder shall
not be a waiver of L's right to the full amount, or L's right to declare a default for failure
to pay or perform. Notice may be served on L at the above address, and upon T at the rented
property by certified mail, the registration slip, and not the return receipt shall be conclusive
evidence of the proper service of such notice. T shall be responsible for keeping appliances in
working order, repairing stopped up drains, garbage disposal units, broken windows, damaged
counter tops, fixtures, walls or ceilings or floors. Working light bulbs will be provided by
L at move-in, and must be supplied or paid for by T at move-out. T agrees to furnish property
attractively. Waterbeds are OK only if T agrees to take full responsibility for any damage or
leakage & to use only underwriter approved waterbeds with innerliners. L is responsible for
roof leaks and exterior painting only. T CAN TERMINATE THIS AGREEMENT UPON 60 DAYS' NOTICE, OR
30 DAYS IF HE GETS A REPLACEMENT TENANT. L CAN TERMINATE THIS AGREEMENT UPON 60 DAYS'NOTICE,
FOR ANY REASON, OR NO REASON AT ALL AT HIS SOLE OPTION. Interest on the security deposit at
6% per year will be paid to T only if T has promptly paid the full (undiscounted) rent for the
duration of the tenancy. T agrees not to remove or damage the following items on the property,
and if he does, to pay the amounts set forth next to the item named: $500 for any tree cut down
or killed, $50 for any shrub or plant or the actual replacement cost, if lower, of any fixture.
Control of insects or animals on property shall be T's sole responsibility, except for Termites,
which shall be L's responsibility to eradicate. Procedure on REPAIRS: T should get bids from
2-3 repairmen of his choice. L will pay for any repairs that are his responsibility after work
has been completed to satisfaction of T & L. It is expected that T will handle all his own
minor repairs (under $30) and will treat the property as his own. A HIGHER LEVEL OF TENANT
RESPONSIBILITY IS EXPECTED IN THE RENTAL OF THIS HOME THAN IN AN APARTMENT BUILDING WHERE A
RESIDENT MANAGER IS ON THE PREMISES. T UNDERSTANDS THAT PROPERTY IS OWNED BY AN ABSENTEE LAND-
LORD AND NO READY STAFF IS AVAILABLE FOR REPAIRS. IF THE TENANT IS NOT READY TO ACCEPT A VERY
LOW LEVEL OF SERVICE, HE SHOULD NOT SIGN THIS RENTAL AGREEMENT. T agrees to keep roof and drains
clear & if he does not, L may have the work done once a year at T's expense ($9 per hour estimated)
L WILL GENERALLY PAY FOR MATERIALS IF T WISHES TO PAINT (WHITE) OR MAKE PERMANENT IMPROVEMENTS TO
THE PROPERTY. ALL SUCH WORK OR ANY CHANGES ON THE PROPERTY MUST BE APPROVED IN WRITING BEFORE
ANY WORK IS STARTED. This sheet constitutes the entire agreement between the parties except for
additional provisions written here:_____

Sally Dentary   *12/25/1979*   *Mary Tenant*
_____   _____   _____
Phone: 383 3229   DATED   TENANT
AGENT FOR LANDLORD   _____   _____
                                        TENANT

APPLICATION TO RENT

	TENANT ONE(NAME)	TENANT TWO(NAME)

Anticipated length of stay

Full Name & Date of Birth
Present Address
How long there
Office Address
How long there
Office Phone
Present Home Phone
Name of Immediate Superior
Company Name & Division
    Job Description
Approx. Salary

Marital Status

Proposed Occupants of Unit
    (give names & ages)

Pets? Give Name and Description

IT IS CLEARLY UNDERSTOOD THAT $300 PER MONTH PER DOG ON PREMISES FOR ANY PART OF A MONTH, OR
OTHER PET, WILL BE DUE, UNLESS OTHERWISE AGREED on this sheet, right here: <u>NO PETS ALLOWED !</u>

Cal Drivers License

Social Security #

Car License Plates
    Give State & Number

Make/Model car, Year and color

Nearest relative in area
    Name/Add/Phone

Closest personal friend in area
    Name/Add/Phone

Business or Credit reference
    Name/Add/Phone

NAME & PHONE OF LAST TWO LANDLORDS
& DATES YOU WERE THERE(Give add)

Bank & Branch (Checking)
Approximate balance

Bank or S&L(Savings Account)
Approximate balance

Parents name & address & phone
Use guardian or older relative
you want notified in case of
accident or death

Were you ever evicted from any
tenancy?
Were you ever bankrupt?

Have you ever not paid rent when due?

I DECLARE THE ABOVE APPLICATION INFORMATION TO BE TRUE UNDER PENALTY OF PERJURY AND AGREE THAT
MY LANDLORD MAY IMMEDIATELY TERMINATE ANY TENANCY ENTERED INTO IN RELIANCE UPON MISINFORMATION
GIVEN ON THIS APPLICATION.

I agree to lease the unit on the terms on the reverse of this sheet, and agree that in the event
I have been accepted by the landlord's signature on the reverse, and I <u>change my mind</u> and do not
move into the premises or stop payment on my initial deposit check, the sum of one month's rent
will be due as liquidated damages since other prospective tenants will have been turned away, and
it will be necessary for L to readvertise the property, and re-evaluate other tenants.
DATED: _____
    SIGN HERE ON THIS SIDE FOR APPLICATION TO RENT. OTHER SIDE IS LEASE TO BE SIGNED ALSO.

Applicant   Applicant   Applicant

THREE DAY NOTICE TO PAY RENT OR QUIT THE PREMISES

&

NOTICE TERMINATING TENANCY

To:_____ & all others in possession of the premises
    name of tenant(s)

at: _____, California
    Street Address, Apt.#, City or Town, County

Take notice that rent for the above described premises amounting to $_____

is now past due for the month(s) of _____, _____.   Year 197____

 The period for which rent is now past due is _____ to _____.

You are notified that if the amount of $_____ is not paid within three

days after the service of this notice upon you, and/or you do not deliver

vacant possession to the owner within three days, an action in UNLAWFUL

DETAINER will be filed against you together with an action for damages as

provided by law. California Laws provide for the recovery of treble damages

in the event that rent is wilfully and wrongfully withheld.

In addition to the foregoing notice, and without prejudice thereto, you

are also notified that in any event, your tenancy of the above premises

is terminated thirty days after the service of this notice, and you are

required to vacate at the expiration of said period of time .

Dated:_____

Served on:_____

By:_____

Date & Time:_____

Place:_____

_____
Signed by Owner

Copies: 1. Tenant(s)
        2. Court File
        3. Owner's File

I declare under penalty of perjury that I served the above notice
as indicated above, and that I am over 18 years of age.

_____
Signed by Server of Process

I could write another whole book about managing property effectively, avoiding problem tenants, and dealing with problem tenants. But I'm happy to say that someone else did a fine job of writing such a book, which is the ideal companion volume to TWO YEARS FOR FREEDOM. Once you own real estate, the book LANDLORDING, by Leigh Robinson, and my cassette tape will be indispensable.

LANDLORDING

A Handymanual for Scrupulous Landlords and Landladies Who Do It Themselves

LANDLORDING is available by mail order from me, Bill Greene, at $13, postage and tax paid. If you would like to purchase a cassette tape covering DO IT YOURSELF EVICTIONS, together with all the proper forms, it will be included with the book LANDLORDING for an additional $10.

Please send me, postage and tax paid:

☐ Landlording $13   ☐ Cassette Tape on $10   ☐ Both $23
                                Problem Tenants
Send check and order to: Bill Greene, Box 408, Mill Valley, CA 94941

KEEPING A LOW PROFILE

PAY NO TAXES EVER AGAIN, LEGALLY!!

If someone told you that Bill Greene could wave a magic wand to help you manage your financial affairs so that you would never need to pay income taxes again; you'd say they were crazy. But I'm going to show you how to do just that; Pay no taxes, ever again, for the rest of your life, -- Legally!

I am writing this chapter in the fall of 1978. For ten years, in spite of intensive scrutiny by the Internal Revenue Service, I've paid no taxes, while accumulating several million dollars in assets. The methods I am about to outline will show you how to do it too, in simple non-technical terms. With minimal effort on your part, you can not only eliminate all future income tax liabilities, but also get a refund of taxes you have paid during the past three years.

Our well-intentioned but somewhat naive President, Jimmy Carter, claimed during the presidential campaign that "The income tax laws of America are a disgrace to the human race". During this period he frequently maintained that our income tax laws were unfair and unduly complicated. He promised vast reforms that were necessary. Yet, after his election, the 1976 reforms introduced by him -- the so-called 'Tax Simplification Act' - only made things more complicated. Accountants and

MY ACCOUNTANT AND LAWYER CELEBRATING THE 1976 TAX
SIMPLIFICATION ACT. "REFORMS" LIKE THIS JUST MAKE OUR
TAX CODE LONGER, MORE COMPLICATED AND MORE UNFAIR.
THAT'S GOOD FOR LAWYERS, ACCOUNTANTS AND BUREAUCRATS.

lawyers lovingly call it their Full Employment Act'!

In many ways the 1976 reforms made taxes even more burdensome to the ordinary middle class wage-slave. More than ever, productive working people are getting taxed to death by a system nobody likes. The IRS, in its collection and enforcement proceedings, often operates like the Gestapo or Secret Police; incorporating in its methods midnight raids, rewards to informers, burglars, and female secret agents who use sex to pry out information from suspected tax evaders.

These days the IRS is even trying to pass regulations taxing people for such things as the 'value' of the parking space they get when they park! Our Constitution and Bill of Rights have been so eroded by IRS practices that our founding fathers must be turning over in their graves.

We might as well be living in a totalitarian dictatorship, for all the voice we have in our tax system. Certain politicians express wonderment that over-taxed, basically honest citizens are turning to any device in their fight for survival. Even the lunatic fringe tax rebels who refuse to pay any taxes and file blank returns have over a million supporters these days. The growing subterranean economy of non-taxpayers who earn money but don't file any returns or even officially exist "on paper" is estimated to produce one tenth of our Gross National Product. It's all cash, no questions asked. No W-2 forms, no checks please.

Of course, the members of the subterranean economy are tax-evaders. There's a risk of actually going to jail if they are informed on and caught. But legal tax avoidance - what we talk about here - for many people is a game with no risk. The rules guarantee you will win. You simply learn the rules. Find a good coach and manager, your lawyer and your accountant, and get on with the game. Look for openings. Never give up. Hang tough. Play to win. Beat your opponent. You can't lose. You don't have to pay any taxes again ever! You never go to jail in this game unless there is an intent to defraud. Everything I'm going to tell you about and everything I do in my personal life involves no intent to defraud the IRS - I am merely using the present laws as they stand, these same laws which our President declares a disgrace to the human race. These same unfair laws allow big corporations like Syntex, the

oil companies, the coal companies, and rich guys like me, to earn millions and pay no taxes whatsoever.

The IRS doesn't like the Bill Greenes of the World telling Mr. Average taxpayer these secrets. They've tried to shut me down instead of the loopholes. But I contend the loopholes I talk about will stay. Why? Because most Senators and Congressmen use them. They pay no taxes. If you play by their rules, you won't pay taxes either. When Ronald Reagan was govenor of California there was a flap because he paid no Federal or state income taxes. Nixon managed to keep his taxes at zero by falsifying deductions (clearly tax evasion) for which he quietly received a full presidential pardon.

You might remember from the papers that during his first year in office, Jimmy Carter made a small cash gift of $6,000 to the U.S. government because he was so 'embarrassed' at having no taxes due. As if he hadn't planned it that way! I submit that a large proportion of our Senators and Congressmen enjoy allowances and incomes of $500,000 a year from the public and most of them pay little or no taxes. I certainly pay no taxes. After reading this, if you ever pay any income taxes you deserve a dunce cap. America today is like France before the French revolution; A few aristocrats and politicians control 95% of the wealth and they pay no taxes. The workers and small businessmen pay all the taxes. But you can get smart and join the tax free class now!

I'm going to show you how to get on the band wagon. In just one chapter, I can't cover every detail. But by making you aware of the opportunities, the different tax shelters, the books and literature available, I can enable you to get out in the world to ask the right questions. Then you will be able to make these tax avoidance principles apply to yourself. Remember, you can only become a millionaire quickly if you don't pay any taxes.

Let's run through a basic outline of one way to eliminate, or at least save substantially, on your taxes. It will also make you considerably richer because the main focus of the plan saves taxes but represents a very good investment. Let's take an example. We will assume that it is January 1979. You're a working person, or couple, and you make

around $25,000 a year. You don't own any small businesses or invest-
ment property. You are that unenviable person - the wage-slave, the
consumer, the taxpayer. You are a person who goes to a regular job
at 9 a.m. and gets out at 5 p.m. You get a paycheck and find that about
one third of it is deducted for federal tax, maybe 10% for state tax,
another 10% for Social Security and other deductions. Little or no
chance to finagle. What do you take home? Less than half your earnings.
A large part of that goes for sales taxes, gasoline taxes, property taxes
on your home and so on. Worse than that, even if you get a salary raise
of 10% every year, the extra wage throws you in a higher tax bracket
resulting in more taxes than ever.

Combine the evergrowing tax burden with the fact that inflation
continuously reduces the purchasing power of every dollar you receive.
The net effect of all this is that your standard of living declines every
year even with cost-of-living raises from the boss. What can you do
about it? There's a hell of a lot you can do about it!

Following the procedures taught in my Tycoon Class and explained
in this book or on cassette tapes, you can negotiate your way into the
purchase of real property. You'll end up reducing the tax on your
$25,000 regular income job to zero. For example, take a $100,000 fourplex
located in Anytown USA. This fourplex you select is old, grungy and
in need of lots of cosmetic work, like painting, repairs and maintenance.
It also has worn carpets and drapes, and if you're lucky perhaps some
scruffy furniture. These physical defects are the ideal ones you are
seeking. Financially, the closer you can get to a no-money-down deal on
the fourplex, the better your tax benefits will be.

In connection with our $100,000 fourplex example, let's assume you
bought it with no-money-down because you got an $80,000 first mortgage
from a savings loan association. You got a $24,000 second loan from the
seller of that property. The extra $4,000 over cost was to provide enough
to cover the closing costs. So, on January 1, 1979, you take title to this
income property without taking a dime out of your pocket. We'll assume
that rents covered expenses during 1979, your first year of ownership.
Now let's skip to April 15 of the following year, 1980, and look at your tax

return. Remember that tax return is a summary of your income and expense for the year ending December 31, 1979. Let's see what the effect of buying this one property has had on your income tax.

First of all, you must be aware that the IRS has a concept known as depreciation. Even though the value of your building may be going up by 20% per year in the real world, the IRS, for tax purposes, will let you write off, as a tax deductible expense, between 4 and 10% of its value per year, as if it was losing cash money. The IRS ties in allowable depreciation with the concept known as 'useful life'. What this means is that the IRS allows you to take a loss based upon your original cost of $100,000 spread over each year of the 'useful life' of property. The fact that you did not spend a dime of your own money, but used only borrowed money to buy this property, is totally irrelevant to the depreciation you're allowed to take.

Let me show you how this first property (and others like it that you might buy this year) will be a magic wand to eliminate your taxes. Because of depreciation allowances, and a few other goodies you can legally claim, you won't have to pay any taxes this year or over again. In fact, if you do two or three real estate deals this year you'll get a refund of all the taxes you have paid for the past three years as well. I'll run through it now to show you exactly how the system works.

The first thing you do after you have closed your deal is set up depreciation schedules.   You select a 'useful life' for each component of the property - that is, the structure, the roof, the carpets, drapes, stoves, furnishings and so on. These depreciation schedules have to be reasonable and the IRS does publish certain guidelines. But it is up to you to either use these schedules or to create shorter ones if you feel you can justify selecting a shorter 'useful life'. The IRS will try to change your figures only if they are judged unreasonable. Of course if you're not audited within three years your figures stand and can't be challenged. This is due to the three year statue of limitations.

Now, as I said, I like to buy older, rundown structures because with such buildings the 'useful life', in my reasonable opinion, may be as little as ten years or less. Of course you as a taxpayer always want the shortest possible life because that generates maximum depreciation. In one case, I actually bought a building so run down that it was condemned one week after I bought it. In that instance I gave it a 'useful life' of one year. I don't see how the IRS can complain about that, because I did in fact have to rebuild it completely in order to get a permit of occupancy.

The 'useful life' concept does not mean the time remaining until the place will fall down but rather the time span during which it will lose its useful or economic value. For instance, if you have a run down, worn out building which will have to be substantially remodelled within a 10 year period, then a 10 year 'useful life' on that property for tax purposes is fine. It is strictly a matter of opinion. Your opinion, if at all reasonable, is just as good as an IRS agent's opinion. They want a long life. You want a short life, to get the largest possible depreciation deductions.

Now, the purchase price of the example property was $100,000. You must break it down into various components. First of all, estimate what represents the value of the land. You want it to be a low percentage, say, 10% of the total. The IRS would like it to be high, because you can't depreciate land. In our example, let's give the land a value of $10,000, the structure $70,000 and the furnishings (drapes, carpets, stoves and refrigerators) another $10,000. The important thing to remember is that you want to choose a value for the structure that is relatively high as compared with the land value. Obviously you couldn't get a 10% land/90% building ratio if you were dealing with a little old farm house on a 50 acre farm. The value of the land would probably exceed the value of the building by far.

What do you look for to get the best depreciation? Small lots with tall buildings, not too much land, plenty of bricks and wood. With urban property where you have a structure that occupies most of the lot you will find that the IRS will go along with your setting a land value of around 20% of the price you paid with 80% allocated to the building and furnishings. Who sets up this allocation? YOU DO. This allocation will be challenged by the IRS only if you are audited, only if they look at it, and only if it is unreasonable. Once you come up with any evidence showing that your estimate was based upon a reasonable set of assumptions, the burden is on the IRS to show that your estimated 'useful life' and allocation of land value to building value is unreasonable. If you want to be totally on the safe side and allocate in a way that will never be challenged, your county property tax bill generally values the structure and the land separately. If you use their ratio, the IRS will seldom question a ratio set by these independent 'experts'.

However, with many properties I feel the ratio arbitrarily selected by the county assessor is wrong; often in our favor with a low land value, sometimes in favor of the IRS. You are free to develop a ratio which is more favorable to you. What's all this for? Once you've estimated the land value and deducted it from the cost of the property, the remainder is the value of the structure and contents. Valuing the structure itself at, say, $70,00 and setting the useful life of that structure at ten years, then (straight line depreciation) on your tax return gives you a $7,000 per year depreciation loss which you can use to offset other income on your tax return. Even though that building may be going up in value by $10,000 or $20,000 a year in the real world, for tax purposes you're allowed to depreciate the building - that is take a loss on your tax return - just as if your salary was reduced by $7,000. Depreciation gives you a loss that isn't really a loss. It is a loss for accounting purposes only.

Let's assume that with the deal you got drapes, carpets, furniture and removable fixtures (such as refrigerators) that you and the prior property owner by contract agreed were worth another $20,000. Getting a high value on any personal property is best for you. You can also depreciate these fixtures and furnishings, but the estimated useful life of personal property is much shorter than the useful life of a structure. So, let's say you bought this fourplex and allocated $70,000 to the value of the structure and $20,000 to the value of the personal property inside the building.

You will notice that this leaves $10,000 for the value of the land. Land according to IRS rules does not depreciate at all. Therefore, one thing I like to look for is real estate on leased land. Actually, if that lease at a reasonable 'ground rent' runs for a very long time like 99 years, you than have the use of that property for as long as you live but you get maximum depreciation. Why? Because the entire cost of the deal was all for depreciable assets.

Let's get back to the depreciation on personal property. Say you give the personal property a life of six years. Actually that's a very conservative (long) estimated life for used carpets, drapes, stoves, washers and dryers. The IRS would probably let you get away with three years. But, for the sake of this example, let's use six years. The cost or basis of the personal property is $20,000. On any personal property with an estimated life of at least six years, the IRS will let you take 20% extra depreciation the first year.* Why? I guess the IRS wants to encourage the purchase of used junk. That's the rule. That 20% of $20,000 obviously gives you an extra $4,000 in first year depreciation on the personal property. That too will be a loss deductible from your regular other income even though it's all on paper. So you see how a $11,000 depreciation loss was created: $7,000 on the structure, $4,000 not even counting regular depreciation on the contents of another $3,000 or so.

The next thing to do towards the yearend is to arrange for an improvement loan. You borrow $10,000 for repairs and painting on your fourplex.

BORROWED MONEY IS NEVER TAXABLE INCOME

You can do what you want with it, but by definition, borrowed money is not income and therefore not taxable. So here we are on December 30. You borrow $10,000 and on the same day you write out a check to the Victorian House Painting Co. for a $10,000 interior and exterior paint job. Guess what that accomplishes? You've got a $10,000 deduction for the money you've borrowed to repair, cosmetically improve, or paint the property. Out of pocket you've spent nothing. But now, in addition to the $11,000 depreciation deductions, you've got another $10,000 deduction: Total $22,000!

That's only the beginning. Perhaps you bought a new car or pick-up truck in 1979. Before you got into the real estate business a car used for pleasure or driving to and from work wouldn't have resulted in any deductions at all. But now that you're in a business where that car is used, you will not only be able to deduct most or all of your car expenses, you'll be able to get an investment tax credit! What is an investment tax credit? Very simply (and brushing aside a lot of the bull) an investment tax credit gives you a bottom line deduction from your taxes of approximately 10% of the cost of that car. Your accountant will do the paper work. So, assuming you bought a relatively cheap car, a nice economical Honda for $5,000 to use in connection with looking around for properties and managing the properties

*Limited to $2,000 per person, per year. Our example assumes a couple filing jointly.

purchased in 1979 you get $500 off you tax bill plus 17¢ per mile. If you drove 10,000 business miles, that's $1,700. But more about your car in a few pages.

So here it is, December 30 and you have generated these deductions: $10,000 repairs, $11,000 depreciation, $1,700 car expense, $500 tax credit and you have reduced the tax on your $25,000 regular job income to zero. If you had earned more than $25,000 you would have just bought a more expensive building or two or three more properties.

As you see, the acquisition of one small piece of real estate generated enough deductions to save you around $7,000 in taxes.

What was the secret? What was the formula? Acquire run down buildings, not vacant land, but income property with as little as possible of your own money into the deal. You'll get the same deductions even if you put your own money into the deal, but from an investment point of view, aside from tax considerations, the less money you have into a project the less you can lose and the less risk you have. For that reason I emphasize making no-money-down deals. These deals can usually be structured so you have no personal liability. As a result, if the project doesn't work out you can always walk away from the property and you have lost nothing except your credit rating.

Once you own property you will collect rental income. You will use rents to pay your loans and expenses and in a year or two all sorts of magical things will happen in terms of making tax free money. First, when a tenant moves out and you get another one, you're going to get from the new tenant a very big security deposit. The old landlord probably made the mistake of getting a deposit for what he called 'first and last months' rent. Thus, for example, he got $300 for the first and $300 for the last months' rent and that counted as taxable income to him. But, you put in your rental agreement that you'll give the tenant the first month free. Then you take an amount equal to the first and last months' rent plus $150 as a security deposit (in this case $750). Guess what? Any 'security deposit' you take in is tax free money. Why? Because it's not income you are collecting. At least as far as the IRS is concerned, you're going to have to return it some day!.

In the real world, will you ever have to return it? No! "someday" will never come! When that first tenant moves out and a new tenant moves in, the new tenant's security deposit will replace the deposit you have to return.

In other words, when 'Tenant 2' moves in many years from now, he'll be obliged to give you an even larger security deposit and you'll use that new deposit to pay off the $750 that's due to 'Tenant 1'. Result? All security deposits collected by you will, in effect, be tax free money.

One IRS agent, auditing a friend, took the very unreasonable position that for security deposits to be tax free money, the landlord had to keep them in a separate segregated trust account. Such Bullshit! But, if you want to be super conservative and meet the IRS's latest brainstorm, setting up a trust account really doesn't cramp your style much. All you have to do is put that money in a savings loan association at 6% interest, say, and keep it nicely segregated from your operating funds and play money. As a matter of course, the savings and loan will allow you to borrow against that money immediately. They'll give you the money right back at one point higher than they pay you. So, if you deposit it in the savings and loan at 6%, they'll lend you that money back indefinitely at essentially 1% a year. In the case of our $750 security deposit example, the net loan cost of $7.50 a year will be fully deductible, of course, so you get the use of $750 indefinitely as your play money. The interest income isn't taxable because it is held 'in trust' for tenant claims while you borrow and use it. The tax benefits of a property owner are just beginning for you now.

Let's go back to auto expenses. When you were a wage-slave you drove your car to and from work; you got no benefits and no deductions whatsoever. But now that you are in the business of owning and operating property, a certain large percentage of the use of your auto will be applicable to your business. The IRS makes it easy for you. It says take 17¢ per mile as a deduction. Once again, this is an arbitrary figure set by the IRS, just like the depreciation figure. Let's say that in the course of a year's time, you drive 20,000 miles in your car. A certain amount of that will be personal use. You have a social life and you drive over and pick up Suzy to go dancing. That is not business mileage. However, if it is reasonable to assume that you use your car 50% for business (which you should document in some way, either by keeping records in a dairy or however you want to do it) then you take 17¢ a mile or $1,700 as a deduction allowed off your other income. Now we assumed that you bought a Honda. Remember? That particular car at 45 miles per gallon is cheap to run and doesn't need any repairs. The cost of the gas and oil and very minor repairs will average 3¢ a mile. In our inflation-ridden world Honda's don't go down in value when you sell - their value usually goes up 20% per year. The real cost to you in running that car for a business is at most 3¢ x 10,000 miles or $300. The real cost doesn't make any difference to the IRS. The government says you can take $1,700 and of course you should take it. The rule as I understand it (and I always stand ready to be corrected) is that you get a deduction of 17¢ a mile on the first 15,000 miles regardless of the fact that your actual costs may have been far less and your car appreciated in value during the year. When you were a working stiff there was no way that you could deduct car expense as a business expense. Now you can legally deduct five times what you actually spent. *

Another good deduction is your telephone bill. Most of us get phone bills of $40 or $50 a month. Once into real estate or any small business you can deduct a reasonable percentage (shall we say half?) of your phone bill. Why? Because you've been calling people who might want to sell or trade their building. You've been calling tenants. You've been calling plumbers, suppliers and workmen all in connection with your business. Those are all deductible business calls. As a result, a reasonable portion of your phone bill is now also deductible for income tax purposes.

There are lots of other deductions such as depreciation and investment tax credits on that portion of your home furnishings set aside exclusively for your property management office. These deductions are limited only by your imagination and resourcefulness. As long as they come within the IRS definition of having been ordinary and necessary to the sort of business you are in, they are legal and you should take them. When you were a working stiff you had a shop in your basement. Suppose you wanted to buy a lathe or expensive wood working equipment to make yourself a desk or piece of furniture. You spent $5,000 on the wood working equipment - hammers, nails, drills, and that sort of thing, none of which was deductable because it was a hobby. Now it is because you use it to fix up your investment property. The cost of small tools is immediately deductible. If you were to buy a $5,000 Shopsmith drill press, lathe and hand saw, you could possibly borrow the entire purchase

*If you own an expensive American car, taking depreciation and actual expenses may be more tax advantageous than the mileage allowance.

price and have the loan payable over a long period of time. You'd get an immediate investment tax credit and a deduction for tax purposes that would save you several thousands in taxes.

You can even deduct the cost of some clothes. The IRS can get a little picky on this. You can't deduct the cost of a suit, tie, vest and white shirt. The rules say you can't deduct the cost of clothes you can wear outside the particular requirements of your profession or trade. Thus you still can't deduct the cost of a new suit you could wear to church on Sunday. However, if you bought a pair of studded bib overalls - which are very fashionable with the Disco set - for the specific purpose of working on your building, this clothing expense is (in my opinion and according to cases I've studied) another deductible expense. Then, of course, there's the typewriter, furniture and all the supplies you would need in the course of running your real estate business.

Can you deduct your groceries? Lunches? Certainly you can deduct cleaning supplies, soap, and what you feed prospective tenants and business contacts. I'll tell you how. At Christmastime, if it is your custom to give your tenants a bottle of wine, there is no reason why you can't deduct the cost of a case of wine as a business expense. If it is your custom to invite prospective tenants to your home for lunch to gain their goodwill before renting an apartment, there is no reason that drinks or food you serve at home (or pay for in a restaurant) can't be deductible. Certainly if you invite your handyman out to lunch or entertain a potential secretary, or a person who might be interested in renting your property, these outlays are all deductible business expenses.

How about a trip to Mexico? Unfortunately, if you fly to Puerta Vallarta with the idea of looking at property that you might buy, the IRS won't let you deduct the cost as a business expense. However, you do get the deduction if you go to a meeting of the California Apartment Owners Association, or a Bill Greene Tycoon Class that happens to be held in sunny Puerta Vallarta.* Many organizations hold conventions or educational seminars in resorty locales. With certain minor limitations, these travel expenses for 'education' are deductible.

Now let's assume you purchased another fourplex or even two fourplexes in the course of the following year. That shouldn't be too hard. You can acquire three properties in a year with ease. During my very active period

*Be sure to get on our mailing list for tax deductible junkets. I plan a series of tax avoidance seminars.

Once you own real estate, you can deduct many expenses to reduce your income tax, and the I.R.S. Vampires can't do a thing about it.

I did as many as three deals a <u>week.</u> Most of them required little or no money. Sometimes I was able to walk away from a closing with the proceeds of overfinancing. It was as easy as falling off a log. Every deal generated more and more tax losses till I had far more than I needed.

You'll note than even if you buy property on the very last day of the year, you still get the extra 20% first-year depreciation on personal property. In our example, that was a $4,000 bonus depreciation loss you took on carpets, drapes, furniture, and appliances. The $10,000 loss you generated by borrowing money for repairs or painting could have been done on the last day of the year. Also there is the investment tax credits on basement power tools or the car used in your business. All these tax benefits can be obtained by purchasing 'capital assets' up to the last day of the year. Straight line depreciation on the <u>structure itself</u> has to be allocated equally throughout the useful life of the property, so you get the <u>most</u> depreciation if the property is purchased on January 1st, and only 1/12th as much if you bought on December 1st. How to account for all this is explained in my chapter titled Getting Organized as a Tycoon, and in more detail in the Landlording book sold by us (by mail).

In my hypothetical example I presumed that your job-related income was $25,000 per year. You saw how easy it was to shelter that entire income from tax by merely acquiring one property. If you bought three more properties, assuming the same facts, you'd generate tax losses in excess of $74,000. Why bother? What can you do with excess or "overflow depreciation" that more than shelters all your current income? Simple! You can use the excess depreciation generated by real estate acquisitions to get a refund of all taxes you've paid in the past three years. Here's how: Let's suppose that in your first year you bought several small buildings to generate accounting "losses" of $75,000 more, for a total of $100,000.

If you earned $25,000 a year during the past three years, guess what? That $100,000 of losses can not only shelter your current year's income of $25,000, but can also be <u>carried back</u> three years. You don't pay any tax this year, and you also get back every cent you paid in income taxes for the past three years. Not only that, you get <u>interest</u> from the Federal Government along with your tax refund. The interest varies with the market rate, but is in the area of 6% to 9% per year. These are the current interest rates on refunds: July 1, 1975, through January 31, 1976 - 9% a year; February 1, 1976, through January 31, 1978 - 7% a year; Beginning February 1, 1978 - 6% a year.

245

So let's review the assumptions:

1. You earned about $25,000 this year and in each of the past three years.
2. On the average you paid a $10,000 Federal and State Income Tax in each of the past three years.
3. This year you acquired (with little or no investment) one or more older income properties that break even financially, but generate a total of $100,000 in overflow depreciation or "tax shelter."
4. You file your current year's tax return showing the $100,000 "loss."
5. On your tax return your $100,000 "loss" gets you a refund of all taxes paid during the past three years.

Result?

1. No tax due for the current year. The $10,000 that was withheld or prepaid is returned to you in full.
2. The $10,000 that was paid in income taxes last year comes back to you in the form of a U.S. Treasury check for $10,000 plus about $900 in interest.
3. The $10,000 you paid in taxes two years ago is also mailed to you in the form of another U.S. Treasury check for $10,000 plus $1,800 (two year's) interest.
4. The $10,000 you paid in taxes three years ago is refunded with about $2,700 in interest.

What you want is to plan and structure losses so they always just balance your income. In the beginning you'll need to take maximum allowable depreciation and create deductions that can carry back for three years. After a while, though, what you want is just enough losses to cancel out your income. That way, total earnings from your outside job and rents would just equal losses and you wouldn't waste depreciation you might need in the future. In other words, why take more than you need?

In my own case, because of the large number of properties I owned, I could (by taking shorter lives or accellerated depreciation) generate two or three times as much depreciation as I needed to shelter all my income. By taking less depreciation than what was legally allowed, I saved it up to shelter future profits. Accounting is not a science, it is an art. At first you'll need the help of a Certified Public Accountant. Later you'll develop all the required talents yourself. The art of filing a proper tax return lies in constructing reasonable depreciation schedules that will be honored by the IRS which, at the same time will, put you in a position of not having to

246

pay income taxes.

Everything I have been talking about so far is strictly legal tax avoidance. Some people would call it tax deferral. It's very different from tax evasion, which is illegal. You can go to jail for evasion if the blue meanies catch you. Let me give you an example of tax evasion: Assume that you collect $25,000 in fees, and you intentionally do not report it. If you really owe a tax on that money (because you don't have any tax shelters), and your lover or spouse gets very mad at you, that person could report you for the standard IRS 10% Blood Money Reward. For this money, the ex-lover might testify in court that you intentionally did not report $25,000 in income. With an informant's fee at stake, he/she may even amplify or lie for the IRS. That's the sort of thing you could go to jail for. That's tax evasion.

Avoidance is legal! Taking a 10-year life on a property, that the IRS feels you should have taken a 15-year life on is not tax evasion it's just a matter of differing opinion. You're not anywhere near the grey area of criminal prosecution. If you are audited the IRS likes to argue almost every aspect of your return. Once you become a large-scale property owner, expect to be audited almost every year. IRS agents will probably fiddle around with your depreciation schedules and suggest all kinds of inane and typically bureaucratic changes they want to make on your return. However the rules of the game are on your side. If you take straight line depreciation, for say, 10 years, and the IRS insists on a 15-year life, then you can take component depreciation. Component depreciation is where you set up a separate useful life for the roof, the windows, the floors, the pipes, etc. You can then get exactly the same total deductions as before.

If the IRS does get tough about your taking too short a life on property, you can always increase deductions dramatically by 'breaking up' property into its various components. For accounting purposes, you would get up on the roof and say, "This roof is already 10 years old and probably has only a 12-year life," so you take the value of that roof -- say $4,000 -- and break it down so that you take $2,000 (2-year life) depreciation on that. You can use this method with every window, stove and floorboard, carry it to any extreme and always come out with the desired result deduction-wise. As I mentioned, in your first year of operations, high deductions might be more significant because you want to generate enough depreciation losses to carry back three years in order to get that big refund. But, once you've got a substantial number of properties you will find that overflow depreciation will be so much that you can become very conservative and still have all the depreciation you need. Strangely enough, the IRS never fights when you use conservative figures. If the IRS says the life of the building is 20 years and you take a 30-year life they don't argue. But if they say it's 20 and you take 10, they may give you some static. When push comes to shove, if you really need that high depreciation and they do knock out the figures you chose, then threaten to use either component depreciation or accelerated depreciation to come out with the same result you had before.

In the example I just gave you'll have many other deductions too:

1) interest paid on money borrowed

2) real estate taxes

3) maintenance expenses.

The taxpayer in the real estate business is in a game rigged in his favor. If he knows the rules. In the course of being in this business a lot of other tax opportunities will come your way if you keep up with the latest gimmicks by reading books like this one, taking courses like mine and keeping up with all the current literature in the field. For instance, "The Wall Street Journal" has a 'Tax Tips' column appearing on its front page once a week. Read it! Apply it!

I'm assuming that in all the buildings you buy, rents and expenses are just about even. Thus for tax purposes it's the depreciation figures that loom important. This depreciation never catches up with you. Conventional wisdom goes something like this: You can shelter your outside (non-real estate) income with the real estate overflow depreciation. Your ordinary income from your job or outside earnings would have been taxed at ordinary income rates, but you sheltered all the income. Later on when you sell the property you must recapture the tax savings, but you do so at the (lower) capital gains rates. For instance, if after ten years you sell the property for what it cost ($100,000) and you had depreciated it to zero, you would have to pay a tax on the whole $100,000 received as capital gains. However, as I say, this is conventional wisdom. The $100,000 profit would be theoretically taxed at capital gains rates or half of your ordinary income tax rate. The IRS rules say that each year you take $10,000 in depreciation, your "basis" goes down by $10,000. So if you sell it in year one for $100,000 after taking $10,000 depreciation, you would have a $90,000 basis and a taxable capital gain profit of $10,000. If you sell it in year two after taking $20,000 in depreciation, you'd have a capital gain (profit) of $20,000. This is, of course, if you sell at the price you bought it at.

Most accountants will say that the net effect of investing in real estate is that "today's income escapes current taxation to be taxed later at capital gains rates." But I say you'll never have to pay any taxes during all your life because, like Vincent Astor, you should never sell your properties! Ever! You can pull money out by tax free refinancing. The IRS will allow you to go through a maneuver called 'trading up'. This is covered quite clearly by (for a refreshing change) Internal Revenue Code section 1031. For all practical purposes, this law tells you to find a new property and arrange for the sale of old property to close the same day. If you do the paper work right, there is no tax consequence whatsoever. I cover this in great detail in the chaper on Exchanges. But for now let me show you how it works: Let's assume that a few years ago you bought a fourplex for $100,000. You depreciated it to zero but it's still really worth $100,000. You now find a building that is worth $1,000,000 that requires a $100,000 downpayment. You arrange for the sale of your $100,000 building to be simultaneous with your purchase of the million dollar building. The $100,000 cash you get for your old building goes to the seller of the million dollar building as his downpayment. If you do it just that way there is no tax consequence to you.

Instead of starting depreciation at one million on the new building, you start at $900,000 because you carry over the used-up ($100,000) depreciation or basis from the old property into the new. In real life the figures would never be simple but I'm giving you this only as an example.

249

Let's recap. The original property bought for $100,000 you depreciated to zero so $100,000 depreciation was used up. When you buy that new million dollar building the depreciation that you took on the orginal property is taken off the price you pay for the new building. This is called a $100,000 reduction in basis. Your "basis" for depreciation starts at $900,000.

When you trade up you should try to trade up in value as dramatically as in this example. Let's look at what happens if you go from a $100,000 building to $1,000,000 building. From the $100,000 building you took $10,000 a year depreciation each year for ten years. At the end of the ten years, if you buy a million dollar building (without a dime out of your pocket) you begin to generate $90,000 a year depreciation, assuming a 10-year life on the trade up property. Can you see how trading up gives you new depreciation everytime you do it? The depreciation in the new deal can be many times more than what you had before. That's why any real estate investor who has been at the game for a while keeps trading up regularly.

Actually, the rules of the tax game as they now stand force you to trade up. If you don't trade up and your depreciation runs out, all those rents coming in become taxable income. A tycoon wants to shelter all his income all the time. Real estate is tax shelter that you can create for yourself.

Now I have given you the basics let's get a little more sophisticated and go into the subject of generating maximum deductions in real estate.

Suppose that one of your tenants puts an unsightly chip in the bath-tub. You have to spend $60 to replace that broken bathtub with a new one. Because it's a relatively small expense I'm quite sure the IRS, even if fully informed, would not make you capitalize the bathtub and depreciate it over six years at $10 per year. As picky and unreasonable as they are they'd probably allow you to write off the entire $60 in the year the broken bathtub was replaced. Likewise if in a later year the same thing happened to a commode or a toilet fixture, you could probably replace it and write it off immediately.

Bear in mind that if you were to do a major remodeling job all at once-- take out the fixtures, retile, put in new fixtures, and basically build a brand new $5,000 bathroom -- the IRS would say that's a capital improvement. Remodeling must be depreciated over the life of the new bathroom, which might be 20 years. Therefore, remember to get maximum deductions you want to expense the costs of improvements, that is, write it off immediatley as a repair. However, once you have all the losses you need you may want to drag out those deductions by capitalizing them. The IRS will never argue if you capitalize a repair but they will fight you if you are trying to expense something they think is a capital improvement.

The IRS does issue guidelines and there are books to help you decide what's a capital improvement and what's a repair. In those years you need deductions be sure to classify expenses as repairs, not capital improvements. Is there a choice? Let me give you one example: If you have a house with a four sided roof and you repair or replace all four sections at once, that's clearly a new roof, a capital improvement. If you put on a brand new roof which will last ten years you can write off only 1/10 each year. But, suppose only a quarter of it was leaking and you just got that quarter fixed and the roofing bill said clearly "Roof Repairs, $200." The IRS couldn't get you to capitalize that because you didn't get a whole new roof. You only took care of one section needing an emergency repair. Of course if it is an old roof the chances are that next season another section will leak and you can fix that up. It can then be expensed as another repair. If, in the third year you have another leak, you'll expense that. In the fourth year the same. The net result is that in four years you have a brand new roof but you've been able to expense it off right away instead of writing it off over ten years. Remember, if you want write-offs, do repairs and do them piece-meal, not as part of a general remodelling plan - - or at least not as part of any plan the IRS can ascertain.

Now let me introduce you to the concept of the tax lottery system. It works like this: The IRS does not audit everybody. It does not even audit all landlords. Often audits are aimed at one specific enforcement problem which the President has thought up in that particular year in order to get a few votes. For example, a directive may come down some year that property owners should get a rough treatment because it is thought that

they are expensing too many four-martini business lunches. The IRS
will pull your tax return to see if you wrote off a lot of lunches. That
year taxmen may not even look at your depreciation schedules because
they are only interested in one little area - how many martinis you drank.
The agent may say you should have charged off only $500 for lunches and
you charged off $1,100. The IRS wants to knock $600 off your expenses.
Most taxpayers don't argue because they don't want the agents delving into
every single accounting entry. As I told you, accounting is an art, not
a science and the IRS could take you to court over every single expense if
it wanted to be nasty. Since court lawyers and accountants are expensive
($50 - $100 per hour) even if you win and keep your $600 expenses, it
would probably result in a couple of thousand dollars thrown away in legal
costs. Not to mention fooling around for months and going to countless
meetings and conferences. Generally if you are audited, give in, settle
fast and keep expenses down. If possible keep the IRS agents out of your
hair. If you are argumentative they may start going over everything.
But remember, not everyone is audited. The IRS uses the lottery system.
If your name is not pulled and three years pass, you're home free. The
statute of limitations says that the IRS can question your return for
only three years after it's filed. However, if they suspect you of tax
evasion, they have up to seven years to investigate.

If you've been audited once for a particular year, they generally don't
come back at you for the same year. Even if during the first audit, they
just asked about one very narrow issue (such as the yacht you kept to
entertain your tenants.) If you gave in on the yacht maybe they will
let you keep your 10-year depreciation schedules.

Once you own real estate there are many gimmicks you can use that
are entirely legal. Let me give you one more: Suppose you have a teenage
kid who goes to high school. I'm not sure what teenage kids get as an
allowance these days, but let's say you give him $100 a month. If you give
your kid $100 a month for his albums, gasoline and baseball uniforms, of
course there is no deduction - - you don't get any tax benefit. So, why
not <u>hire</u> your kid instead of just giving him that money? Let him do
minor jobs around the property you own. Keep a record of what those

duties are: wash the windows, paint the walls, vacuum, clean the yard. Give him $100 a month for that. What can happen here? What if you had your own kids or three or four kids to whom you previously were giving money without getting any tax benefit. Suppose you now _pay_ those kids $750 a year? That $750 x 4 kids is now deductible to you as an expense! It's not taxable to the kid however, because people don't have to pay income taxes if they earn under $2,950 a year.

Here's another advantage to owning real estate: If you have a windfall in your non-real estate business (whatever that business may be) there are a few maneuvers to shelter that unexpected income. They are legitimate and at this point perfectly legal and ethical. Owning real estate makes it possible for you to shift income and losses to different years. Suppose you got a $5,000 bonus in December from your regular business. You hadn't planned on that, right? Now you need to generate a $5,000 loss if you want to avoid paying tax on that bonus. One thing you can do is pre-pay your real estate taxes, insurance premiums or any other expenses in connection with real estate. That way you generate a $5,000 loss when its needed. Another way to do the same thing is to pre-pay any legal or accounting fees. Or almost any expense for that matter. Of course if you don't happen to have the cash you can always borrow to pre-pay bills. Once you are a real estate owner, lenders realize that we do this sort of thing and are quite accommodating about making loans in December to be paid back the following year. As a result, you shouldn't have any difficulty shifting expenses (or income) back and forth between the years to keep your income tax at zero, regardless of unexpected factors.

A logical question at this point is, "Since you have now exposed all these loopholes to the unwashed masses, don't you think this in itself might cause Congress to clamp down and make it impossible to do in the future what you have done in the past?"

There is that risk of course, but if any logic or sanity exists in Washington (and I usually doubt there is) they must realize that housing and construction are two of the most vital sections of the economy, right up there with food production and distribution. Farmers get all sorts of subsidies and benefits to encourage them to work long hours at physically difficult and somewhat unpleasant tasks. Likewise, real estate has to get some special encouragement from government if money and effort is to flow into buildings and homes. There are negative factors involved with real estate (look at the chapter on problem tenants!), so there must be something to make it more attractive than Swiss bank accounts, gold, fine art or antiques. That 'something' exists in being left alone and being able to defer taxes. Without the benefits of overflow depreciation and trading up tax-free, you can be sure I'd walk away from my holdings tomorrow. I'd let the lending institutions take over my empire. The Government could have it all if they wanted it. If the rules were changed, money would flow out of real estate in a flood the likes of which haven't been seen since Noah's days. We'd follow England down the tubes -- creating the European situation where there is virtually no new construction except for inefficient public housing erected at government expense. Of course, 'government' expense is always taxpayer expense. Congress often enacts British socialistic legislation here almost exactly a decade after it proves to be unworkable in England. This indicates that there may be no logic or sanity in Washington.

The present system of no-government-meddling, plus tax breaks for real estate investors, works. Whole cities could be housed in the projects built by wealthy investors who backed ventures solely for their tax shelter features. The present system of a relatively free economy in real estate, works. It delivers reasonably priced dwellings, factories, warehouses, offices and stores to the people who use them.

The United States is the only country in the world with no housing problem. Housing here is abundant, with an existing housing stock supplying per person double the square footage of other developed countries. Our low costs for finished housing is a marvel to the world. In Denmark, Sweden, France and England there are ten year waiting lists for apartments. All but the most expensive housing is built wastefully by governments at substantial cost to the taxpayers. Homes or apartments are simply not available.

In the States the only problems exist in places like Manhattan where local governments have instituted high taxes or rent controls or both. In New York no new residential construction takes place unless it is super luxurious condos or public slums erected and maintained at enormous taxpayer expense. Some areas in New York look like Dresden, Germany after the bombings. The strangulation of private real estate in New York has made it the most unliveable city in the world and has played a large part in bankrupting the city. Even talk by politicians of the elimination of the tax shelter features from real estate will cause a rapid outflow of capital from this industry just as surely as presently existing tax incentives have caused wealthy people to invest in real estate tax shelters.

I feel that the unhealthy socialistic trends of the past fifty years are finally being reversed. The successful taxpayer revolt in California - led by property owners - reduced real estate taxes by two thirds. If that can be done nationally, you and I can spend less time working on loopholes, and more time being productive. With income taxes at a maximum of 20% I'd be more than happy to pay my share - wouldn't you?

Until then, lets play by the present rules, take advantage of the laws as they stand and pay no taxes at all - - legally.

SPECIAL NOTE

THIS CHAPTER IS REPEATED IN
BILL'S BOOK ON TAX AVOIDANCE

This new book, "Welcome to the Taxpayer's Revolt" should be published in late 1979. Price about $16. Get on Bill's mailing list (free) for an announcement of availability.

NOTES

1031 EXCHANGES
"Buying & Selling"

Knowing how to make a tax free real estate exchange is extremely important. I'm going to tell you what a tax free trade is, why you should trade, when you should trade, and how you should trade. As a result of this information, instead of selling property and paying up to 65% of your profits in Federal and State taxes, you will be able to make deals and save substantial amounts of money. This involves big money that would otherwise have been squandered in taxes. The net result of your mastering the technique of trading up will be to increase your net worth at tremendous speed. This will give you a fast, clear path to financial independence. With financial freedom you gain control over your own destiny.

What we are covering specifically is the use of Internal Revenue Tax Code: Section 1031 relating to tax free, or more accurately, tax deferred exchanges. After reading this you will be able to mastermind your own tax free trades without a lawyer or CPA at your side. In addition, you will understand exchanging better than a vast majority of lawyers, accountants, and real estate brokers.

First of all, let's clear up the biggest misunderstanding concerning trades of real property. Most people believe if you own a small property, and you want to trade up to a bigger property, you have to find someone with a big property who is willing to take your smaller property in trade. Nothing could be further from the truth. Here is what really happens:

You want to trade up from a single family home you own (as a rental unit) to a bigger property, say a twenty-unit apartment building. The owner of those twenty units doesn't want your single family house because it is smaller. He wants to trade up himself. In the real world the owner of the larger piece of property you want almost always wishes to trade up himself. He will seldom want to sell for cash, and will rarely, if ever, want to trade down.

"But," you may say, "You are not talking about trading after all, are you? Because I always thought that when you traded you gave something other than cash and you got something other than cash in return from the person you traded with." But here is where I will clarify a common misconception about real estate trading. Exchanges or trades under Section 1031 of the IRS Code are never really trades or exchanges of property A for property B. Section 1031 - tax free exchanges - are simply paper exchanges done solely for tax purposes. 1031 exchanges are a completely legal IRS approved way of legally avoiding taxes when you sell property at a profit and immediately invest in other property. What this 1031 exchange really is, is a way to "sell" your property without paying any capital gains tax, any ordinary income tax, or any tax at all!

There are three main requirements for such tax free exchanges. The fourth requirement (an immediate reinvestment of proceeds) has some flexibility. First, there must be like property sold and like property acquired. But "like" property for the IRS has a very special meaning I will explain later. Second, the property you are buying must have a bigger price tag than the property you are selling. Third, the property you are buying must have a bigger mortgage than the property you are selling. And fourth, this is where some flexibility comes in. There should be a simultaneous closing of the two deals. But, if you structure the "trade" carefully you can sell now and reinvest several months or even several years later.

The "trading" is all done on paper. There is no real trade. There is just an elaborate fiction to avoid taxes. The Section 1031 deal is an artificial method of selling and buying that would never exist but for the Tax Code. It's a way that you and I can "sell" property by meeting requirements set forth by a certain very important federal law known as Section 1031 of the Internal Revenue Code.

If you have ever looked up anything in the Tax Code, you know the Code is indeed Code. It is difficult to understand, uses obscure language, and is almost impossible to read. But in contrast to most other sections, 1031 is relatively clear and is only one paragraph long. It says:

"No gain or loss shall be recognized if property held for productive use in trade or business or for investment is exchanged solely for property of a like kind to be held either for productive use in trade or business or for investment." Specifically excluded from this section is stock in trade, property held primarily for sale, stocks, bonds, notes, claims against other people, certificates of trust, or other securities.

To have your deal meet the code requirements it is necessary to previously establish an intent that the property you own and the properties you are acquiring are for investment, not for a quick resale. Then, all you have to do is adhere to the three main requirements for a 1031 exchange. As I said:

It must be a like for like exchange.

The new property must have a bigger price tag.

The new property must have a bigger mortgage.

The fact that your intent in doing a 1031 exchange is solely to avoid taxes cannot be held against you and will not invalidate the tax free status of your trade. Actually, you could broadcast on national network and place an ad in the New York Times saying that your whole, exclusive, and only purpose in doing a section 1031 exchange was to avoid taxes. And, if the IRS heard that announcement and knew your intention, your exchange would still be tax free - as long as you followed the exact provisions of section 1031. Under existing USA tax laws, almost any other tax saving business transaction could be disregarded by the IRS if tax avoidance was your main motivation.

The only reason for doing a 1031 exchange is to take advantage of a legally approved method of avoiding taxes. This section is one of the few of the tax code that have been interpreted in favor of the taxpayer in many court cases. For perhaps the first time in your "tax planning" you do not have to go through elaborate shenanigans to manufacture "evidence" to convince the IRS that what you did was a bona-fide business transaction without tax avoidance motives. It is sufficient that your exchange was done for no other purpose than beating the IRS out of taxes.

Normally in other areas of tax law, if you arrange almost any transaction for the purpose of avoiding taxes, you will achieve the opposite result. The IRS will say "any transaction you did just for tax benefits is not bona-fide and we will tax you anyway." But 1031 is different. Just follow the three rules, like for like, bigger price, bigger mortgage, and you are home free, free of taxes that is. You will notice 1031 does not apply only to real estate. Before I elaborate on how to use it in real estate let's take some other examples. First, gold coins and foreign money; second, antique cars. Last, we'll look at real estate.

Suppose in your opinion, Austrian Corona gold coins will go up in value faster than South African Kruger Rand gold coins. You have a thousand dollars worth of Rands, ten coins that you bought for $100@. You swap them for a thousand dollars worth of Coronas, also ten coins. In a few days your prediction comes true, and the Coronas are in fact worth 20% more than the Rands. By trading, you accomplished what amounts to a tax free sale of your Kruger Rands. You acquired 10 Austrian Coronas with 10 Rands. Had you paid a capital gains tax on the sale of your Rands, you would only have been able to buy 5 Coronas. Now that the Rands went up by say 20%, you trade back for 12 Rands. If you had paid taxes you would be down to 5.5 Rands from the 10 you started with. Now, let's say you own Swiss francs today but you feel that German marks will go up at a faster rate. You can exchange your Swiss francs for German marks, tax free.

If what you did was a sale instead of an exchange – what would your tax situation look like? Say you bought marks for $10,000. They now have a market value of $20,000. If you sold them for dollars you would have a $10,000 gain and a tax to pay of around 50% of that $10,000 gain. You would lose $5,000 of your capital and would only be able to spend $15,000 on German marks. So by trading your Swiss francs for German marks you keep your profits and do not have to pay any tax! In effect, you have used your entire $20,000 worth of your Swiss francs to get $20,000 worth of German marks. If the marks go up relative to the francs (which is what you thought they would do), you can trade back and forth indefinitely, and thereby keep increasing your wealth, at least in dollar terms. In real terms, all paper money is depreciating.

Where do you get the money to live on in the meantime? You could borrow dollars against your foreign money - tax free!

Next, assume you had an antique 1910 Buick. Why would you want to do a tax free exchange? Because you would avoid the capital gains tax that would otherwise be due if you merely sold the car at a big profit, took the money and then went out to buy another car. So you can do a three way exchange of the car you own for the one you want to buy - and thus avoid any taxes. But like in real estate, the owner of what you want probably doesn't want what you have to trade - so a three-way deal is needed. Let's see how a three-way trade works in real estate.

REAL ESTATE TRADES

Now, you will recall that the property eligible for a tax free exchange had to be property held for productive use in a trade or business or for investment and could not be property held primarily for sale. How do you make sure that the IRS cannot establish that you were holding the property, the gold coins, foreign money, antique cars or real estate, for sale?

At the outset you should form the required intention with regard to every piece of property that you ever buy or ever consider buying. Your intention must be that you are buying for the long term, that is, you are buying "it" for a long term investment. You have no intention of selling. You will not sell. I repeat, you will not ever sell that property. That must be your intention if you want to own property that qualifies for trading.

It is necessary and essential that at the time you buy the property you write everyone who might possibly be interested in your intentions, and also everyone who isn't interested, that your intention with regard to that specific piece of property is to never sell it! Got that??? Keep carbon copies of those letters. You tell everyone in sight and you even write on your offer form, "this property is being purchased for investment and not for resale." Nobody cares except the IRS and it is they you have to convince that any trading property you own was bought for investment, not stock in trade. It is going to be considered stock in trade if you are willing to sell it at a profit the minute a good offer materializes.

You might consider creating plenty of evidence of your investment inten- tions by asking a broker you know to write you a letter asking you if your property is for sale. Then you can reply in the most strongly imaginable terms that you are outraged that they would consider offering you mere money for your property. Rant and rave a little: "I would never consider selling my property to you or to anyone else! I bought this for investment purposes and I am not of a mind to sell that property just because somebody offers me a quick profit." Be irate. Be firm!

With five or six file copies of similar answers to inquiries about a possible sale, the IRS will be hard put to classify that property as dealer property because, by their definition "dealer property" is property which you bought with the intention of reselling to someone else, not as a long term investment. So, to summarize, it is very important to form the proper intention at the time you buy any property that you are going to hold that property as a long term investment and you are not going to sell it - unless your circumstances change drastically. You are going to buy that property for investment.

Another reason that is acceptable to the IRS is that you bought the property for the production of income and not for resale. As another example, let us say you bought a building for the purpose of manufacturing rubber tires. You buy a tire factory with the intention of manufacturing tires, not to resell the building at a profit. Now, of course, use in trade or business may be interpreted another way. Your trade or business could and should be owning and operating warehouses or other income property such as apartment buildings or stores. But the important thing is that if the IRS suspects that you were a (shudder) speculator and just bought to resell, they will hit you with an ordinary income tax and won't let you do a tax free exchange. The important thing is to, at every stage of your operations, make it very clear to everyone that you are not in the business of buying property to sell at a profit.

Why? Well, to have that intention - to buy property with the intention of selling it at a profit - and then to reinvest the money would be stupid. These days ordinary income is taxed at approximately 30% by the Feds.* California State tax adds another 15%. For example if you bought property with the intention of selling it for a quick buck, then you would also have the intention of giving 45% of your profits away to Uncle Sam and your State. (You can adjust the figure to meet your state tax.) That would be a pretty stupid intention when the law as expressed in 1031 gives you the opportunity to dispose of your property in a tax free exchange.

The only motive for doing a 1031 exchange is tax savings, and as

*The effective tax rate was reduced from 50% to 30% for transactions after November 1978.

262

Why is the I.R.S. like the Catholic Church ?

Your lips tell me "NO-NO" BUT THERE'S "YES-YES" IN your eyes!

Both find "sin" in what you were THINKING.
not in what you DID.

SECTION 1031 EXCHANGES ARE ONE OF THE FEW EXCEPTIONS
TO THE GENERAL RULE THAT A TRANSACTION ENTERED INTO
PRIMARILY FOR TAX AVOIDANCE REASONS IS DECLARED VOID
BY THE I.R.S.

I've said that is considerable. There is really no other motive. Naturally it would be much easier, even if you wanted to acquire other property to merely sell your first property, to take that money and buy property number 2, the bigger and better property, because then you wouldn't have to worry about doing all the paperwork that is required for a 1031 exchange. But, with a big potential tax bite involved, obviously it is better to take the time and take the effort to do a 1031 exchange rather than to merely sell your property, take the proceeds, and invest it in other properties. Why? Because if you do a sale and repurchase the Federal and State governments could take as much as 65% of your profits from the sale!

Now you want to know, when should I exchange? When should I start trying to arrange an exchange under section 1031? The answer is: Any time you find a bigger and better property than the one that you own and it's for sale at a fair price, consider arranging a 1031 exchange.

I have heard some so-called authorities say that you start looking for an exchange only when your depreciation runs out. That may be anywhere from 10 to 15 years after you have acquired the property. Don't tell the IRS - but you should be ready to exchange one-day after you get the property, just as long as the new deal is better than the one you're getting out of. The prospective trade property must have the magic three factors - 1. like for like 2. bigger price tag 3. bigger loan.

Don't wait until depreciation runs out. If you want to be a Tycoon always keep your eyes open for good real estate deals. Be prepared to use the equity in property that you already own as the down payment on property you hope to acquire. Are there any alternatives to a 1031 exchange that you should consider? Of course there are.

If it's possible to make a No Money Down Deal for the place you are acquiring and not dispose of the place you already own, then hold on to good investment property. If you are able to acquire property number two without trading for a low down payment that you have or can borrow try to hold on to it. Remember one of the greatest real estate fortunes of all time - that of Vincent Astor; was built on the motto "Never sell the land" if you don't have to. And he formed that intention even before the Tax Code made it even more necessary.

With that, I will show you how a classic "1031" trade works. In the real world, every trade involves at least three people. There are never just two people because in the real world there has to be a cash buyer, that is someone who comes into the deal with money and no property to trade. At the other, or upper, end of the trade, there is usually someone who is selling real estate for cash. "He" may be a tax free entity like a pension fund, foundation or charity. Or he is cashing in his chips and willing to pay the tax on the sale. More than likely the seller is going to arrange for his own trade up. Getting all these characters together might seem like a tall order, but we are going to see what happens in a typical trade deal - the 1031 exchange that goes on every day between sophisticated large-scale real estate investors - the likes of which you will be within the next 3 years.

Let's dissect a typical simple tax free exchange. There are three characters in our drama. We will call you Mr. Dumpy because many years ago you bought "El Dumpo," a little house in the Oakland ghetto, cost: $2,000. Today it is worth $10,000. It brings you $100 per month in rent. You have a potential $8,000 profit or capital gain on the house. If you sold it outright, you would have to pay a capital gain tax on the $8,000 profit you would make. Depending on your tax bracket, that could be up to $4,000 or more.

You have been looking around at various real estate deals and you've found Mr. Classy who owns a $100,000 apartment house of 4 units in a nice section of Reno, Nevada. He has it up for sale and will take $100,000. Step number one is for you to go to Mr. Classy to negotiate price. We will assume that Mr. Classy agrees to sell you his 4-plex for the sum of $100,000 payable in cash, within 90 days.

But, you write on your offer to Mr. Classy, after you have put in all of the standard other terms you write: "This acquisition subject to buyer being able to find a buyer for 23 El Dumpo Lane, Oakland, at a price of $10,000 or better and structuring this deal as a tax free exchange under section 1031 IRC." Now, Mr. Classy, if he is not a sophisticated investor, will want to know why you put that sentence in this contract. And then you are going to show him this chapter. You show him that if you are able to close the sale of your house and buy Mr. Classy's house on the same day, and you do all the paper work just right, then you will not have to pay any tax on the sale

Mr. Classy, upon learning about exchanges will think trading is so clever that he will want to do a simultaneous trade of his property so that he can get the same benefits. Actually, in the real world, Mr. Classy and people like him, have already arranged for an exchange just like you are doing except that Mr. Classy is probably buying a million dollar property. The owner of the million dollar property is in turn probably arranging to trade into a 2 million dollar property. And that seller of the 2 million dollar property is moving up to a ten million dollar shopping center and so on up the line.

In the real world, when you close your first trade you may well find that not only your trade, but also 6 or 7 or 8 other trades all in the same chain must close simultaneously with your deal. Now that, of course, involves a lot of fancy footwork. And if you have ever been in any real estate deals at all, you know that even simple deals seldom close on time. So you can just imagine the postponements that will occur with a large number of closings all having to be done on the same day. Some people have conflicting appointments and medical problems. There are spouses who have to be brought in to sign papers, some may be involved in divorce proceedings. It should be obvious that in your typical exchange there are normally all kinds of special problems. Exchanges rarely, if ever, close on the day scheduled.

That is one reason why real estate brokers do not like trades. When you mention trading to a typical real estate broker, they will do all they can to discourage it. They will lie and tell you that the tax saving really is not significant. They will advise "just sell your property and forget about the fancy complicated trading business". But what these brokers are really saying is that they don't want their commission delayed. Since brokers don't like their commissions to be postponed and they like a deal to close as quickly as it can, that is the real reason they will discourage you from doing a tax free exchange. Whether you pay zero tax or a half million capital gains tax is of little concern to a real estate broker. Their commission is the same regardless of your tax liability. Obviously the broker would rather have you do a simple deal and pay a big income tax rather than do what from their point of view is a complicated deal just to save you a great amount of money in taxes. Moral: Don't let anyone talk you out of it. It is your money, your future, and your freedom!

Let's get back to our example. Your first trade will be very simple and very easy to understand. Your first step as an exchanger was to go out and find a bigger property that you wanted to exchange into.

Step number two is to *find a cash buyer for your property*. Now that doesn't mean the cash buyer has to have all cash but he has to be able to raise a down payment plus financing so that, at the close, he will come up with a total of $10,000 in cash to be able to cash out Mr. Classy.

Now what do I mean by "cash out" Mr. Classy? Well, look at Mr. Classy's motivation for a minute. He doesn't really want your little dumpy house. If anything, he wants a much bigger and better apartment building than the one he is selling. But for the moment, assume that Classy just wants to cash out. In real life you will find that cashing out is often the motiviation of the person with the bigger property. He may want to cash in his chips and retire, or maybe it is an estate sale. But seldom, if ever, does the owner of a bigger property want to trade down into a little dump.

I won't say it never happens but I have just never seen a "trade down" and I have been involved in a hundred or more trades. As I say, I've never once seen the owner of a bigger property who wants to trade down into a littler one. The only time something like that happens is with residences where parents formerly had a large family. The kids went off to school or got married. Now they want a smaller house. When we are talking about residences or owner occupied homes, a whole different set of trading rules apply and we will cover those later. But the point is we are here learning about exchanging <u>investment</u> or <u>income</u> property. It could be vacant land, held for investment, farms or factories but not homes or principal residences.

Getting back to our story of Mr. Classy and Mr. Dumpy and Mr. Cash, Mr. Classy wants to cash out by selling you his four-plex. Mr. Cash wants to buy El Dumpo. You are Mr. Dumpy and you won't sell your property to Mr. Cash just outright because if you did you would have to pay a substantial amount of capital gains tax. So here is what you do. This is how you arrange your exchange:

You go to your favorite escrow company. You tell them that you want them to arrange a tax free 3-way exchange under section 1031 of the Internal Revenue Code. Give them the prices, names and addresses involved and they will do all the paperwork. As always it is your responsibility to make sure that they don't foul up. So you know how to check on them, this is what the title company should do. Prior to the day set for closing, they should ask you for a deed to El Dumpo. This deed should transfer title to El Dumpo to Mr. Classy. Then they will get a signed deed from Mr. Classy covering El Dumpo, transferring title to Mr. Cash. They will also need a deed from Mr. Classy for his big apartment building transferring title to you, Mr. Dumpy.

When the smoke clears on the day of the closing this is what happens. Mr. Classy technically (and always technically) "buys" El Dumpo, but it is done with the understanding that he will simultaneously sell it, or deed it, to Mr. Cash. Mr. Cash will deposit in escrow $10,000 - part of it may be coming from a mortgage and part of it is his own money - but in any event, $10,000 will be deposited with the title company and that $10,000 will be handed to Mr. Classy in exchange for his deed to the apartment building and the deed to El Dumpo. Now, Mr. Classy has to get one other thing and that's $90,000 so that his total receipts for the day will be $100,000.

Where does he get the $90,000 from? Well, you, Mr. Dumpy, have arranged for a $90,000 loan in connection with buying Mr. Classy's apartment house. Perhaps you got $80,000 from a savings and loan and $10,000 from your mother in law or a hard money lender, or even $10,000 from Mr. Classy himself who carried back a second. In any event, Mr. Classy now has the $100,000 he wanted in the first place. Mr. Classy walks away from the deal with money. He does not own El Dumpo. That has been sold out of the trade to Mr. Cash. Chances are, in the real world, Mr. Classy will have arranged a trade up and his $100,000 will be used as the down payment on a still larger property, but that is no concern of yours.

To summarize, Dumpy, that's you, ends up with title to Classy's $100,000 4-plex. Mr. Cash ends up with the title to, and ownership of, the $10,000 El Dumpo. Mr. Classy walks away with a total of $100,000 in cash or paper he's carried back. As mentioned, more than likely he's arranged his own trade to close the same day. Classy will probably "trade-up" and buy an even bigger and better property, perhaps an 8-plex or 16 units.

You saw how, for an instant, Mr. Classy did in fact own El Dumpo. He

A THREE WAY TAX FREE TRADE

① MR. DUMPY OWNS 'EL DUMPO'   MR. CLASSY OWNS THE CLASSY APTS.   MR. CASH HAS $10,000   BANKER HAS $90,000 CASH.

② $100,000   THE BANK PUTS 90,000 IN THE POT. MR. CASH PUTS 10,000 IN THE POT.

③ MR. DUMPY DEEDS EL DUMPO TO MR. CLASSY

④

MR. CLASSY DEEDS EL DUMPO TO MR. CASH. AT THE SAME TIME HE DEEDS
THE CLASSY APTS. TO MR. DUMPY

⑤

MR. CASH OWNS EL DUMPO   MR. DUMPY OWNS CLASSY APTS.   MR. CLASSY WALKS
AWAY WITH $100,000

THE BANK KEEPS AN
IOU FOR $90,000

This is what the I.R.S. gets in a 1031 Exchange   !

(THE SHAFT)

sold it immediately, to Mr. Cash. Now it is very important that in an exchange the person with the big property takes title to the property at the bottom end of the trade. There are no tax consequences to Mr. Classy for having bought and simultaneously sold the dump. He bought it for $10,000 and he sold it for $10,000. Whether he was a dealer or not is irrevelant because there was no profit. He bought and sold at the same price.

You, Mr. Dumpy, were the owner of El Dumpo and you now have achieved your objective, which was to use your entire $10,000 equity in that house (assuming there was no mortgage) as if it was cash, as a down payment to buy the 4-plex, the bigger building you wanted to go into. You had a $10,000 property free and clear and you used that property, just as if it were cash, to make the down payment on the bigger property you are going to move into. If you had not done it as an exchange there would have been a capital gains tax of up to $4,000 on the profit resulting from a cash sale of the dump. But no tax at all was due because you did a 1031 exchange. It's really quite simple, isn't it?

Now that you understand the concept, let's talk in detail about the requirements of a 1031 exchange. First of all, there must be "like property for like property". What does the IRS mean by that? Does it mean you can only trade a 4-plex for another apartment building? Not at all. You could have a single family rental home (not your principal residence) that was worth half a million and you could trade it for an apartment building of 20 units that was also worth any amount more than half a million.

You can trade ANY sort of real estate that is held for investment purposes for any other sort of real estate that is held for investment purposes. A farm for a store. Store for office buildings. Offices for land. Land for homes. Don't let anyone tell you that you can't trade a farm for an apartment building, or an apartment building for a shopping center. Shops can be traded for homes or homes for farms; apartments for vacant land - all of that is like kind property, just so long as it is held for investment purposes OR for the production of income OR for use in your trade or business.

What is not like for like? Assume you bought vacant land, created a sub-division and then you built 20 homes on it. If you had advertised those 20 homes for sale to whoever came along, then the IRS would say that these homes were your inventory. It would be just like a jeweler's inventory of diamonds. If he made a profit on jewels he'd have to pay ordinary income tax on his profit. More importantly, because it was stock in trade, he could not TRADE that property tax-free at all. Therefore, you cannot trade so-called "dealer property" for investment property.

Is there any other kind of un-like property that you might get in trouble with? Certainly there is. Your primary residence is governed by a different set of rules. You cannot trade your primary residence for an apartment building or for another house which you are not going to move into. How can you get around that rule?

Is there a way to trade your primary residence for income property? Well, that's very simple. All you do is move out of your primary residence and rent it out. Once it has been rented out for a reasonable period of time (at least six months) it is no longer your primary residence. It has been trans-formed into income property. You can then trade it for other income prop-erty. But a residence can be sold for cash tax free and need not be traded, under a different tax rule. Using that option you'd have up to 18 months to reinvest cash received from the sale of a residence into a more costly residence.

What's the next requirement for a tax-free exchange? The first was 'like for like'. The second one is 'bigger price'. The place that you are trading up to has to have a higher price tag than the place you're getting out of.

Supposing in our example you own a $10,000 dump and you are going to trade but you're going to wind up with a $9,000 dump plus $1,000 cash. That would be called 'trading down' and in that case you would realize $1,000 tax-able cash. That $1,000 cash would be taxable to you, either as ordinary in-come or capital gain. Had you traded for an $10,000 deal you could have worked things out so that there was no tax. The whole purpose of making an exchange in the first place is to avoid any tax.

To review, the place that you are trading into should have a bigger price tag, and common sense should require that it's a bigger and better place than the one you are disposing of. Naturally the place you're trading into (not a tax requirement, but is just common sense) should be a better VALUE than the place you're getting out of. Obviously if you think you are getting less than fair market value for the place you are getting rid of and you are paying over market value for the place you are getting into, then I can think of no reason to do an exchange. What would the purpose be? Besides tax benefits, always look at basic economics before you exchange or before you do any deal for that matter. After the exchange is over, you should make more money. You should be getting more cash flow. Cash flow as you remember is the net money left over after you pay mortgages, expenses and real estate taxes. If you would have more cash flow from staying in the old property than from the one you're buying, stop and think it over. The improved cash flow doesn't have to be immediate but you certainly should have the prospect of making more money (after taxes) out of the new deal than the one you're getting out of.

The final requirement of a tax-free exchange is that the place you're getting into should have a bigger loan on it than the loan on the place you are selling. That's pretty straight forward. In the case of our example, El Dumpo had an $8,000 loan against it. But the place you're getting into is going to have a $90,000 loan against it. No problem there.

What happens if the loan on the new place, for some reason, is smaller? Then you have to take the smaller loan on the new place and subtract it from the larger loan. The net "loan relief" figure that you get constitutes taxable income to you. How do you avoid that problem? You arrange things so that the place you are going to buy has a bigger loan than the place you are selling. You can do it by refinancing the old place before you trade. Simple!

Can you do an exchange like for like, bigger price and bigger loan and on the day of the closing take out a lot of cash? The answer is no. If you do that, there will be tax consequences. You always have to arrange your affairs so that you do not take out any cash on the day of the exchange. There are plenty of other ways to get cash out of an exchange.

You can refinance the old property and take out cash before the deal closes. Remember, when you refinance property you already own, any money you borrow is tax-free money. The fact that you trade up later, as long as you follow the rules (like for like, bigger price, bigger loan) doesn't result in the money you got in an earlier "refi" becoming taxable.

What if you do not refinance? In a proposed trade you meet the three

274

requirements. Like for like, bigger price, bigger loan. You close the deal and trade up into the new building. Assume for the moment you had a very big equity in your original property, so the loan on the new property is less than 80% of the value. For example, you had a $50,000 free and clear duplex and you are using that equity as the down payment on a $100,000 free and clear 4-plex. You would have a $50,000 equity in the new 4-plex after the deal closed. The way you would get tax-free cash out of that deal is to wait a respectable amount of time (30 days anyway) to refinance.

After the deal closed, then you'd arrange to refinance the new property with an 80% or an $80,000 loan, thereby raising $30,000 additional tax-free cash. The IRS rule on the subject is that the refinancing of the place you end up with cannot have been arranged prior to the exchange date. So, even if it is your intention to refi, you should not tell anyone your intention nor arrange refinancing until after you have taken the title. Don't send in any loan applications. Don't start that until after you close the deal or the IRS might try to tax the refinancing proceeds. The same rule would apply to refinancing the place you are about to get rid of in an exchange. That should be done on a date prior to the date of any of your negotiating or signing papers with the seller of the big property. The IRS rule is, if you take money out of a trade as part of the trade, that money will be taxable.

Refinancing negotiated as part of an exchange can give rise to tax consequences. I will not go into the formula of how it's taxed because I advocate structuring every deal so you don't have to pay any tax at all. You can do that by simply exchanging like for like, paying a bigger price and taking over a bigger loan. If there is no loan on either property that's OK because you can always add cash to close a trade-up without tax consequences to yourself.

Suppose that the only property you have is a single family residence and you want to do the equivalent of a section 1031 exchange getting yourself a bigger and better residence. Actually, that's covered by a different section of the Internal Revenue Code, Section 1034. That section provides you do not have to go through the rigamorole of a simultaneous trade and transfer of title. These complexities are eliminated. All you have to do is sell your residence. Then you have 18 months to take that money and find another house. The same three rules apply. But with Section 1034, like for like means when you sell a primary residence you must buy another primary residence. The new place has to have a bigger price but the loan amounts are irrelevant with residences. As a result, you can come out of the sale of a residence and acquisition of a new one with a lot of cash.

Let's see how it works: Suppose you own a $100,000 house free and clear. You bought it cheap 30 years ago. You now sell your home for $100,000. Now you've got $100,000 cash. Next, within 18 months, you buy a $101,000 house with a $10,000 cash down payment. Assuming a $10,000 down payment on a $101,000 house, that leaves you with $91,000 cash, tax-free, to use for speculating in real estate, or whatever you want to do with it. So you see, section 1034 is actually considerably more liberal than section 1031 because you don't have to do any same-day close and you can pick up a lot of cash by heavily mortgaging your new home. You can sell, have use of the money while you take 18 months to look around for a new place. It's 24 months if you build a new home. The 24 months from the sale date applies to the date when you actually physically move into a new property, not when you pay for it. You have to be physically residing in a newly built place 24 months from the time you sell the old place. With new construction you can also move into the new place 24 months before you sell the old one and get the same benefits. If you're over 55, the first $100,000 in capital gain on a residence is tax free, even if you don't purchase another house.

If you want to trade from an expensive residence into income property, you have to move out of the residence, rent it, or at least try to rent it, thereby, converting it to income, or investment property. Then, of course, you can do a 1031 exchange by arranging simultaneous closes of escrow . . . just as we did in our example with Mr. Cash, Mr. Dumpy and Mr. Classy.

Is there any disadvantage to exchanging? Yes. It's a very minor disadvantage. It results from the rule that you MUST carry forward the depreciated basis of your old property into your new property. Now, that was a big mouthful of words. Let me explain how the accounting works.

In our example, to keep the math simple, assume that the $10,000 dump you bought was on land of little or no value. You bought it ten years ago for $10,000 and over the years, since it was run down rental property, you depreciated it down to zero. So, although your original cost was $10,000 your basis (that's what the IRS people use to describe the net figure you get when you take cost less depreciation over the years) was zero. As you remember, if you bought something for $10,000, depreciated it down to zero, and then sold it for $10,000 you would, for tax purposes, have a $10,000 profit. This is the tax consequence even though your actual profit, since you bought and sold at the same price, was zero. Why would you have a $10,000 "profit"? Because the IRS let you use that depreciation - let's say for ten years, $1,000 a year - to shelter your outside or regular income. They do not let you get away with sheltering your ordinary income for 10 years and then sell the property and pay no tax at all. No, they make you recover that depreciation when you sell, giving rise to the accountants' saying "this year's depreciation is a future year's taxable capital gain."

So, you had a $10,000 property. You depreciated it down to zero. Now you're going to buy a $100,000 property. In an exchange you must now adjust the basis of the new property by taking the depreciation that you have already taken on El Dumpo and carrying it forward into the price of the Classy apartments. Now it is really pretty easy to do because in our example you're using that fully depreciated $10,000 property as a down payment, just as if it were $10,000 cash on the new property for $100,000.

Since you're fully depreciated that $10,000 property what you do is treat the new $100,000 property as if you had already depreciated $10,000 of it. You acquired the $100,000 property in an exchange. You used your fully depreciated $10,000 property as your trade in. Assuming you have a ten year useful life expectancy on the new place, you start with a tax basis on the new property of only $90,000. You do not get to take depreciation on the full $100,000 price because you are carrying forward the used up depreciation. But now you deduct from the depreciable basis of the new property the $10,000 depreciation you already used up on the trade in. As a result you only get $9,000 a year depreciation on the Classy apartments instead of $10,000 per year depreciation.

I hope that teaches you the principle of the "carry forward of basis." With multiple properties and the various complicated deals we go into these days the actual accounting can get a little hairy. But now that you know the principle, you can probably figure out your carry forward basis on a simple deal. On your tax return I'd advise you to get a C.P.A. to look your figures over!

In most trades you will be getting a lot more in depreciation deductions after the trade than you were getting before the trade. If the price of the property you are getting into is a lot more than the price of the property you are getting out of, you'll always have plenty of over-flow depreciation. Let me explain how that works.

If you had a $10,000 property, assuming your depreciation hadn't run out and it was being depreciated on a 10 year life, you were getting a $1,000 a year depreciation allowance. But if you go to a $100,000 property, even if the $10,000 property was fully depreciated, you would get $9,000 a year annual depreciation allowable out of the new property. That means you're exchanging a zero or $1,000 a year depreciation allowance for a $9,000 depreciation allowance. So obviously one advantage of trading up is that you can, without laying out any cash, increase your depreciation deductions drastically. If you own a $10,000 building that had a 10 year life and you were in your 9th year one of the classic reasons for looking for a trade is to generate new depreciation when your old depreciation schedule is about to run out. You can shelter all your outside salary or professional income with depreciation as more fully explained in "Pay No Taxes Ever Again."

Another reason for trading up is to take your profits out of old deals, tax free, acquire new larger properties and then raise more cash by re-financing the new property after the close of escrow. You don't pay any ordinary income tax or capital gains taxes when you exchange, and of course borrowed money is never taxable.

You can also use a trade to get out of 3 or 4 small slummy properties into one bigger property. You can consolidate small holdings by trading up into one big project. Just arrange for our Mr. Classy to take title, only for a second, to your three, four, six or ten dumps. You can get out of slumlording; sell the whole mess at a stroke and move into "Pride of Owner-ship" deals. Of course you have to pre-arrange for the sale of your dumps to Mr. Cash buyers. In this way you can exchange a lot of little scattered junk properties into one first class apartment complex or shopping center.

Another reason you might want to do a trade is to generate a larger scale of operations. In other words, on day one you had half a dozen single family homes you were renting out. Because the rental income was marginal you had to do everything yourself: maintenance, repairs and collecting rent. That took up a lot of your time. But if you could trade those small homes up into a 100-unit apartment building, then the cash flow and the rents from that 100-unit apartment building will support a full-time manager and a handyman who could run the place without you. You would then become more of an executive and less of a janitor. No more stopped up toilets or unpleasant details.

When you trade up into bigger properties you generate a larger amount of cash flow. There is money for staff and, of course, larger amounts of borrowing power. In a few years you become a much more important individual to bankers, suppliers and everybody else when the rents you have coming in are $900,000 a year rather than $9,000.

Some people exchange because they want to change location. For instance, you may think that the property you own in Los Angeles or San Diego is overvalued. Property in Palm Springs, Sacramento or Placerville is, you feel, going to increase in price at a much more rapid rate. Hopefully you will be getting much more appreciation by reinvesting in another location. You can trade out of property in one city and go to another city. Not only that, you can trade US property for non-US property OR you can trade your foreign property for US property. There are no geographic requirements under Sections 1031! You can trade into or out of any type of investment property in the world. And, of course, if you trade up at regular intervals you will go from being a small property owner to tycoon status.

Now that you know the basics of exchanging let me pass on just a couple of warnings so you don't screw up. First of all, there is a good form some folks use called an 'exchange agreement'. The IRS, when they are giving somebody a real thorough audit, like to review all the papers. If they find a "buy and sell" agreement (an agreement that shows you are buying Mr. Classy's place and you are selling your place to Mr. Cash) they may try to dis-allow the exchange because they say you didn't do the paperwork properly. But you are home free if Mr. Classy actually took title to

El Dumpo. You should have some sort of agreement covering the mechanics. Here is one suggestion:

ADDENDUM TO DEPOSIT RECEIPT
OFFER TO PURCHASE THE CLASSY APARTMENTS,
DATED JUNE 1, 19XX

The undersigned Mr. Classy does hereby agree to take in trade for the Classy Apartments title to El Dumpo for the sole purpose of effecting a Section 1031 tax deferred exchange for Mr. Dumpy. Mr. Classy agrees to immediately convey title to El Dumpo to Mr. Cash, or such other buyer out-of-trade as may be found. It is understood that this exchange is being made as an accomodation to Mr. Dumpy and shall not result in any additional costs, risks or liabilities to Mr. Classy. All such costs or risks shall be born by Mr. Dumpy. In the event Mr. Cash is unable to complete the purchase of El Dumpo by September 1st 19XX, it is agreed that on that date Mr. Dumpy will purchase the Classy apartments at the price and terms agreed upon in the attached Deposit Receipt.

_____   _____

DAVID DUMPY   CALVIN CLASSY

_____   _____

MRS. HUMPTY DUMPY   MRS. CORRINNE CLASSY

(All contracts should be adapted to your own deals with the help of a competent attorney)

The crucial thing in a tax free exchange is the taking of title to the smaller property by Mr. Classy before it is deeded to the cash buyer. To do it exactly right you should create some sort of exchange agreement, making it obvious to an IRS agent what was done. You need only have a letter that you and Mr. Classy sign showing your intention to do a proper 1031 exchange. You both understand that you are really just selling El Dumpo to a third party and buying the Classy place. Mr. Classy understands that he is just taking title to the dump as a convenience to you, but the IRS (if they want to give you a hard time) will insist upon seeing an exchange agreement. The example on the prior page should do the trick.

Let's assume another problem: For some reason Mr. Classy at the closing doesn't want or isn't able to sign a proper deed to El Dumpo. The most common reason - he is not getting along with his wife. A divorce may be pending. As a result Mrs. Classy won't sign papers for him. Under the law of most states a wife has an automatic interest in any real estate that her husband owns. But if the wife will not sign or Mr. Classy cannot sign the deed there's a solution. It is possible for the owners involved to deed all the properties in the trade to a title company as nominee or straw man. The title company then completes the trade and deeds out El Dumpo to Mr. Cash and the classy apartments to you. This is an alternative way of doing a legal tax free exchange.

Once again: Both properties in the trade are deeded to a title company. The title company, acting as an agent for Mr. Classy, conveys to Mr. Cash. Remember, in real estate (or in any other business), wherever there is a problem there is always a way around it. I certainly hope that my Tycoons never assume that all is lost. If Mrs. Classy refused to sign the trade papers for El Dumpo, you would simply have asked the title company if they know any other way of doing it. They probably would have told you they could take the title as just explained. If they didn't make any useful suggestions, it would be up to you to go to another source for ideas. Never give up until you have exhausted every title company, every lawyer, every accountant and every trade broker in your city. Get the deal to close - one way or another. It's easy to give up! But tycoons are a different breed. They always close their deals. When the going gets tough, the tough get going. A cliché, but apt!

Another problem that often comes up is that the chap taking the role of Mr. Classy in our agreement says, "Look, I'll cooperate with you in doing a tax free exchange. I'll do whatever you want. I also want a real firm deal on my sale so if you're not able to make an exchange I want you to personally guarantee that you will take the property anyway." If that happens, you have a decision to make. Are you willing to take the property even if you do not sell your old place? Can you raise the money to close the deal? I would generally prefer to put into my exchange agreement that if I do not sell El Dumpo to a third party I would deed it to Mr. Classy and buy it back myself within a year at the exchange price. Or as an alternative I might try to get a concession from the seller; he would take back a big enough second mortgage to cover the smaller amount of cash I would have had to make up for if El Dumpo could not be sold. I would also see how much cash I could get out of a refinance of El Dumpo and try to renegotiate either price or terms to fit the realities of my pocketbook.

The best possibility is that you might be able to talk Mr. Classy into really taking title and possession of El Dumpo, especially if you guarantee rents at a certain level satisfactory to Mr. Classy. You can, if you have to, guarantee to manage El Dumpo. You can further guarantee to sell it for him within a year, or whatever time period you both can agree upon. If it can't be sold, you can buy it back yourself.

In case you are ever audited by the IRS and they find you've used our sample contract, to the effect that if an exchange could not be arranged, you as buyer would pay cash and take over the property anyway -- the IRS agent may not know his law very well. THE AGENT MIGHT TRY TO DISALLOW THE TRADE saying there really was not an exchange. "You just wanted to buy his place and sell your place", says the IRS. "All your agreements were buy/sell agreements, not exchange agreements." The IRS agent may wrongly try to disallow the tax free exchange. If that happens, you just tell the IRS agent that there was a case in 1935 called the Mercantile Trust Case. It was a very famous case for exchangers. In that case there was an agreement to exchange with a 'sale in lieu' provision just like in our sample form. The deal was approved by the courts as a tax free exchange! In other words, there was contractual language between the parties in that particular case that if the property was not in fact exchanged the deal would go through anyway and the property would be bought for cash. The IRS tried to say that even though there was an exchange later, the Mr. Dumpy of Mercantile Trust did not really have any intention to do a 1031 exchange. The good old IRS was trying back in 1935 to say that a secret intention to buy rather than trade resulted in a "non tax free exchange". But the court said as long as the parties go through the motions required by Section 1031 it doesn't really matter what was in their heart of hearts.

There was another interesting twist in 1962 in the Baird Publishing Co. case. It involved a delayed exchange. A religious organization wanted to acquire a building that was owned by Baird Publishing Co. A church seems to have owned all the property on the block except Baird's factory and wanted it all for their new church. Baird didn't particularly want to sell his little printing plant until the church agreed to build Baird a brand new building nearby. But they wanted to buy the Baird building immediately. Since Baird didn't want to pay taxes a trade was written up on paper. The deal was to give Baird a new building built to his specifications a little distance from the old one. The exchange contract provided that Baird could stay in the old building rent free until the new one was finished. Only when the new building was finished would Baird move all his publishing equipment over to the new place. So what essentially happened in the Baird case was: The church bought Baird's property on day one. Considerably later, the new building was completed. Baird moved, and title was then conveyed to Baird. He got his new publishing company building, worth considerably more than the old one. The IRS, as you might imagine, said this was not simultaneous exchange and disallowed it as a tax free exchange. When it got to court, the judge decided that even though legal title to the trade-in property passed long before title to the new place passed to Baird, Baird still had the use of the old place rent free and the "equitable" title remained with Baird. In other words, the court felt "real ownership" passed to the church only when Baird finally moved out of El Dumpo and moved into the new building. So they let Baird have a delayed tax free exchange.

Now, let me tell you how you could possibly use that case to your advantage. You've got a red hot buyer for some property that you own and they want to tie up your property. They want it badly and are willing to pay you a very good price. You think your building is worth only $70,000 but the buyer is willing to give you $100,000. The only problem is that you haven't found a suitable property you want to trade up into. You could, of course, have the buyer build for you. But here is my suggestion how you could structure a variation on the Baird delayed trade to still come within the rule of the Baird Publishing Co., case. You sell your property to the new buyer. We will call them the "Church" just to make the example tie in with Baird. You sell your property to Church, but do it on a Contract of Sale. That is, you give possession but keep title. Church "agrees to buy" but does not close the deal by taking title. Your keeping title and giving up possession would probably be construed as you keeping a substantial interest in the property just like Baird who, in his case, gave up title while he kept possession.

I think if you, as seller, kept title to your property and delivered physical possession to the buyer and then had Church put $100,000 cash or an I.O.U. for $100,000 into a title company escrow to be held until you found a suitable trade property, I believe you would have the makings of a good deferred tax free exchange. You would go out and find the trade property. When you do, whether it is 6 months later or 5 years later, it shouldn't matter to the IRS. Once you have found the trade-up property, have the title company use the $100,000 on deposit as the down payment on the place you are buying. Now, very important: Church should take title to the new property and a second later convey to you. Simultaneously, you convey a deed to El Dumpo to the Church. Both titles change hands at the same instant. It would seem to me that the Baird Rule provides a way for you to take advantage of a situation where you find somebody who really wants your property and will pay a premium price at a time you haven't found "trade-up" property.

Another famous case for traders was the Starker case. Up until 1977, every "trader" was going crazy using the so-called Starker Rule. Everybody in the business thought it stood for the proposition that if you found a buyer for your property all you did was sell your property to him, transfer title and tell that buyer to put the money into an escrow company (not to give it to you). Then you both gave the escrow company instructions that that money could only be taken out to buy suitable exchange property. The new trade-up property would be purchased years later in the name of your buyer who would simultaneously deed it to you, thereby accomplishing a tax free exchange. That was a pretty good rule while it lasted. But, in the state of Oregon, Judge Solomon, who decided the original Starker case, in a different case came to the conclusion that he had made a mistake. The net result is that many knowledgeable people in real estate feel that the Starker rule is dead, and title to all properties in a trade should pass simultaneously.

I believe that without simultaneous transfer of titles, or a Baird situation, the IRS would take the position that you had constructive receipt of the money. That is, you controlled the sale proceeds even though you had not physically put your hot little hands on the check. The IRS would consider a deal like that just a sale of the old property. They would say the new property purchase was a separate and distinct deal. The IRS would probably not allow it to be a tax free exchange. Who knows what a court would decide?

As a conclusion, I would have to join in the view that the Starker Rule is unreliable if not dead. But the law is a very funny thing and since every case is a little bit different, and the intention of the parties is always a little bit different, who knows? You might fight your Starker-type-trade out with the IRS and get your transaction ruled to be a valid tax free exchange. Disputed real estate trades seem to be one of the few areas of the tax law where the taxpayer often prevails against the IRS.

In summary, it is best to follow approved established procedures. But if you have created something that looks vaguely like a trade, you might as well risk treating it tax-wise as a tax free exchange. The worst that can happen is that the IRS will disallow it. If your tax free exchange is disallowed, you may be able to settle the tax they claimed is due for a small percentage on the dollar. If the IRS will not be reasonable, you can fight it out in court where the odds are the court will side with you. In any event, you have got the use of the money for half a dozen years until your case is decided.

NOTES

BECOMING AN INSURANCE CO.

Riddle: What is the ideal business to be in?

1. Costs little to nothing
2. Takes little or no time
3. Provides big after tax return
4. Reasonable risk

Answer: Lloyd's of London

If you are rich (millionaire or better) of good reputation (no Mafia ties) and go for the above, becoming an underwriting partner at Lloyd's will in effect make you a medium sized insurance company. By becoming a partner or "name" at Lloyd's, you sign on for selected risks, collect premium income, and on the average, will earn between $30,000 and $180,000 per year for the rest of your life.

Of course, insurance is a <u>risk</u> business and if London, New York, San Francisco, Tokyo, Rome and Johannesburg simultaneously had earthquakes you would owe Lloyd's policy holders everything down to your last shirt button.

You have heard of Lloyd's as the insurance group that will insure anything, including a movie star's bottom. Lloyd's will insure almost anything, anytime, anywhere for almost anybody. You probably guessed that this centuries old insurance underwriting group is very profitable for its owners, but if you have a solid net worth of around a million or more U.S. Dollars. you could become a partner at Lloyd's -- without investing anything except your good name (and credit) plus small investigation fees amounting to under $5,000.

Becoming a partner at Lloyd's is relatively easy. First, you must find a sponsor to nominate you. Your sponsor must be an existing partner at Lloyd's or "name" as Lloyd's refers to its underwriting members. Lloyd's publishes a directory of members and has 12,000 names. They are the wealthy people of almost every non-communist country, including the U.S. I became a Lloyd's name in 1976.

For the past five hundred years, practically every aristocrat in the British Empire was a Lloyd's name. Lloyd's, until recently, was exclusively a gentlemen's club where the Very Rich Men of Great Britain checked in on their visits to London. But don't worry, you don't have to be an aristocrat or male anymore -- just wealthy and of good reputation. Mafia and Terrorist Types (even if rich) Need Not Apply.

Now that the Fuzzy Thinking Leftists have eradicated wealthy aristocrats from Great Britain by forcing them to emigrate or be taxed into oblivion, Lloyd's was forced to seek an infusion of new blood by accepting rich foreigners and women. I personally sponsored one of their first Black partners -- a brilliant real estate tycoon from California. Lloyd's needed to change with the times because its capital base was eroding as the British rich were decimated by taxes both on their income and on their capital.

This is the way Lloyd's works in theory, although in fact the details are handled by agents on the trading floor at Lloyd's of London.

Mr. Oil Tanker Owner wishes to insure a million dollar oil cargo being shipped from Kuwait to New Jersey. He drops in at Lloyd's of London and approaches a big table around which are seated 12,000 assorted Lloyd's partners. Since the going insurance rate on such a trip is $100,000 (actually it is much less, but this is an example only) the risk is offered to the Lloyd's names. Assume that 10,000 Lloyd's partners agree to sign on for the risk with each one taking .01% of the premium (or $10) and each one assuming .01% of the risk of loss. (Obviously a maximum of $100 on that particular voyage.) If the ship makes it and discharges the oil without mishap, each Lloyd's partner gets to keep $10, but if the ship sinks, each partner returns the premium and contributes $90 to reimburse Mr. Oil Tanker Owner for his $100,000 insured loss. Mr. Owner obviously wouldn't insure with Lloyd's unless he was sure that every partner could come up with $100 on demand.

That is the theory of Lloyd's, but since Lloyd's members are from all over the world, they don't actually get around the table personally. Instead, they give their power of attorney to active Lloyd's underwriters who select the types of risks and percentage of participation that each "name" indicates he would feel comfortable with. Theoretically, at least, every single risk written by a name could result in a loss. If that happened the Lloyd's name could by contract, be liable to lose the shirt on his back to pay the claims. But the nature of the insurance business is that by spreading risks, that is, by issuing a lot of different types of policies all over the world, there should almost always be a net underwriting profit at Lloyd's. There is also additional earnings from investment of the "float" or premiums received and invested before losses and claims are paid out.

In our example, the $100,000 premium received on the oil shipment would be received the day the policy was issued. If the claim drifted in and was paid two years later, the interest on the $100,000 at 10% per annum might be an accumulated $20,000. Besides the large annual float of premium income, there is additional income from reserves built up in prior years. Even in bad insurance years, when underwriting profits are small, Lloyd's partners do fairly well. What is fairly well? ....between $30,000 and $180,000 per year, just for signing your name and in effect, lending your credit standing to Lloyd's. The book Hazard Unlimited (see book list) contains all the information about Lloyd's you will need to know.

It is theoretically possible to go bust because of your participation in Lloyd's, but the reality is substantial profits for Lloyd's names in most years. In bad years a Lloyd's partner just does not make as much. It is extremely rare that he will have to come up with actual "out of pocket" cash -- but it has happened from time to time and could happen again.

Insurance is, after all, a risk business and if you want to average $35,000 per year in extra income by just signing your name, you will have to be comfortable with a small risk factor. You may have to give part of your profits back now and then.

WHEN THE GOOD TIMES ARE OVER

In 1976 my true love dumped me. Even though I was making over half a million a year, without LOVE I was ready to jump off the Golden Gate Bridge. But, as in other times of crises, I fell back upon my favorite method of coping. I asked myself, what product or service (preferable profitable) might I offer to other people suffering through similar situations? Trying to think creatively, to solve my own problem, I jotted down a dozen ways of getting through a traumatic break up. There might be specialized counselling, or a new kind of seminar for the recently divorced. A book perhaps.

It took me only a day of bouncing these and other thoughts off other people to discover a neighbor who had also gone through a recent break-up. He must have asked the same question. This neighbor, Mel Krantzler, a psychiatric social worker, started by giving group counselling for the recently separated. He called his sessions "Creative Divorce". His thoughts and observations developed into a book. Krantzler's Creative Divorce became a runaway best seller. My neighbor was already meeting most of the eligible women in the county through his local sessions, but when he went on lecture tours and promoted his book, he started making big money as well. I wondered if I could somehow repeat his success - both with women, and in finding fame as a minor-celebrity.

Seeing no need for competing classes in Marin County, California, I flew to Hawaii and planted myself on an empty beach and scribbled for two weeks. What came out was an "epic limerick". It was good therapy if not good poetry. Just writing down on paper how I felt set the worst of my wounds to healing. The doing of something creative was a move in a positive direction. Here's some of the poems.

A YEAR IN THE LIFE OF A LANDLORD

She called me at my house one day,
To rent a little place to stay
But I had nothing that was nice
At anything close to the price
that she could then afford to pay.

Still on the phone I had a hunch,
so I asked her out to lunch.
The hunch was fantastic
For she wasn't plastic
As we munched, I liked her a bunch.

Bright and so cheerful,
an eyeful, an earful.
Her story hit like a punch...
A mother quite drunk
Her husband a skunk
A baby real small
and no one at all
to care for her needs
or her fears

She hugged me and felt me
'til she did melt me
while I was sipping a beer
She truly was as you can see,
a sweet and helpless deer.
We smoked a little grass,
she shook her little
That day she moved in here.

I didn't fall in love I slid,
'Cause she was such a lovely kid,
Shopped for the best prices,
didn't smoke or have vices.

For me it was 'for keeps' I knew
I hoped some day she'd love me too.
She said she did
and in passion was wild
I knew she did
when she wanted my child.

The baby came and life was tame,
with pleasure we invented
We stayed high, a year flew by,
I was never so contented.

I wish the story could have ended there
A love affair you might compare,
To the best you've heard of anywhere.
But life is contrary
and I'm glad we didn't marry.

Divorce can be an expense
Only a year did we tarry
before things got hairy,
For a year I had been dense.

THE BEST DAY OF MY LIFE

I woke up, well loved, feeling good with my lover's leg around me.
With the sun shining many colors through the stained glass
of our bedroom window.
And just looked at her.

Two gigglers, one who couldn't even talk yet, planned an attack.
With a YELL they CHARGED and JUMPED on the bed.
Two naked bodies attacking with nonstop kisses, demanding a story.

While the tale of the tiger with removable spots is read
for the hundredth time, they squish around the water bed,
not really paying attention.

My lover makes breakfast:
Cream of Wheat with lumps,
orange juice with seeds,
burned cocoa, and toast to match.
Served in bed, it's the best breakfast I ever had.

The four of us take a warm shower,
And giggle
And grab ass
And splash,
and sing songs, rubbing lather on each other.

And this perfect morning is not really marred,
when the littlest member gets soap in her eyes, and cries,
just for a minute as we all help her with clear water
and sympathy.

We dry off and dress quickly.
The boy climbs in my truck for a day of high adventure
(for a three year old).

I forgot to put out the trash,
So we careen madly down the hill chasing the garbage man
until we catch him.

My son turns to me with admiration and says:

"With me helping, we can catch anybody in the whole world,
can't we Daddy?
We can beat anyone,
We can do anything you and me,
can't we Daddy,"
"We sure can." I said,
And for a long time, I believed we could do anything.
At least anything anyone would ever want to do,
me and my little family.

I sent the verses to potential publishers. It was soon apparent there was no commercial market for poetry. One publisher told me, "the only place that people buy poetry is Russia. But if a super successful guy like you could write an inspiring book on HOW TO GET RICH then you would have a best seller."

But at the time, ending my loneliness was far more important to me than locking myself up with a typewriter. So I went to the local pick up bars. When I told women that my idea of a great weekend was looking at real estate they thought I was some kind of nut. I had more money than I would spend in a thousand years, a presentable appearance, and some intelligence. Yet finding a replacement for my lost love was nowhere on the horizon.

Then I had a brainstorm. I sent this ad to the local paper:

BECOME A LADY TYCOON
Millionaire bachelor will show you how
to get filthy rich in real estate, start-
ing with nothing. Bring Lunch. Vin-
tage wine & snacks supplied. All day
Saturday Class at Mill Valley mountain-
top retreat. Five Bucks. Call 383-3229

The initial response was good. Fifteen women appeared on my front lawn. They laughed when I told them the vintage of the wine -- last Thursday.

For five or six hours I ad-libbed about my techniques for buying and managing property. Vigorous applause ended every session. The "Tycoon Classes" caught on. Dinner invitations poured in from lady students who wanted private consultations. Some wanted me to take a piece of their action and sometimes they came up with good deals too.

What happened then shouldn't have been a surprise, but it was. My social life had improved so much that I seldom thought about the girl who had left me several months earlier. Then SHE called. There had been a fight with her new boy friend. Would I take her back? Had things not been going so well, I might had been like the hero in OF HUMAN BONDAGE - right back on the emotional roller coaster with her. But scheduled dinner dates with a dozen lovely Lady Tycoons enabled me to decline the offer - graciously.

When the good times are over, it's a good time to quit.
When the fighting is constant, to say, "This is it."

It's hard to adjust, but certainly true
Cut your losses real fast, go on to something new.

When the spouse really bugs you, say, "This is it."
When the good times are over, it's a good time to quit.

Later I found that rule applies to business situations just as well as personal situations.

What happened next was inevitable in view of the success of the class and the success of the students. Two of my star pupils, Babette Donaldson and Joan Shiels made me an offer I couldn't refuse. For a generous cut of hoped for profits, they would organize and handle all details of transforming my informal front lawn sessions into a "Tycoon Seminar" to be given at major hotels. Tricia Britt was employed to handle public relations. They got me on television and in the papers. The four person staff did a fantastic job. Without any seminar experience, without free lectures or previews of any sort, the first Bill Greene Tycoon Class opened in Spring 1977 to a sold out grand ballroom at the Mark Hopkins Hotel. The audience of nearly 300 was pleased and the comments were universally favorable, even though the tickets were priced at a hefty $250.*

Like the front lawn students, many of the attendees at my first "Hotel Seminar" did very well too. At least one guy, barely 21, acquired a million dollars worth of property within a year. Almost everyone bought one or two

*Since then prices have gone up.

properties with my No Money Down system. Many came to advanced sessions at my home. I gave them for recreation. At sessions like those, my Tycoons got together to meet each other, to trade and tell war stories. The tycoon techniques definitely worked. I was now ready to follow the publisher's advice. I would write the book.

A good snappy title was a problem, but eventually I settled on TWO YEARS FOR FREEDOM. (If you have a better title idea for the next printing, let me know. An autographed copy of the next edition from me to you if I use your title.)

The original poetry was still in a drawer. Without seeing it, the publisher said, "Keep that poetry out of your book. Nobody is interested", they insisted. In spite of those objections I included some of the poetry here. My literary efforts might not help anyone make money, but readers might appreciate it if I passed along this comforting concept:

ALL TROUBLES, NO MATTER HOW BAD THEY SEEM,
WILL PASS. CREATIVE SOLUTIONS WILL LEAD YOU
IN SATISFYING NEW DIRECTIONS.

NEW DIRECTIONS

I've taught you how to make a million dollars in two years, and no doubt a substantial portion of my readers (hopefully you among them), will have the stamina to achieve financial independence in the near future. What will you do then? From my life you can see that merely being well off didn't insure happiness. But like May West said, "I've been poor and miserable and I've been rich and miserable, and rich is better." Not that I'm particularly miserable. Things are going rather well lately.

I learned that once you've obtained financial independence, you can do whatever you want. You can move out of undesireable situations to a climate or among people you find more enjoyable. The world is wide open. You can write, teach, or politic. And if you are rich, people listen. You might go back to Page One of this book and start doing all those things I told you were a waste of time (before you were rich) -- like getting high, buying a terrific car, going around the world. You can be promiscuous or even get drunk until you tire of it. But you will have freedom in a world that permits very very few people to be free. YOU CAN DO AS YOU WILL WITH ALL THE DAYS OF YOUR LIFE.

You've read through my book now. Perhaps you wonder how I spend my personal time and my freedom: I've avoided the trap of being tied down by business ventures and properties. I hired a bright associate to handle rent collections and administrative details. I'm free to come and go as I please. I give my Tycoon Class Seminars twice a year because I enjoy meeting new, interesting, ambitious people. I zip off to Europe, Africa or Asia several months every year. I explore new investment opportunities or look after old ones. Every deal I make now has to involve those I enjoy working with. Every venture has to have a minimum of aggravation and maximum of fun for me.

Right now I'd like to get all or a part of a resort in some friendly tax-haven country like the Cayman Islands, perhaps Hong Kong or Thailand. To be of interest, a deal has to be financially sound, but maximum profits is no longer my primary goal. A pleasant climate, meeting attractive, intelligent women, good food, a government that doesn't hassle me -- that's all I ask for in a business venture.

Animals have been eating other animals since the beginning of time. Civilized Americans now consume each other with due process of law: The "poor" majority steals from a productive and harder working minority. Learning and teaching ways to preserve the products of ones own enterprising -- our hard earned money -- has been my most recent project. If you're ambitious and hard-working you will have the same problem. How can you keep what you've worked for from a cynical, rapacious government?

When I am treated unfairly by some petty bureaucrat in the Internal Revenue Department for instance, I no longer have to cringe and give in to avoid crippling legal expenses. I can fight back. For starters, I can afford to hire the best lawyers. It's unfair that you have to be rich and prominent to have a chance at justice, but that's the way it is. Best of all, like other Tycoons, I have the luxury of having little or no personal contact with the unreasonable I.R.eSSers. I can join and even run for office with the Libertarian Party whose main goal is the abolition of the Income Tax. I can fight an unfair and inhuman system with my books and lectures. It is possible for me to render public service by exposing stupidities that need to be exposed.

I just finished writing an informative and useful book on the American Income Tax System called, WELCOME TO THE TAXPAYER'S REVOLT - HOW TO PAY NO TAXES, LEGALLY.[1] I am self-publishing because I don't want a big book company censoring what I have to say. Also by publishing directly, I get to keep more of the sales price. The new book covers every

---

[1] How to get it? By writing me and enclosing your $16 check (Visa or Master Charge number).

scam, legal and otherwise, known to modern man, and is full of humor and cartoons. You got some of the flavor of the new book from the "Pay No Taxes" chapter. If you want ten times as much information, send for the new book.

As you see, I am getting my kicks by solving my problems (and yours), having fun and making money doing it. By the way, there is never an end to problems no matter how much money you have. Having "do it yourself" projects, preferably projects that will also help other people, filling needs, keeps me truly happy. I am happy and satisfied. I'm no longer looking for any guru to give me a life plan. Nor do I want to be your guru or leader. Life is a do it yourself project. I do want to help you be self sufficient, busy, productive, and adding a bit each day to the collective wealth of the world and the comfort, pleasure and FREEDOM of everyone in it.

Once you've made it financially, I think you'll become a much better person. You can be generous with your time and money in a way that was not possible before. Self indulgence in illegal, immoral or fattening pleasures isn't as much of a thrill as it once was. It's there for the taking. Ho Hum! So what do you do for encores? You think about public service. You think about how you can give something back to Society. You think about getting your message out to the fuzzy-thinking Leftists who want a revolution that will make America an unfree country, a "Socialist Paradise" where anyone with an original idea goes to jail. And that is where I am starting. Jail. As this book goes to press, I have been accepted by San Quentin Prison to give my Tycoon Classes to inmates due to be paroled in the near future. I won't make a dime, but maybe it will help some bureaucrats and fuzzy-thinking Leftists realize that there are other possibilities, and the Free Enterprise System, if left alone, can still produce the best products, the best people, and the best Society that this world has ever known.

Hopefully you have enjoyed this book and will drop me a note letting me know how you felt about it, and how later versions could be improved. I hope it will help get you where you want to be!

READING LIST

You don't make a dime sitting home and reading, but you can't go off half-cocked either. Here's Bill's list of the best books for you to read. The first two are essential:

REALTY BLUEBOOK, c/o Bill Greene, P.O. Box 408, Mill Valley, CA 94941. $11.00
This book contains loan amortization tables, contract forms, checklists to use when buying property. It summarizes laws affecting real estate and gives tax hints. It is the "Bible" of the real estate world. Very technical material is made simple. We got it for our readers "wholesale."

LANDLORDING, by Leigh Robinson, c/o Bill Greene (as above). $13.00
This book is so good Bill wishes he had written it himself. It is full of entertaining practical knowledge of tools, eviction techniques, and forms. It contains all the practical information you need to manage property effectively. A MUST for any landlord. It's always "sold out" at stores, so we've laid in a supply just for our readers -- at a little discount.

DON'T GO BUY APPEARANCES, by George Hoffman, Woodward Books, Box 773, Corte Madera, California. $2.95
All you will need to know about making an intelligent physical appraisal of real property by an unusally intelligent former local building inspector. Highly recommended! The price is 1/1,000th of what it will be worth to you.

HOW TO USE LEVERAGE TO MAKE MONEY IN LOCAL REAL ESTATE, by George Bockl, Prentice Hall Inc., Englewood Cliffs, New Jersey. $2.95
When you feel yourself running out of steam, this will give you another shot of adrenalin -- lots of new ideas. An inspiration from a Milwaukee real estate man who started from scratch to make over a million in real estate.

HAZARD UNLIMITED (The Story of Lloyd's of London), by Antony Brown, Peter Davies Publishing, 15 Queen St., London W1X 8BE, England. $10.00 should cover cost of book plus postage.
This book is recommended for those with a net worth of one million or more, and who are considering joining Lloyd's. Call me if you still want to join after reading it.

ART LAW (1977) Duffy, $40, deals with tax shelter aspects of art. It would be well worth the money--but only to artists or serious collectors of books, coins, manuscripts, paintings, sculpture, etc. Other publications of Practising Law Institute reviewed by me seem too technical or too specialized for the average reader--but if you are concerned with condo conversions, estate planning and tax shelters other than real estate, write Practising Law Institute, 810 7th Avenue, New York, NY 10019 c/o June McDonald, Book Sales Manager, for their complete list of titles.

THE VERY, VERY RICH AND HOW THEY GOT THAT WAY, by Max Gunther, Playboy Press. $1.95 At most bookstores.
While this book is not about real estate (except incidentally) it is another inspirational pickerupper to read when the pipes break, the boiler explodes, or your property is condemned. It will convince you that it's all worth it, and give you some fresh ideas.

HOW TO GET RICH IN REAL ESTATE, by Robert W. Kent, Prentice Hall Inc, Englewood Cliffs, New Jersey. $2.95 At most bookstores.
This guy thinks that "Aunt Tobys", his nickname for small urban apartments, are the only way to fly, so if three to twelve unit buildings in the city are your bag, read this. This book deals with the real estate market in various cities.

TENANTS RIGHTS (CALIFORNIA TENANTS HANDBOOK), M. Moskovitz, R. Warner and C. Sherman, Nolo Press, Occidental, California. $3.95 At most California bookstores.
Used by all fuzzy-thinking leftists, you had better read this before your first appearance in court. It will tell you what your tenant is up to.

SUE THE B*ST*ARDS, by Douglas Matthews, Arbor House, New York. $2.95 Out of print. Get it at the public library.
An entertaining book about how to use the small claims court. Well worth reading.

HOW I TURNED $1000 INTO THREE MILLION IN REAL ESTATE - IN MY SPARE TIME, William Nickerson, Simon and Schuster, Oakland, CA. $10.95 At your public library or bookstore.
Truly one of the books that turned ME onto making it in real estate. A bit dated now since the days it was a best seller in the '50s.

CALIFORNIA REAL ESTATE HANDBOOK, Dept. of Real Estate, State of California. $5.00 Order from California Dept. of Real Estate, Sacramento.
An annually published (by the State) summary of laws, current thinking and lots of excellent information on real estate in California.

THE MONOPOLY GAME, Dave Glubetich. 1601 Oak Pk. Blvd. Pleasant Hill, CA $7.95
Written by an East Bay realtor who has a lot of common sense. This 110 page book is easy, quick reading by a guy hung up on single family homes. As a realtor he spouts the line you'll hear from the best members of his profession. He tells me he is aiming his work toward the average guy with limited horizons. He doesn't mind negative cash flow.

WINNING THROUGH INTIMIDATION, by Robert J. Ringer, Los Angeles
Book Publishers, Los Angeles, CA. In most bookstores. About $4.95
Paperback best seller that will help you psyche out the other side in
negotiations. More amusing than really useful.

HOW TO BECOME FINANCIALLY INDEPENDENT BY INVESTING IN REAL
ESTATE, by Albert J. Lowry, Simon and Schuster, New York. $9.95
Currently in most bookstores, this is an excellent reference book, even if
it is written by the competition.

CRIMINAL TAX FRAUD, by Crowley. $30. Tricks of the trade used by high
priced tax lawyers to keep their clients in the chips and out of the Pokey.
Despite the high price of this book, for those worried about IRS persecution,
it is the best investment you'll ever make. It shows how NOT TO GET CAUGHT;
the basic rule being "Keep your mouth shut" when the IRS comes to call and
don't give them any leads, clues or ex-lovers to interview. Tho written for
LAWYERS, it reads like a novel and is very FUNNY. Get it ! Also get on the
mailing list for the Practicing Law Institute's many seminars and publications
on Tax Shelters, International Tax Havens, Real Estate, etc. Write: Mrs. B.G.
McDonald, Book Sales, PLI, 810 7th Avenue, New York, NY 10019.

MASTER TAX GUIDE, Commerce Clearing House, 4025 W. Peterson Avenue,
Chicago, IL 60646. $7.50
A 500 page "Bible" of Federal Tax Accountants. CCH publishes a number
of books, educational cassettes and newsletters, primarily for lawyers and
accountants. All very helpful. Especially good is their cassette course,
"Fundamentals of Partnership Taxation" by Kess for $27.

HOW TO SAVE MONEY BY INCORPORATING IN A TAX HAVEN, Paul Harris,
Box 613, Grand Cayman Island, British West Indies. $8.50 postpaid
The ex-president of a Cayman Island Bank gives 200 pages of fact-filled
information on all the tax havens of the world: geographics, risks, costs.
Definitely good reading if you are thinking of leaving the States for a
little grass shack on a coral beach permanently or temporarily.

WAKE UP THE FINANCIAL GENIUS INSIDE YOU, Mark O. Haroldson, mail
order from 4751 Holladay Blvd., Salt Lake City, UT 84117, $10
Short, good and very inspirational. Easy, worthwhile spare time reading.

THE INTERNATIONAL MAN, by Douglas Casey, c/o Kephart Communications,
901 Washington St., Alexandria, VA 22314 $15.00
This will tell you more about the freedom you can enjoy after you are rich.
Learn how a Libertarian thinks; which countries are good places to live in
and/or invest.

NEWSLETTERS AND OTHER PUBLICATIONS

Skousen, Mark, Editor, PERSONAL FINANCE, $48 per year (24 issues).
Mention me and send $2 for a sample issue: PO Box 2599, Landover Hills, MD
20784. Aimed at the hard money enthusiast (coins, gold & Swiss Francs) it's
far more intelligently written than most of the doom predicting Howard Ruff
type publications. Some ideas could be worth far more than the cost of a subscription. Ideas on real estate tend to be too general or too impractical (Example:
Aug. 1979: "Now is the time to invest in single family homes in Rhodesia/Zimbabwe).
But stuff like that does tend to open your eyes beyond the City Limits of your
own home town. They are on top of current events and their analysis of trends
is penetrating. I'm sure that physicians and dentists go right out and buy what
is advertised: Diamonds, gold, books on tax avoidance & coin collecting. But these
ads are a good way to see how the winds are blowing. The best material on taxes
finds its way into the highly recommended sister publication, TAX ANGLES (below).

Skousen, Mark, Editor, TAX ANGLES, $24 per year (12 issues) Sample: $2-.
A truly excellent service and good value for money. It's a 4 page newsletter
and unlike most of them that are 89% B.S., this one often has useable hard info.

Revel, Chase, Publisher, INTERNATIONAL ENTREPENEUR'S ASSOCIATION, monthly
bulletins & "Special Reports." These are NOT about real estate, but are concerned
with starting or acquiring small businesses. Membership is $55 per year, and I asked
for a deal on a sample issue, but they haven't returned my call after two months of
trying. So why not pretend you heard somewhere that they'd send a sample for $4
and see what happens. I know you can get on their mailing list free -- and you'll
be deluged with brochures on "The Hottest New Franchising Ideas of 1980" and similar stuff. I found it useful to know what businesses are dying and what is up and
coming. I have some (rental) stores and have used the IEA materials to select my
tenants -- for instance a roller skate rental shop that I'd otherwise have rejected
looked good to me when I read in the IEA materials how much money they made.
Write direct: 631 Wilshire Blvd., Santa Monica CA 90401

Haroldsen, Mark O., Publisher, FINANCIAL FREEDOM REPORT, $36 per year and
well worth it. You may subscribe thru me, Bill "Tycoon" Greene, Box 408, Mill
Valley, CA 94941 (Visa or MstrCg by phone 415-383-8264). This fat MONTHLY
magazine is the largest circulation real estate periodical in America. Aimed at the
"embryo" tycoon, it has inspirational success stories, lots of "how to do it" tips,
and interesting ads for real estate deals and business gadjets unobtainable elsewhere.
Some have said that Haroldsen makes more money talking and writing about it than
doing it. They are probably right. But Mark DID very well in real estate before
he turned his interest to writing his best seller "Wake Up the Financial Genius..."
(see book reviews.) He's found a NEED, and he fills it very well. Highly recommended

Kessler, A.D. ,Publisher, CREATIVE REAL ESTATE, $27 per year, sample issue
$2.75 if you mention Bill"Tycoon" Greene. This monthly magazine is aimed at the
"Big Shot" Tycoon who already owns a million in property -- or the Broker who
handles very big deals. I get some of my best ideas from this publication. But
it's quite technical and definitely not for the beginner. Box 2446,Leucadia CA 92024

Glubetich, David, Publisher, IMPACT REAL ESTATE REPORTS, $99 per year.
Very useful material. Not quite for the novice aimed at by Haroldsen, and not as
stratospheric as CREATIVE REAL ESTATE. Each month he does a different report.
Get a sample report for $5 from among these titles: Buying Single Family Homes,
Syndications, Rennovating Rundown Properties, or (my favorite) Using Options in
Real Estate. Write: Impact Publishing, 1601 Oak Pk. Blvd.,Pleasant Hill CA 94523

BILL GREENE'S TYCOON CLASS:
How To Make A Million By Really Trying—

Bill Greene conducts an *al fresco* money-making session.

He had been to the National Theatre the night before and was enthusing about it. 'I stuck to my principle of asking for the cheapest tickets – in this case standing room only – and sure enough, I found I could slink into a good seat when the lights went out. Great play. Especially since it cost me so little to see it'. This from Bill Greene, a man who gets his kicks by spending as little, and making as much, money as possible. A Chicago-born lawyer, he has amassed a vast fortune in Californian real estate over the past four years.

His disguise, as a man of meagre means, is not trendy affectation. He lets slip no hint of wealth: no Cartier watch peeping out of his frayed shirt sleeve, no Gucci loafers under the tatty jeans; he writes with a cheap ball point pen and eats in the cheapest places in town. In short, he is true to his 'Five Per Cent rule', which, he explained, means never spending more than five per cent of his gross income on consumer goods.

Greene's rigid rules in the game of making money are more than talk. He not only tests them and enacts them in his own business affairs, he is currently teaching aspiring millionaires in California, and his Tycoon Class has become so popular that he has to hire a conference hall seating some 250 at each session. Ironically, this latest Greene money-spinner was originally devised as a means of finding the ideal woman. Or, as he put it: 'a woman under 30, who does not smoke or get into hard liquor or hard drugs, is pretty and sexy, highly intelligent, and who enjoys making money almost as much as making love (and not spending it).

His 'How to be a Lady Tycoon' class was indeed no more than a tender trap. But in the end it trapped him, engaging him in current plans to publish a handbook on his golden rules,

Although his speciality is property investment he maintains his rules can be applied to any business venture, tempered with common sense.

In a characteristically generous mood, he outlined some of his rules (free of charge) to *Guest & Host* readers:

1. The Red Ribbon rule

This says that if you spend time waiting for a deal with a red ribbon around it through which you can double or triple your money, you are on to a sure fire loser because such deals do not exist and you will mistake a bad proposition for a winner.

2. The Hundred House rule

If you look at a hundred properties of the type you are thinking of purchasing and do not offer for any of them – thereafter making an offer for everything you see – you will not fail to find a good property and offer a keen price for it. This is because in your round of a hundred houses you will have acquired detailed knowledge of the market and when you come to offer you will do so at prices just under market levels with skill and confidence. This rule can be applied to businesses other than just property.

3. The Never Pay Any Taxes rule

Study tax law, then arrange your affairs in such a manner so that you pay the minimum tax. Everything you pay in tax has absolutely gone. My philosophy is to defer tax or if possible avoid it altogether. In America this can be done quite legally:
Borrow to the hilt and never sell the property, thus accumulating wealth and gearing up against that.

4. The Five Per Cent rule

Never spend more than five per cent of gross income on consumer goods. You can get round rent by, for example, finding an apartment building and managing the flats, thereby living in it free of charge. Businesswomen can act as hostesses in restaurants in their lunch hours in order to obtain free meals and other services. As for clothes, as a landlord you will find that tenants leave stuff behind that can be used, be it furniture or clothing. In other words, I am advocating bartering your services and time to cut your consumer spending to the bare minimum.

5. Leverage (or 'Gearing')

Anyone who makes big money has acquired the technique of unlimited credit. This boils down to inspiring confidence in bankers. It is a process that takes six months. I can guarantee that within that time I am able to tap any banker for unlimited funds. One golden rule is 'never screw your banker'.

How he came to devise these rules is a humorous story which he told me with much candour during a recent trip to London.

'Just a few months before January 1976 I had everything: a real estate empire of 60 properties that I had built from nothing in three years. A sexy, pretty little "old lady". Two healthy toddlers. An office that practically ran itself and provided me with more money than I could ever hope to spend. A new Rolls Royce convertible, a 90 foot sailing yacht with a fireplace in the master bedroom, and a mansion with adjoining stables and a view of San Francisco Bay.

'My mail box was always stuffed with invitations to "society" parties, and offers of directorships, honorary titles; listings in *Who's Who* and other such publications were coming my way with monotonous regularity.

'It was a situation where I felt as if in a dream and in the back of my mind I suspected that one day I would awake to some different reality. My mornings were spent splashing about in a redwood hot tub with my lady and kids, Japanese style. The rest of the day I wheeled a few deals in the property market.

'I was, in short, terribly pleased with all my accomplishments. After all, only a few years earlier, I was a little nobody from the slums of Chicago. Hard work and sacrifices put me through a prestigious "Ivy League" university and gave me a law degree. I served my time in the US army and thereafter made a fair amount of money tracing missing heirs to large estates – claiming a reasonable cut of the action for my work.

'But the big time began for me when I moved to San Francisco. There in 1973, working on borrowed money, I began picking up properties just as prices began to shoot upwards at a rate of 30 per cent a year. In a short time I was very, very rich.

'Millie, a prospective tenant with a small son, moved in with me and we had a daughter together. To keep from making shock waves in some elements of society she introduced herself as my wife, but the informal "marriage" was permanent as far as I was concerned. I just felt that after one divorce it was financially and psychologically a better deal to keep things informal.

'One day the dream was shattered. Millie said "bye-bye" and took the two kids and moved in with a clothing salesman she had been seeing secretly for some time. She did not have anything against me. She was just "in love", that's all. To me it was the end of the world. I cried. Then I went to a beach in Hawaii where I met old girlfriends. It just made me feel worse. I considered jumping off the 45th floor balcony of the Waikiki Beach Hotel.

'Then one day I pulled myself together and I said: "I am 37 years old and this is not the end of the world, and I am going to do something constructive. I am going to replace Millie with someone (or ones) even better." I would not make the same mistake again. What went wrong between us was that I had a lot of enthusiasm and energy to put into my business and she did not know (or care about) the difference between a real estate deed and a share certificate. Her successor, I determined, would be more turned on by the process of making money than spending it.

'How to find large numbers of young, attractive women on this wavelength? The solution was simple: I placed an ad. in the local paper:

HOW TO BE A LADY TYCOON.
37 year old bachelor millionaire teaches course every Saturday morning, $5. Full money back guarantee if not satisfied for any reason. Bring your own lunch. 10 a.m. to 2 p.m.

'The first Saturday about 20 women and five guys showed up. Having always been a ham and in fact knowing my subject very well, I gave the audience a fire and brimstone lecture about the evils of the tax man and how to achieve financial independence through real estate and by exploiting opportunities around you. My audience applauded warmly and I picked out the best looking women to go and look at properties with me that afternoon.'

While the unsuspecting aspiring millionairesses surveyed Greene's assets he evaluated them as prospective replacements for Millie: 'The search for a new woman was so much fun I was not sure I wanted to find one!'

His course went up in price to $25 until the crowds multiplied to 75 and then 100 and the Tycoon Class was conducted on his front lawn, now no longer simply restricted to women. Greene received invitations to appear on television chat shows, newspaper articles were written. The American tax authorities began to nose around – see rule three – but Greene told them to take the course instead of spending some $250,000 investigating them. One or two exposes were written up in local papers but did not bother Greene who is 'on the way to making my third million'. He met up with a public relations consultant in San Francisco, who told him 'go big time and do a weekend Tycoon Class on nationwide tour at $250 a throw'. To Greene's utter amazement his first class drew in nearly 300.

Unexpectedly, he has had many endorsements of the value of his golden rules from past students who have in fact become tycoons. One young girl, a schoolteacher from the early front lawn days, has developed her own real estate empire worth almost a million, says Greene. 'I get regular calls from female students inviting me to participate in business deals or to meet them socially. That is pretty good for a bald, slightly stout, rather un-romantic fellow (now almost 40). A large corporation has asked if I would consider the sale of the Bill Greene Tycoon Class and the inspiring & unlimited gross profits it generates. I am definitely considering it if the tax angles can be favourably worked out.'

EMBASSY GUEST & HOST, London, May'78
Article by Stella S. Dana, Editor.

**BILL GREENE'S
TYCOON CLASS**
P.O. Box 408
Mill Valley, CA 94941

Making $1 million

By PAUL VOAKES
Times Business Editor

Bill Greene made a million dollars in three years, he's a little embarrassed to say.

But he claims he's ironed the bugs out now. He's sure he could do it from scratch in two.

In fact, he's confident enough of his system that he's begun to share it in what he calls a "tycoon class." He believes any student who follows his advice with religious fervor will make a million by the first year.

Tuition for the two-day class? A paltry $250.

The key to Greene's pathway to riches is not much of a revelation: it's real estate investment. Greene has simply developed techniques and uncovered loopholes that enable investors to multiply their holdings by spending very little cash and paying very few taxes.

Real estate is one of the few investments where the investor cannot lose his shirt, he said, and can turn a handsome profit on very little initial capital.

Greene is accustomed to the charge that it is housing speculators in the Bay Area who have driven up home prices to such unaffordable levels. He counters that speculators aren't nearly so much to blame as the "fuzzy-headed leftist-liberals" and environmentalists.

The themes of housing development in Northern California today are low density, open space and special aesthetic and energy-conservative structural features, Greene said. The requirements of municipal planning bodies are so many and so steep, he said, that developers can profit only by building expensive homes.

"It could take up six years to get all the approvals and reports completed," he said, "so he decides to build 10 $200,000 homes instead of 40 $30,000 homes on the same land."

It is that pattern that has created a general housing scarcity, Green believes.

"Theoretically I favor all the environmental concerns," he added, "but people in favor of all those things don't realize that that's what takes the $30,000 homes off the market."

Anyway, Greene insists, he did not get rich by speculating and doesn't tell his students to.

"I tell them not to sell — they'll never get anywhere if they don't hold onto their properties."

Greene counsels people to acquire new properties by using

Bill Greene

rental income and refinancing owned properties.

He also tells them to buy cheap — loans with no down payments are more easily available, he said, when the investor is buying property sorely in need of rehabilitation. The housing market has shown in the past, he added, that cheap properties, "in less than good neighborhoods and in less than super condition," appreciate at a faster rate than better homes.

Greene acknowledged that cheap housing stock for the beginning investor is hard to come by in the Bay Area, and he is telling his students to look into communities in the Central Valley and in the Reno area.

He said he expects few of his graduates to actually make a million in real estate, but he's found that the class has enticed every student to make at least one purchase of property.

The two major stumbling blocks students encounter are sloth and avarice, he said. If one expects to become financially independent in a few years' time, Greene maintains, one must be willing to work during that time harder than he ever thought possible.

"I got into the habit of looking at at least 100 properties every weekend," he said. "That means you give up other pleasures."

What you don't give up is your job, he cautioned, because the job is the requisite credit reference for mortgage purposes. His students find that time is of greater value than available cash, and that if they can devote long hours to the process their rewards will come.

Too many people stop short, often at their first profit, Greene said.

"Never think of what you'll buy after your first profit. Making $40,000 and buying a Rolls-Royce is not what I'm selling. That's not the way to financial independence."

Greene scoffs at cynics who suggest the actual way he's getting wealthy is by charging $250 a student for his sessions. He expects to gross about $10,000 per weekend class, he said, much of which will be consumed by overhead and printing costs. Compared to the hundreds of thousands he clears every year from his own Bay Area real estate empire, he said, the classes mean little income.

He said he is setting aside income from the classes for a future project: a campaign against the "selective enforcement" of income tax regulations.

Greene has been giving "tycoon classes" in his home for several months. His first "public" seminar was given last month at the Mark Hopkins Hotel in San Francisco, and the second takes place this week in Berkeley. The Cabana session will be the third.

BILL GREENE'S TYCOON CLASS

P.O. Box 408
Mill Valley, CA 94941

Those Preachers of Real Estate Profits

For $295 and up, weekend courses proclaim the persuasive gospel of investing in rental property.

by Edward E. Scharff

Since owning a home is the best investment most Americans ever make, shouldn't buying one or more rental properties run a close second? In theory at least, landlords can sit back and watch property values rise, while rents pay off the mortgage and the tenants take care of the lawn. But successful investment in rental properties calls for some business skills—a sharp eye for property value, a cool hand at negotiating for mortgage money, a nose for tax advantages, and an unsentimental sense of when to raise rents.

Amateurism can be risky. One woman in Philadelphia nearly lost her $50,000 property to creditors not long ago when unexpected expenses cropped up and the building didn't generate the rent she'd been told to expect. Many an investor in Florida condominiums took a beating a few years back when demand for them evaporated.

Clearly, there's a need for investor education, and it is not going unmet. Real estate investment courses are now offered at some colleges and adult schools; they are also given by entrepreneurs charging high tuition and claiming to have made fortunes in residential real estate. Of the handful of private courses being offered around the U.S., only one, called the Lowry-Nickerson Seminar, regularly tours the country. Because of the boom in western real estate, most other courses are given in the West. But a sprinkling of them can be found elsewhere.

Money recently enrolled in two weekend-length sessions—the Lowry-Nickerson Seminar and the Bill Greene Tycoon Class (P.O. Box 408, Mill Valley, Calif. 94941), a well-publicized newcomer. Tuition for the 18-hour Lowry-Nickerson Seminar is $395 for early registrants, $495 for late enrollees. The Bill Greene Tycoon Class charges $295 for 14 hours of instruction. So far, this course has not been offered outside California.

Both courses proved to be serious-minded marathons of investment strategy, tax advice and basic real estate terminology. There may be less costly ways of taking in the same information, but courses like these seem well worth the time of any potential investor who feels at a disadvantage in the company of fast-talking brokers and moneylenders. The instructors were enthusiastic and entertaining.

These are strictly stand-up-and-talk lectures delivered in hotel conference rooms. Mercifully steering clear of pseudopsychological hype and gimmicky visual aids, they stick to the matter at hand—making money in real estate.

To be sure, there's some pep talk. Says Bill Greene, 39, once an aide to the late real estate magnate William Zeckendorf Sr.: "In the future, the government will probably fix it so no one can make a million in real estate or anything else, but right now it's still possible in real estate. You can be among the last tycoons."

While both Greene and the Lowry-Nickerson instructors predict that real estate values will continue skyrocketing for a while, both courses outline a strategy that can work even if prices tail off. Students are advised to look for rental properties that may be undervalued because of poor appearance or bad management. Once a shrewdly chosen undervalued building has been brought up to market standards, the strategy is to raise rents; higher rental income should substantially boost the property's market value.

Nickerson's general philosophy, echoed in both the Greene and Lowry-Nickerson courses, is that once you have bought an undervalued property, made improvements and hiked the rents, you don't just watch the rent money roll in. Instead, you try to pyramid profits by selling, trading or refinancing the property at its new, enhanced market value in order to buy additional property. You repeat the cycle until you become rich.

Profitable losses

Nickerson's apostles preach the considerable advantage of "leverage"—harnessing small amounts of capital to far larger amounts of borrowed money. When an unleveraged investment such as a stock bought outright rises from $100 to $110, its owner has a 10% profit. But real estate worth $100,000 can be bought for, say, $10,000 down. If the property rises in value to $110,000, the owner has a profit before commissions of $10,000—or 100%—on his $10,000 investment.

The teachers hammer away at the luxuriant tax advantages that come with real estate ownership. Homeowners are well aware that interest payments on borrowed money are tax deductible. But real estate investors are granted yet another tax break—depreciation. Thanks to depreciation, profitable ventures can often be made to show a paper loss for tax purposes. A portion of the purchase price of an investment property can be written off each year on the theory that the building is gradually wearing out. Of course, most buildings become more, not less, valuable over time.

Savvy investors refrain from taking cash out of a successful property by selling it, say the lecturers. Instead, they go to a bank and take out a larger loan based on whatever value the property has acquired since it was purchased. The loan can be used as tax-free spending money. Although the capital-gains tax on the building's appreciated value has only been deferred, students learn how to minimize or put off paying that tax almost indefinitely.

If the courses have a common fault, it is that they skim over some hazards. They could have underlined more strongly, for instance, that each property invested in should be potentially self-sustaining. That is, the income should cover all operating expenses. Rents can't always be raised, and investors who try to support a money-losing investment with a moneymaking project risk losing both. Most of history's spectacular real estate debacles have befallen investors who leaned one weak investment against another, like a row of dominoes.

A second point that needed more attention is that real estate fortunes can look deceptively large on paper, just as they can be made to look small at tax time. Owning a lot of valuable but illiquid real estate is not the same as having cash to pay the electric bill.

The most frequent criticisms leveled at Greene, Lowry-Nickerson and their imitators are that their courses are inordinately expensive and that most of the information could be gleaned from books. Both criticisms probably are justified. There are adequate books on real estate. But most tend to be slow going for anyone not already versed in the subject. The courses do an admirable job of packaging the subject matter and making the most important points easy to remember.

The only good deals

Unfortunately, there are relatively few communities with inexpensive investor-oriented programs

Most courses are designed to help real estate brokers pass state licensing exams; their content is usually irrelevant to investing. Some laymen's courses are taught by real estate brokers or savings and loan executives, whose inclination may not be to place investors' interests first.

The Securities and Exchange Commission cautions that some real estate courses may be little more than pretexts for selling questionable investments to gullible participants. Greene also tells his students to be wary of investments that come tied in red ribbon. "You should never depend on others to bring you a good deal," he says. "The only real estate investments that are good deals are the ones you ferret out for yourself." END

Money OCTOBER 1978

EXCERPT

BILL GREENE'S TYCOON CLASS
P.O. Box 408
Mill Valley, CA 94941

PRICE LIST

COMPLETE HOME STUDY COURSE
   Includes 8 cassette tapes, Tycoon Workbook, Landlording,
   Realty Bluebook, Two Years For Freedom and UPS delivery.............. $185

OR ORDER SEPARATELY

TWO YEARS FOR FREEDOM... $16

THE REALTY BLUEBOOK... $11

LANDLORDING... $13

INDIVIDUAL CASSETTE TAPES....................................... $13

Think Like A Tycoon	Handling Tenants*
Finding Super Deals	Pay No Taxes Ever Again, Legally!
Getting Organized	Advanced Tax Avoidance
No Money Down Deals	Trade Up Tax Free - 1031 Exchanges

* Handling Tenants uses and refers to legal forms and documents in the Landlording book, so you will need that text if you order this tape.

SPECIAL INTRODUCTORY TALK: "Buying Your First Investment Property" on cassette. General summary of the Tycoon Class with detailed instruction on how to use the standard offer form (included). This tape will be included as a gift to all those who order the Home Study Course

THIS TAPE ALONE - SPECIAL .... *$ 9*

* * * * * * * ORDER FORM * * * * * * * *

PLEASE SEND ME:

____ COMPLETE HOME STUDY COURSE
      $185 each.
____ TWO YEARS FOR FREEDOM $16 each

____ THE REALTY BLUEBOOK $11 each

____ LANDLORDING $13 each

____ BUYING YOUR FIRST INVESTMENT
      PROPERTY. $9 each
____ INDIVIDUAL CASSETTES $13 each
      (designate titles desired)

_____

_____

_____

_____

NAME_____

ADDRESS_____

CITY/STATE/ZIP_____

Check enclosed _____ Charge me _____

Visa # _____

Mastercharge # _____

Expiration Date _____

TOTAL OF YOUR ORDER _____

TAX AND POSTAGE
(other than Home Study)
add $1 for each item   _____

TOTAL ENCLOSED _____

PLEASE USE BILLING ADDRESS OF YOUR CARD WHEN CHARGING MERCHANDISE.

PHONE ORDERS ACCEPTED WITH CHARGE ORDERS AT (415) 383-3229   9 am to 4 pm.

X1179Y